Your PREGNANCY Questions & Answers

GLADE B. CURTIS, MD, OB/GYN

FISHER
BOOKS™

Publishers:	Bill Fisher	**Library of Congress**
	Helen Fisher	**Cataloging-in-Publication Data**
	Howard Fisher	
		Curtis, Glade B.
Editors:	Judith Schuler	Your pregnancy questions &
	Sarah Smith	answers / Glade B. Curtis;
		illustrated by Les Young.
Book Production:	Deanie Wood	p. cm.
	Randy Schultz	Includes index.
		ISBN 1-55561-150-8
Cover Design:	FifthStreet*design*	1. Pregnancy—Miscellanea.
	Berkeley, CA	2. Childbirth—Miscellanea.
		I. Title.
Cover Photo:	©The Stock Market	RG125.C88 1995
	Nancy A. Santullo	618.2'4—dc20 95-24480
		CIP
Illustrations:	Les Young	

Published by Fisher Books, LLC
5225 W. Massingale Road
Tucson, Arizona 85743-8416
(520) 744-6110

©1995 Glade B. Curtis and Judith Schuler
Printed in the U.S.A.
Printing 10 9 8 7

Contents

Acknowledgments

I have the honor of sharing in the joy, the excitement and even the heartbreak associated with the miracle of childbirth on a daily (and nightly) basis. I thank my patients and their families for allowing me to share in their experiences. I have answered many of these questions hundreds, if not thousands, of times, yet to the person asking the questions, the answer is critical.

My thanks to my wife, Debbie, and our family who have supported me in the pursuit of a profession that requires me to give a lot of time and energy to my patients. Their unfailing support, which is an inspiration to me, has continued during this and other projects. My thanks also to my parents for their endless love and support.

Judi Schuler's insight, persistence, commitment to excellence and accuracy continue to inspire and to challenge me. I appreciate her drive and ability to "pull things together" and keep me focused.

For help with the cover photography for this particular book project, I wish to thank Ludmilla Campbell, Lisa Wong and Kim Kacic. I also appreciate the input and assistance from Cynthia Deines, Nancy L. Thompson, Janet L. Hawley, David Fischer and Dr. Ted Noon.

About the Author

Glade B. Curtis is board-certified by the American College of Obstetricians and Gynecologists. He is in private practice in obstetrics, gynecology and infertility in Sandy, Utah.

One of Dr. Curtis' goals as a doctor is to provide patients with many types of information about gynecological and obstetrical conditions they may have, problems they may encounter and procedures they may undergo. In pursuit of that goal, he has written this book. It is a companion to his best-selling book, *Your Pregnancy Week by Week* and to his latest book *Your Pregnancy After 30*. He has also co-authored a book on female surgeries.

Dr. Curtis is a graduate of the University of Utah and the University of Rochester School of Medicine and Dentistry, Rochester, New York. He was an intern, resident and chief resident in Obstetrics and Gynecology at the University of Rochester Strong Memorial Hospital. Dr. Curtis lives with his wife Debbie and their five children in Sandy, Utah.

To the Readers of this Book

I have endeavored to include all the questions that have been posed to me (and other physicians I know) dealing with every aspect of pregnancy and childbirth. If you have any questions I haven't covered, which might be of interest to other pregnant women, I would appreciate your sending them to me in care of the publisher, Fisher Books. If possible, I will include your question and my answer in subsequent editions. Use the Reader Reply at the back of the book.

Pregnancy is a special time in a woman's life—and an enjoyable one. By being informed and working with your health-care provider, you can provide your baby with the best possible start in life.

✧ *1* ✧
Preparing for Pregnancy

The other day I read about the "12 months of pregnancy." Pregnancy only lasts for 9 months, doesn't it?

The actual length of a pregnancy (the growth of the fetus into a normal-size baby) is only 9 months. What the author was referring to was the concept of *preparing for pregnancy.* The few months before you get pregnant can be as important as the 9 months the fetus develops inside your womb. Adding the two figures together gives you the concept of 12 months of pregnancy.

Why are these 3 or 4 months before pregnancy so important?

With good preparation your baby will get the best start it can toward a healthy life. These months give you time to prepare your body for conception and pregnancy. You can eat nutritiously, cut out alcohol and tobacco use, begin an exercise program, get your weight under control and address other medical concerns such as diabetes or lupus.

What should I do to prepare for pregnancy?

You can do many things to prepare for pregnancy.

- ✧ Exercise regularly.
- ✧ Find out if medications you take on a regular basis can be decreased or discontinued. Ask your physician if they are safe to take during pregnancy.
- ✧ Have your weight under control. Pregnancy is not the time to lose weight.
- ✧ If you need X-rays or medical tests, get them done before trying to get pregnant.
- ✧ It's a good time to control or eliminate tobacco, alcohol or drug use.
- ✧ Decide who will deliver your baby. Check on your insurance coverage.

Attention to these details *before* getting pregnant makes your pregnancy safer and more enjoyable.

Should I see my doctor before I get pregnant or wait until I am pregnant?

Seeing your doctor before you get pregnant helps you prepare for pregnancy. A visit before pregnancy clears up questions about medications you are taking. You can have a Pap smear and any other tests your health-care provider decides are necessary. You and your health-care provider can evaluate your current weight and set a target weight gain for a pregnancy. You will know you're in good health before getting pregnant; if you're not, you can make plans to get into the best shape you can before you get pregnant.

Are there lab tests I should have done before I get pregnant?

Your health-care provider may order a range of tests for you. These include:

❖ Pap smear
❖ Rh-factor test
❖ blood typing
❖ rubella titers
❖ mammogram, if you are 35 or older

If you know you have other specific or chronic medical problems, such as diabetes, have these checked. If you have been exposed to hepatitis or AIDS, tests should be done for these.

My last two pregnancies ended in miscarriages. Should I talk with my doctor before I get pregnant or can I wait until my first visit when I am pregnant?

The history of previous pregnancies can be very important in the success of your next pregnancy. It's true that in many situations nothing can be done to help or to avoid problems. The safest thing to do is talk with your doctor before you try to conceive. Tell your doctor what has happened in the past. Find out if there is anything you can do now or if there are risks you may have to deal with.

Your Body in Pregnancy

I've heard that a woman's body during pregnancy is very different from one before pregnancy. What changes can I expect?

The changes your body goes through during pregnancy are incredible! Your breasts enlarge and the number of milk ducts to produce breast milk actually increases. Your organs become crowded by your enlarging uterus, which may cause more-frequent urination, heartburn or indigestion. Your legs, feet and hands may swell. Your hair and skin often undergo changes. Compare the illustration on this page with that on page 169 to see how a woman's body changes in pregnancy.

What is the purpose of the menstrual cycle?

During your menstrual cycle, your body prepares for the possibility of pregnancy. An egg is released from one of your ovaries, and changes take place in the lining of your uterus to provide an environment for the development of a fertilized egg. If fertilization does not take place, the enriched lining is discarded through the menstrual flow.

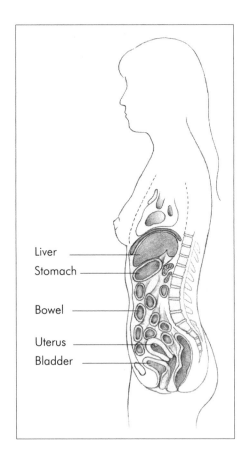

This illustration of a woman's body shows a non-pregnant uterus and various organs. Pregnancy causes many changes! Compare this illustration with the one of a pregnant woman's body on page 169.

Liver

Stomach

Bowel

Uterus

Bladder

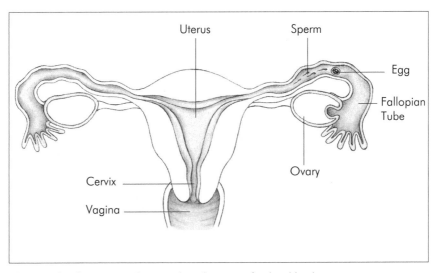

The miracle of pregnancy begins when the egg is fertilized by the sperm.

I've heard that fertilization is almost like a miracle. How does fertilization of the egg occur?

Fertilization is believed to occur in the middle part of the tube called the *ampulla (Fallopian tube)*, not inside the uterus. Sperm travel through the uterine cavity and out into the tube to meet the egg. See the illustration above.

What happens after fertilization?

The fertilized egg begins to divide and to grow. Within 3 to 7 days, it travels down the tube into the uterus and attaches to the wall of the uterus. The developing baby is now called an *embryo.* (After 8 weeks it is called a *fetus.*)

By about the 12th day, the amniotic sac begins to form around the developing embryo. The sac contains fluid in which the baby can easily move around. The amniotic fluid also cushions the fetus against injury and regulates temperature for it.

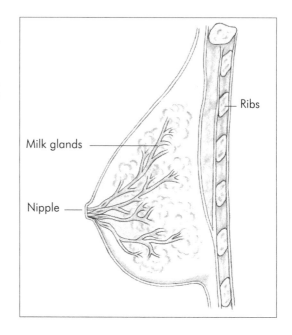

Your breasts go through many changes during pregnancy. Compare this illustration of a breast in a non-pregnant woman with the illustration of a pregnant woman's breast on page 189.

Ribs

Milk glands

Nipple

What is the "bag of waters"?

This is another name for the membranes of the amniotic sac. When it is time for the baby to be born, these membranes must be broken so the birth can take place. If this does not happen naturally, the doctor will break them.

What is the placenta?

The placenta is a flat spongy structure that grows on the wall of the uterus and is attached to the baby by means of the umbilical cord.

What is the purpose of the placenta?

The placenta carries oxygen and nutrients from the mother to the fetus, and it carries carbon dioxide and waste products from the fetus to your body for excretion. It also produces hormones called *HCG (human chorionic gonadotropin), estrogen* and *progesterone*.

What is an ectopic pregnancy?

An ectopic pregnancy is one in which the fertilized egg is implanted outside the uterus and starts to grow there. This is also called a *tubal pregnancy* because 95% of the time it occurs in the Fallopian tube. However, it may also happen in the ovary, the cervix or in other locations in the abdomen. Because there is no way to nourish an embryo in these locations, an ectopic pregnancy must be ended. See illustration on page 246.

Where is the cervix?

The cervix is the necklike opening from the uterus into the vagina. Normally it is closed or very small (0.4 inch; 1cm), and its tissue is firm and thick. It begins to enlarge, or dilate, when it is time for the baby to be born. It also becomes much thinner and softer, which is called *effacement*. The goal of labor is for it to become 100% effaced and about 4 inches (10cm) dilated.

What is the birth canal?

The birth canal is the passage through which the baby travels to be born. It consists of the cervix, the vagina and the vulva.

Your Current Contraception Methods

If I want to get pregnant soon, when should I stop my birth-control pills?

Most doctors recommend staying off the pill for two or three normal menstrual cycles before trying to get pregnant. Use some other form of contraception, such as a barrier method (condom), until you want to get pregnant.

How long should my IUD be out before I try to conceive?

The best and easiest time to remove an IUD is during your period. Wait for a couple of normal cycles after your IUD is removed before trying to conceive. Use a barrier contraceptive during the waiting time.

I use Norplant® for birth control. Is it OK to get pregnant right after it is taken out?

Once the Norplant implant is removed, wait at least two or three menstrual cycles before trying to get pregnant.

Your Prepregnancy Health

Can I have a successful pregnancy even though I have chronic health problems?

Yes. Most women with health problems have successful pregnancies and healthy babies. It is very important for you to discuss your particular situation with your health-care provider *before* becoming pregnant. Follow his or her instructions carefully.

I have diabetes, and I really want to have a baby. Is it possible?

Diabetes can have serious effects during pregnancy. Risks to you and your baby can be decreased with good control of blood sugar or control of your diabetes during pregnancy. Discuss your concerns with your physician *before* you try to conceive.

How long must the diabetes be under good control before I get pregnant?

Most doctors recommend 2 or 3 months before pregnancy begins. This helps lower the risk of miscarriage.

Will pregnancy affect my insulin requirements?

It can. Pregnancy can increase your body's need for insulin.

When do most pregnancy problems occur for diabetic women?

Most problems occur during the first trimester—the first 13 weeks of pregnancy. However, problems can occur throughout pregnancy. This is one important reason to have your diabetes under good control for 3 or 4 months before you conceive.

I have asthma. Will pregnancy affect me?

There is no way to predict ahead of time how your pregnancy will affect your asthma. About 50% of those women affected see no change in their asthma during pregnancy. About 25% have improved symptoms, while 25% have increased problems.

Is my asthma medication safe to take during pregnancy?

Most medications prescribed for asthma are safe to use during pregnancy. Discuss your medication use with your health-care provider.

Is there anything else I can do to avoid asthma problems?

Avoid whatever substances trigger your asthma attacks.

I have high blood pressure, and I want to get pregnant. What kind of problems might I expect during pregnancy?

High blood pressure can cause problems for the mother and the baby. These include kidney damage, stroke or headaches in the mother-to-be and decreased blood flow to the fetus. The decreased blood flow can cause intrauterine-growth retardation (inadequate growth of the fetus).

Can I continue my blood-pressure medication during pregnancy?

Some medications are safe to take during pregnancy; others are not. Do *not* stop or decrease any medication on your own! Discuss your situation with your health-care provider.

I've had heart problems for quite a while, but I want to have a baby. Is this dangerous?

Some heart problems may be serious during pregnancy and require special care. Other heart problems may affect your health so adversely that your physician will advise against pregnancy. This serious question must be discussed with your heart specialist and your obstetrician before you make any decision.

I have lupus, and with my first flareup my kidneys were affected. Is this a serious consideration before I get pregnant?

Any situation that results in loss of kidney function can be serious during pregnancy. Be sure your physician knows about this situation before you get pregnant. You will need to make a plan to follow during your pregnancy.

My mother always warned me not to try to have a baby because I have epilepsy. Should I avoid pregnancy?

I cannot answer this question without knowing your full medical history. I can tell you that some seizure medications are safe to take during pregnancy, and I know women with epilepsy who have had successful pregnancies.

What kind of problems can I expect if I have epilepsy?

Mothers with epilepsy have a 1 in 30 chance of having a baby with a seizure disorder. Babies also have a higher incidence of birth defects. Seizures can be dangerous for you and your developing fetus, so it is extremely important for you to take your medication as prescribed before and during pregnancy.

What kind of seizure medication is safest to take during pregnancy?

Research has shown that phenobarbital is safe to take before and during pregnancy. Discuss its use with your physician, but do *not* discontinue or decrease your medication on your own!

I've been told I was anemic in the past. Should I start taking iron now?

Anemia can be easily checked by your doctor. When you're pregnant, there are great demands on your body's iron supplies for the baby. Many women start taking vitamins or iron before getting pregnant. Because you have had a problem in the past, it's better to discuss this with your health-care provider before pregnancy.

I've heard there's a new drug being used for sickle-cell anemia, which I have. Can I use it while I try to get pregnant?

You are probably referring to *hydroxyurea*, which has proved to be the first effective treatment of sickle-cell anemia. It helps reduce the excruciating pain of some sickle-cell attacks, but its use carries some risk and it cannot be given to all sickle-cell sufferers. Because the drug is so new, no one yet knows the long-term effects, so women who are contemplating pregnancy are advised *not* to use it.

I take thyroid medicine for a thyroid problem. Do I need to change the dosage or stop taking it if I want to get pregnant?

Don't make *any* changes without first consulting your physician. Medication for thyroid problems is very important during pregnancy.

Will an occasional bladder infection before pregnancy cause problems during pregnancy?

It shouldn't, so don't be alarmed if you have a bladder infection or a urinary-tract infection (UTI) before or during pregnancy.

What about other health problems? Do I need to see my physician about them before I get pregnant?

Yes, you should. It's best to have any chronic medical condition under control before you get pregnant. You will feel better, and it's better for your growing baby if you deal with these issues before pregnancy.

My friend had surgery for breast cancer a few months ago, and now she's talking about getting pregnant. Is that dangerous?

This is a very individual problem and depends on the seriousness of her cancer and the type of treatment your friend received. It is very important for your friend to talk to her doctor if she is thinking about getting pregnant and she is being treated for cancer. It is much easier and safer for the woman to make decisions about treatments or medications before becoming pregnant than after.

I've been having a lot of back problems, and my orthopedic surgeon wants to do some X-rays, a CT scan and an MRI. Should I have them before I get pregnant?

Yes, these tests should be completed before you consider conceiving. A good time to schedule these tests is right after the end of your period so you know you're not pregnant.

I just got a vaccination for rubella. Is it OK to stop my birth control and try to get pregnant?

No. Some vaccinations are safe during pregnancy, and some are not. Most physicians believe it's wise to continue contraception for at least 3 months after receiving any type of vaccination.

I often have to take medications for various problems. Can you give me some good advice about medication use before pregnancy?

It's best to be cautious with your use of medications while

you are preparing for pregnancy and while you are trying to conceive. Follow these guidelines for safe use:

- ✧ Take all prescription medications as they are prescribed.
- ✧ Do not use medications you used in the past for current problems.
- ✧ Be careful with over-the-counter medications. Many contain caffeine, alcohol and other additives.
- ✧ Never use anyone else's medication for your medical problem.
- ✧ Notify your health-care provider immediately if you are using medication and believe you might be pregnant.

I often take several vitamins and herbs. Can I continue to take them while I prepare for pregnancy?

It isn't a good idea to self-medicate with anything while preparing for or during your pregnancy. In excessive amounts certain vitamins, such as vitamin A, can increase the risk of birth defects. The key to vitamin use and nutrition during pregnancy is balance. A multivitamin is the only supplementation most women need while they are trying to conceive.

I read somewhere that caffeine can make a woman infertile. Is that true?

Studies have shown drinking 8 cups of coffee a day (1600mg of caffeine) is associated with a decrease in a woman's fertility (ability to get pregnant). Some researchers have found an association between excessive caffeine consumption and miscarriage.

Should I Consider Genetic Counseling?

My sister had a baby last year that was born with Down's syndrome. I'm considering pregnancy. Should I have genetic counseling?

This is something to discuss with your doctor. The answer is based on many factors, including your past health, your partner's health and your family medical history.

What can genetic counseling tell me?

Genetic counseling won't give you an *exact* answer, but a counselor can discuss possibilities or probabilities regarding a planned pregnancy and your baby. In a situation like the one you describe with your sister, ask your doctor for advice.

Should everyone consider genetic counseling?

It is not necessary for every woman. If there is a family history of problems, it is probably advisable to seek this type of counseling. Other situations in which genetic counseling should be considered include:

- ✧ women over 35
- ✧ when either you or your partner has a birth defect
- ✧ if you have delivered a baby with a birth defect
- ✧ if you have had three or more miscarriages in a row
- ✧ if you and your partner are related

Pregnancy for Older Couples

I'm 40 years old this month and want to have another baby. How will this pregnancy be different from my earlier one?

There are several advantages to being older. You are more mature and probably have more patience. Your financial situation may be better than when you were younger. On the other hand, problems you have with chronic illnesses such as high blood pressure or diabetes can worsen and affect both you and your baby.

Does this mean I shouldn't get pregnant now that I'm older?

No, but a pregnancy may be more difficult for you. This is a very individual situation that you and your partner should discuss with your doctor.

I am 39 and hope to be pregnant soon. Will I need any special tests during pregnancy?

With increasing maternal age, tests to consider include ultrasound, amniocentesis, chorionic villus sampling, serum alphafetoprotein and diabetes testing. If you haven't had a mammogram, you should have one if you are over 35.

What are some of the possible problems I might have if I am over 35 and get pregnant?

Risks are varied and include:
- ❖ an increased risk of a baby with Down's syndrome
- ❖ a higher risk of Cesarean section
- ❖ problems with diabetes or high blood pressure
- ❖ a harder, longer labor

If you have other chronic medical problems, such as thyroid disease, or take medications regularly, discuss your concerns with your health-care provider before getting pregnant.

My husband is older, and we've heard that his age can affect my pregnancy and our baby. Is this true?

Researchers believe this is true. It has been shown that chromosomal abnormalities occur more often in women over 35 and men over 40. Men over age 55 are twice as likely as younger men to father a child with Down's syndrome.

Nutrition Before Pregnancy

I want to be pregnant soon. I love hamburgers, French fries and other junk foods. Will this be a problem when I get pregnant? I'll eat better then!

The best plan is to start eating nutritiously *before* you get pregnant. By the time many women know they're pregnant, they are 7 or 8 weeks into the pregnancy—or more! These early weeks of pregnancy are important in the development of your baby. Start eating right before you are pregnant.

Can't I just start eating better when I find out I'm pregnant?

It is best for you and your developing baby if you develop good eating habits before you get pregnant. It is important to your health and the development of your baby for you to eat nutritiously for the 12 months of pregnancy.

I plan to start watching my weight once I'm pregnant. Is there a problem with this plan?

Pregnancy is *not* the time to start a new diet or to try to lose weight. Dieting can cause temporary deficiencies in vitamins and minerals that are important to your developing baby. Ask your health-care provider about a good eating plan before getting pregnant, and make necessary changes before pregnancy.

Exercising Before Pregnancy

I don't really like to work out. Is exercise that important?

Exercise is good for you, whether or not you are pregnant. Develop a good exercise program before getting pregnant to help you feel better, control weight and increase stamina. Exercise can also help make labor and delivery easier.

How can I find and maintain a good exercise program?

Find exercise you enjoy and can do in any type of weather. A great deal of information on various types of exercise programs is available from your local hospital, your health-care provider and health clubs. The American College of Obstetricians and Gynecologists (ACOG) has tapes available on exercise during and after pregnancy. Ask your health-care provider for information on ordering them.

I love to exercise but have been warned about doing too much. How can I know if I am overdoing it?

Some general guidelines for exercise before and during pregnancy include:

- ✧ Before starting a new program, consult your health-care provider about past medical problems and past pregnancy complications.
- ✧ Start exercising before you get pregnant.
- ✧ Exercise on a regular basis.
- ✧ Start gradually, and increase as you build strength.
- ✧ Wear comfortable clothing.
- ✧ Avoid contact sports or risky exercise, such as water skiing or horseback riding.

✧ Allow plenty of time for warming up and cooling down.

✧ Check your pulse every 10 to 15 minutes during exercise.

✧ Don't let your pulse exceed 140 beats a minute.

✧ Once you're pregnant, be careful changing positions.

✧ After the fourth month of pregnancy, don't lie flat on your back when exercising. This decreases blood flow to your baby.

✧ Stop exercising and consult your doctor if you have any bleeding, loss of fluid from the vagina, shortness of breath, dizziness, severe abdominal pain or other serious problems.

Substance Use

My friend just found out that she is 8 weeks pregnant. She uses cocaine once or twice a week but says she'll stop now that she's pregnant. Is this bad for the baby?

Any kind of substance abuse or drug abuse can be harmful during pregnancy. A woman should attempt to get these problems under control before stopping birth control or trying to conceive. A health-care provider can help a woman find assistance. (Doctors who deal with these problems are called *addictionologists*.) It is extremely important to stop using cocaine before conceiving. Research has shown that damage to the baby can occur as early as 3 days after conception!

I've tried to stop smoking, but I don't know if I can. Can cigarette smoking harm a growing baby?

We know definitely that smoking affects pregnancy and development of the fetus. Low birth weight and a slow growth rate are problems in babies born to mothers who smoke. For your health and the health of your baby it's essential to stop smoking before you consider pregnancy.

My friend told me she stopped drinking before she got pregnant, but I don't drink very much. I don't have to stop, do I?

In the past, we believed a little alcohol was OK during pregnancy, but times have changed. Most physicians and other health-care providers believe it's best to abstain completely from alcohol during pregnancy. Every time you take a drink, your baby does too! It is wise to stop using alcohol from the time you are preparing to conceive until after your baby is born.

There really aren't very many side effects from marijuana; I always feel relaxed when I smoke it. Is it bad for the baby?

It can be a dangerous drug during pregnancy. Marijuana crosses the placenta and enters the baby's system. We know it can cause attention deficits, impaired decision making and memory problems in childhood years if a fetus is exposed before birth.

Working Before Pregnancy

At work I am exposed to an X-ray machine and chemicals every day. Will this be problem when I am pregnant?

Get answers to these questions *before* you get pregnant. Many workplace exposures, such as X-rays and chemicals, could be harmful. If you wait to ask these questions until after you find out you're pregnant, you have already exposed your developing fetus to various dangers during some of the most important weeks of development.

My job requires me to stand for a 10-hour shift; I'm used to it. Will this be a problem when I'm pregnant?

Studies have shown that women who stand for a long time each day have smaller babies. If you have had premature deliveries or an incompetent cervix in the past, discuss the situation with your health-care provider.

I pay for health-care coverage out of my check at work. Will this cover me when I get pregnant in a few months?

Not all insurance plans include maternity coverage. Some have a waiting period to pay for surgery or having a baby. Some may not cover your doctor or the hospital you want to go to. Find out about these things before trying to get pregnant. Having a baby costs a lot of money; find out ahead of time what your coverage is rather than after you are already pregnant. Planning ahead may save you some money and save you the trouble of changing doctors or hospitals.

Sexually Transmitted Diseases

In the last 2 years, I've had a chlamydia infection four times. Can this cause problems when I want to get pregnant in a few months?

Sexually transmitted diseases (STDs) can damage your uterus or Fallopian tubes, making it more difficult to get pregnant. If you get an STD while you're pregnant, it could affect your pregnancy.

How can I protect myself from STDs?

Having your partner use condoms is a good way to protect yourself against STDs, especially if you have more than one sexual partner.

What are some other sexually transmitted diseases?

Other STDs include gonorrhea, genital herpes, genital warts (condyloma), syphilis and HIV (the virus that causes AIDS). Use a condom before trying to get pregnant if you have a problem with infections or are exposed to infections frequently, even if you use other forms of birth control. If you get an infection, get it cleared up before you try to get pregnant.

❖2❖

Your Health &
Medical Concerns

I think I'm pregnant, but I'm not sure I know all the signs and symptoms of pregnancy. Can you tell me what to look for?

The first sign that you are pregnant will probably be a missed menstrual period. As your pregnancy progresses, you may exprience:

- ❖ nausea, with or without vomiting
- ❖ fatigue
- ❖ breast changes and breast tenderness
- ❖ frequent urination

If I am pregnant, is it true that my health can affect the health of my growing baby?

Yes. Good nutrition, proper exercise, sufficient rest and attention to how you take care of yourself all have an impact on your pregnancy. Your health care can also have an effect on your pregnancy and how well you tolerate being pregnant.

Someone said I should be in good health before I get pregnant. Why?

If you are in good health before you get pregnant, you'll feel more secure about your growing baby. You'll know that you've done your best to ensure a healthy baby.

When should I see my doctor?

It's best to see him or her before you become pregnant. Routine exams will tell you that you are healthy and any problems are under control. If there are medical problems, they can be dealt with before your pregnancy begins.

What is Prenatal Care?

What is "prenatal care," and why do I need it?

Prenatal means *before birth,* and *prenatal care* is the care you receive for your entire pregnancy. You need this special care to help you discover any problems before they become serious. Health-care providers are specially trained to deal with pregnancy and can answer your questions and deal with your concerns during this important time.

How does the care I receive affect my pregnancy?

You want to feel confident the care you receive is the best you can find. If you have confidence in your health-care provider, you will be able to relax and enjoy your pregnancy. It really is a special time in a woman's life, and an enjoyable one. You want to do everything possible to make it the best 9 months for your growing baby.

What can I expect on my first prenatal visit?

Your first prenatal visit to your health-care provider may be your longest. You will be asked a lot of questions, and you will undergo a physical exam. Lab tests may be ordered.

What kind of questions will I be asked?

You will be asked for a complete medical history, including information about your periods, recent birth-control methods and previous pregnancies. Tell your health-care provider about any miscarriages or abortions. Be sure to include information about hospital stays or surgery you have had.

What other things will my doctor want to know?

Your doctor needs to know about any medications you take or any medications you are allergic to. Your family's past medical history may be important, such as the occurrence of diabetes or other chronic illnesses. Be sure to tell him or her about any chronic medical problems you have. If you have medical records, bring them with you.

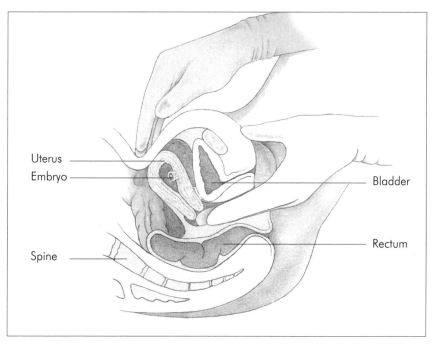

Uterus
Embryo
Bladder
Rectum
Spine

A pelvic exam is a necessary part of your gynecological and obstetrical care.

I hate having a pelvic exam. Will I need one?

Yes, you probably will. A pelvic exam is important because it helps your health-care provider determine if your uterus is the appropriate size for how far along you are in pregnancy. A Pap smear will also be done, if it hasn't been done in the last year.

How often will I have to go to the doctor?

In most cases, you will go every four weeks for the first seven months, then every two weeks until the last month, then once a week. If problems arise, more-frequent visits may be necessary.

What kind of lab tests will I need to have done?

Your health-care provider will probably order several tests during the first or second visit. These may include:

- a complete blood count (CBC)
- urinalysis and urine culture
- Pap smear (for cancer)
- cervical cultures, as indicated
- blood-sugar test (for diabetes)
- rubella titers (for immunity against rubella)
- blood typing
- Rh-factor
- test for syphilis
- test for hepatitis antibodies
- alphafetoprotein test (for possible problems in baby)

Choosing Your Health-Care Provider

I have a friend who says I need to go to a special kind of doctor for prenatal care and delivery of my baby.
Is this true?

You have many choices when it comes to choosing your health-care provider for your pregnancy. You can choose an obstetrician, a family practitioner or a certified nurse-midwife to oversee your prenatal care.

What is an obstetrician?

An *obstetrician* is a medical doctor or an osteopathic physician who specializes in the care of pregnant women, including delivering babies. He or she has completed further training in obstetrics and gynecology after medical school.

What is a family practitioner?

A *family practitioner* is sometimes called a *general practitioner* and often provides care for the entire family. Many family practitioners deliver babies and are very experienced at it. In some cases, an obstetrician may not be available in a community because it is small or remote. In these cases, a family practitioner often delivers babies. If problems arise, your family practitioner may refer you to an obstetrician for prenatal care.

What is a certified nurse-midwife?

A *certified nurse-midwife* is a trained professional who often cares for women who have low-risk, uncomplicated pregnancies. These professionals are registered nurses who have sought additional professional training and certification in nurse-midwifery. They are supervised by a physician and call him or her if complications occur.

What is a "perinatologist"?

A *perinatologist* is an obstetrician who specializes in high-risk pregnancies. Only about 10% of all pregnant women need to see a perinatologist. If you have serious problems during pregnancy, you may be referred to a perinatologist. Or, you may need to see one if you experienced problems with past pregnancies.

If I see a perinatologist, will my doctor still deliver the baby?

This depends on the problem; it may still be possible for you to deliver with your doctor. If you are seeing a perinatologist, you may have to deliver your baby at a hospital other than the one you had chosen. Usually this is because of specialized facilities or the availability of specialized tests for you or your baby.

How can I find the best care giver for me?

If you have an obstetrician you like, you may not have to look any further. If you don't have one, call your local medical society, and ask for a referral. Ask friends who have recently had a baby about their health-care provider. Ask the opinion of a labor-delivery nurse. Sometimes another doctor, such as a pediatrician or internist, can refer you to an obstetrician. Ask your local librarian for publications that list physicians in your area.

Whom can I turn to to talk about my fears and to answer my questions while I'm pregnant?

It's important to establish communication with your health-care provider so you can ask him or her *anything* about your condition. It's good to read articles and books, such as this one and my other book, *Your Pregnancy Week by Week*. They help you prepare questions to ask your health-care provider.

Blood tests will be done to ensure that you and your baby are healthy.

But *never* substitute any information you receive from other sources in place of asking particular questions about your personal pregnancy. Your health-care provider knows you, your history and what has occurred during this pregnancy. *Always* discuss your concerns with him or her!

I feel embarrassed asking some of the questions I have. They seem silly or stupid.

Don't be afraid to ask your health-care provider any question. He or she has probably already heard it, so don't be embarrassed. It's possible a situation is unwise or risky for you, so be sure to check even the smallest details. It's better to take time to get answers to all your questions than to wait until a problem develops.

Dealing with "Morning Sickness"

***I'm nauseated every morning but don't throw up. My friend
had the same thing but had to go to the hospital for I.V.s. Is
this "morning sickness"?***

An early symptom of pregnancy for many women is nausea,
with or without vomiting; it is often called *morning sickness*. A
condition called *hyperemesis gravidarum* results when a
woman experiences a great deal of vomiting and the inability
to eat foods or to drink fluids. If a woman has this problem,
she may need to be treated in the hospital with I.V.s (intravenous feeding) and medicines for nausea.

***I feel so nauseous in the morning that I can't eat anything.
Does this last throughout pregnancy?***

Nausea is typically the worst during the beginning of pregnancy; most often it is bad in the morning and improves during
the day. Morning sickness usually begins around week 6 and
lasts until week 12 or 13, when it lessens and disappears.

What can I do about nausea?

Many things have been suggested to help you deal with the nausea and vomiting related to morning sickness. Try these suggestions, and use what works for you.

- ✧ Spread meals throughout the day so you eat several small snacks instead of one large meal.
- ✧ Eat a snack before you get up, such as crackers or rice cakes. Or ask your partner to make you some dry toast.
- ✧ Avoid heavy, fatty foods.
- ✧ Keep up your intake of fluids—they may be easier to handle than solids, and you want to avoid dehydration.
- ✧ Alternate wet foods with dry foods. Eat only dry foods at one meal, then liquids at the next.
- ✧ Try ginger—it's a natural remedy for nausea. Grate it on vegetables and other foods.
- ✧ Suck on a cut, fresh lemon when you feel nauseous.
- ✧ Avoid things that trigger your nausea, such as odors, movement or noise.
- ✧ Get enough rest.
- ✧ Avoid getting sweaty or overheated, which can contribute to your nausea.

I have nausea and vomiting, but it's only at night. Is this the same thing as morning sickness?

Nausea and vomiting with pregnancy can occur at any time of the day or night; sometimes it lasts all day long. It often begins to lessen after a few weeks and usually disappears around the end of the first trimester.

My sister had to go into the hospital when she had morning sickness. Why?

If a woman gets dehydrated or loses a substantial amount of weight with morning sickness, she may have to be put in the hospital where she can be fed intravenously. Usually it only takes a couple of days in the hospital until the woman can resume eating solids. The main purpose in putting her in the hospital is to keep her fluid intake up and to give her the nourishment she needs through I.V. feedings.

One of my friends told me her dentist warned her to take care of her teeth if she had morning sickness. How were her teeth affected?

When nausea is accompanied by vomiting, the contents of the stomach that enter the mouth can cause a breakdown in tooth enamel. Brush your teeth after vomiting to remove any residue from the vomit.

This may sound weird, but I've heard that a man can suffer from morning sickness when his wife is pregnant. Is this true?

Many fathers-to-be experience some sort of physical problem during their wife's pregnancy. The condition is called *couvade*, from a Carib Indian tribe in which every expectant father engages in rituals that enable him to understand what his wife is experiencing. In our culture, a father-to-be may experience nausea, headache, back and muscle aches, insomnia, fatigue or depression.

How Your Health Affects Your Growing Baby

How does my health affect my growing baby?

Your baby is totally dependent on you for all of its needs. To make sure he or she gets the best possible start in life, it's important for you to eat right, get enough rest and stay as healthy as possible throughout your pregnancy.

I've heard that some infections and illnesses I have can affect the development of my baby. Is that true?

Yes. Some infections and illnesses you experience may affect your growing baby. That is why it is important to remind your doctor that you are pregnant when you call him or her about any medical problems. See the chart on page 40, which lists some of the more common ones, with the effects each illness can have on a developing fetus.

If I have a fever, especially a high one, can it hurt my baby?

Yes, it may. Your baby relies on you for its temperature control. A *prolonged* high fever, especially in the first trimester (first 13 weeks), can affect a developing fetus.

Is there anything I can do, which won't harm the baby, to bring down a high fever?

Drink lots of liquids, take acetaminophen (Tylenol®) and dress appropriately to help you cool down. If your physician prescribes medication for a cold, bladder infection or other illness, take it as prescribed.

I recently read that hepatitis is becoming more serious for pregnant women. What do I need to be aware of?

Hepatitis is a viral infection of the liver and is one of the most serious infections that can occur during pregnancy. Your doctor will probably test you for hepatitis B at the beginning of your pregnancy.

How is hepatitis B transmitted?

Hepatitis B is spread from one person to another by the reuse of intravenous needles and by sexual contact. It is responsible for nearly 50% of the cases of hepatitis in the U.S. This type of hepatitis can be transmitted to a developing fetus.

Are there other types of hepatitis?

Yes. They are named for the viruses that cause them. *Hepatitis A* is usually transmitted by person-to-person contact via poor sanitation or poor hygiene. It is responsible for over 30% of the reported hepatitis cases in the United States.

Hepatitis C, also called *non-A, non-B hepatitis*, is responsible for about 10% of the hepatitis cases in the United States. You can become infected with this type of hepatitis through multiple blood transfusions or the use of intravenous drugs.

What are the symptoms of hepatitis?

Symptoms include flulike symptoms, nausea and pain in the area of the liver or upper-right abdomen. The person may appear yellow or jaundiced, and urine may be darker than normal.

How can hepatitis affect a developing baby?

Hepatitis is a viral infection that affects the liver. A developing baby that gets hepatitis is at serious risk for liver damage or stillbirth.

What can be done about this problem?

If a baby is born to a mother who tests positive for hepatitis at the beginning of pregnancy, it may be necessary to give the baby immune globulin against hepatitis after it is born. It is now recommended that all newborns receive hepatitis vaccine shortly after birth. Ask your pediatrician if the vaccine is available in your area.

I read that Group-B streptococcus infection in a mother-to-be can cause lots of problems for her baby. What are some of them?

Group-B streptococcus (GBS) rarely causes problems in adults but can cause life-threatening infections in newborns, including pneumonia, meningitis, lung damage, kidney damage, loss of sight, hearing loss, cerebral palsy and developmental problems.

How do I get GBS?

GBS is often found in the mouth or lower-digestive, urinary or reproductive organs. In women, GBS is most often found in the vagina or rectum. You get GBS when your immunity or resistance is down. It is possible to "carry" GBS in your system and not be sick or have any symptoms.

What are the symptoms of GBS?

There may not be any symptoms. Sometimes a woman will have a vaginal discharge.

Can it be treated?

Yes, GBS is treated with antibiotics.

Will I know I have GBS?

We do not have an ideal screening test for vaginal GBS. If you become high risk for developing GBS during labor, your doctor will test you at that time and give you antibiotics to help prevent transmission of the GBS bacteria from you to your baby.

Why would I become high risk?

Your risk increases with premature labor, premature rupture of membranes or a previous GBS infection.

Lyme disease is prevalent in our area. Is it dangerous for my baby if I get Lyme disease during my pregnancy?

Lyme disease is an infection caused by a spirochete (bacteria) carried and transmitted to humans by ticks. We know the spirochetes that cause Lyme disease do cross the placenta.

Complications from this infection include preterm labor, fetal death or a rashlike illness in the newborn.

What are the symptoms of Lyme disease?

There are several stages of the disease. In most people, a skin lesion with a distinctive look, called a *bull's eye,* appears at the site of the bite. Flulike symptoms appear, and after 4 to 6 weeks there may be signs of heart problems or neurologic problems. Arthritis may be a problem later.

If I do get Lyme disease, how it is treated?

Treatment for Lyme disease includes long-term antibiotic therapy. Many medications used to treat Lyme disease are safe for use during pregnancy.

How can I avoid exposure to Lyme disease?

Stay out of areas that are known to have ticks, such as heavily wooded areas. If you can't avoid them, wear long-sleeved shirts, long pants, socks and boots or closed shoes. Check your hair for ticks; they often attach themselves to the hair or the scalp.

What is lupus?

Lupus (*systemic lupus erythematosus* or *SLE*) is a disease of unknown cause that affects women more often than men (about 9 to 1). Women with lupus have a large number of antibodies in their bloodstream that are directed toward the women's own tissues. This can affect various parts of the body including the joints, skin, kidneys, muscles, lungs, brain and central nervous system.

Why is lupus a concern in pregnancy?

Lupus occurs most often in young or middle-aged women who may become pregnant. Miscarriage, premature delivery and complications around the time of delivery are increased in women with lupus.

What are the symptoms of lupus?

The most common symptom is joint pain. Other symptoms include rashes or sores on the skin, fever, kidney problems and hypertension.

How is lupus treated?

The drug of choice to treat lupus is steroids; the most commonly prescribed steroid is *prednisone*. Many studies on the safety of prednisone during pregnancy have found it to be safe.

I've heard a lot lately about toxic streptococcus A, the "flesh-eating" bacteria. What is it?

Toxic streptococcus A can cause severe damage to anyone who suffers from it. It is a bacterial infection that usually starts in a cut on the skin, not as a sore throat. It spreads very quickly and can soon involve the entire body.

How does it get into my system?

The strep A bacteria can get in through a very small scratch, scrape or cut in the skin. The skin then turns red and becomes swollen, painful and infected very quickly.

What are the symptoms of toxic streptococcus A?
   ✧ fever above 102F (39C)
   ✧ an inflamed cut or scratch
   ✧ flulike symptoms
   ✧ unusually cold extremities (feet, hands, legs and arms)

Is there anything I can do to prevent toxic strep A?

Yes. Any time you cut or scratch yourself, clean the affected area with soap and water, alcohol or hydrogen peroxide. All are safe to use during pregnancy. After careful washing, apply triple antibiotic cream or ointment (available over the counter) to the area. Use a light bandage, if necessary. Keep the area clean, and reapply antibiotic ointment as needed. These same measures can and should be used with every member of your family.

I've been having some diarrhea lately. Should I be concerned?

It's possible to have diarrhea during pregnancy, and it can raise many concerns for you. If the diarrhea doesn't go away in 24 hours, or if it keeps returning, contact your health-care provider. He or she may decide to have you take a medication for the problem. Do not take any medication for diarrhea without discussing it with your health-care provider first.

Is there anything I can do myself if I have diarrhea?

One of the best things you can do is increase your fluid intake. Drink a lot of water, juice and other clear fluids, such as broth. (Avoid apple juice, though, because it can act as a laxative.) You may feel better eating a bland diet, without solid foods, until you feel better.

Is it dangerous for my baby if I don't eat solids?

No, it isn't harmful for a few days if you keep up your fluid intake. Solid foods may actually cause you more gastrointestinal distress. Avoid milk products while you have diarrhea; they can make it worse.

My vet told me to be careful about caring for my cat. What does caring for my cat have to do with my pregnancy?

If you have a cat, you may be exposed to *toxoplasma gondii*, a protozoa which causes *toxoplasmosis*. It is a disease that is spread by contact with infected cat feces or by eating raw, infected meat. You can pick up protozoa from an infected cat's litter box, from counters and other surfaces the cat walks on or from the cat itself when you pet it.

What problems can toxoplasmosis cause me or my baby?

Infection during pregnancy can lead to miscarriage or an infected infant at birth. Usually an infection in the mother has no symptoms.

How can I protect myself from toxoplasmosis?

A pregnant woman should avoid exposure to cat feces. Get someone else to change the kitty litter. Keep cats off counters and other areas where you could pick up the protozoa. Wash your hands thoroughly after contact with your cat or contact with raw meat. Keep counters clean, and cook meat thoroughly. Hygienic measures prevent transmission of the protozoa.

I've heard about cytomegalovirus. What is it?

Cytomegalovirus (CMV) is a member of the herpes-virus family. It is transmitted in humans by contact with saliva or urine. Day-care centers are a common source of the infection. CMV can also be passed by sexual contact.

How can cytomegalovirus affect me?

Most infections do not cause any symptoms. When symptoms do occur, they include a fever, sore throat and joint pain.

How can cytomegalovirus affect my growing baby?

In an infant, CMV can cause low birth weight, microcephaly, calcification inside the skull, eye problems, mental retardation, motor retardation, jaundice, enlarged liver, enlarged spleen and anemia.

I've heard about a pregnant woman getting rubella. What is it exactly?

Rubella, also called *German measles,* is a viral infection that causes few problems in the non-pregnant woman. It is more serious during pregnancy, especially in the first trimester.

What are the symptoms of rubella?

The most common symptom of rubella is a skin rash. You may also experience flulike symptoms.

How can rubella affect my growing baby?

Rubella infection during pregnancy can increase the rate of miscarriage and cause malformations in the baby, especially heart defects.

I've been exposed to chicken pox. Can they hurt me or my baby?

If you have had chicken pox before, it shouldn't be a problem for either of you. If you haven't had chicken pox, this can be a problem. Exposure during the first trimester can result in birth defects, such as heart problems. Exposure close to delivery (within 1 week) can result in chicken pox in the baby.

How can chicken pox affect me?

Adults don't tolerate chicken pox as well as children. Contraction of the disease can result in serious symptoms, including painful lesions, high fever and severe flulike symptoms.

I'm not sure if I've had chicken pox before. What can I do?

Avoid exposure to the disease, if you possibly can.

I just read about varicella. What is it exactly?

Varicella (sometimes called *varicella-zoster*) is a member of the herpes-virus family, which is the same family as chicken pox. Varicella may remain latent for years, only to be reactivated later as herpes zoster or shingles.

How can varicella affect me?

If you get shingles while you are pregnant, it can be a serious illness, with severe pain and even breathing problems. Fortunately, it is rare.

What are the symptoms of varicella?

Pain is the main symptom of varicella (shingles); this may be accompanied by a rash or lesions.

How can varicella affect my growing baby?

It may cause birth defects. If you are exposed within two weeks of delivery the baby may catch the disease.

Environmental Poisons & Pollutants

I've heard environmental poisons can be dangerous to a pregnant woman. What are they?

Environmental poisons and pollutants that can harm a developing fetus include lead, mercury, PCBs and pesticides.

How can lead harm a developing baby?

Exposure to lead can cause an increase in the chance of miscarriage. Lead is readily transported across the placenta to the baby. Poisoning occurs as early as the twelfth week of pregnancy.

Possible Prenatal Effects of Mother's Illness

Illness in Mother	*Possible Effect on Fetus*
Chicken pox	Heart problems
Cytomegalovirus	Microcephaly, brain damage, hearing loss
Group-B streptococcus	Pneumonia, meningitis, cerebral palsy, damage to lungs or kidneys
Hepatitis	Liver damage, death
Lupus	Miscarriage, premature delivery
Lyme disease	Preterm labor, fetal death, rash in newborn
Rubella (German measles)	Cataracts, deafness, heart lesions; can involve all organs
Syphilis	Skin defects, fetal death
Toxoplasmosis	Possible effects on all organs
Varicella	Possible effects on all organs

How could I be exposed to lead?

Lead exposure may come from many sources, including some gasoline, water pipes, solders, storage batteries, some construction materials, paints, dyes and wood preservatives. You may also be exposed in your workplace; find out if there is a risk.

How can mercury harm a developing baby?

Reports of mercury exposure have been linked to cerebral palsy and microcephaly.

How could I be exposed to mercury?

Exposure usually occurs from contaminated fish. There was also a report of contamination of grain with mercury.

How can PCBs (polychlorinated biphenyls) harm a developing baby?

PCBs are not single compounds but mixtures of several compounds. Most fish, birds and humans have small, measurable amounts of PCBs in their tissues. PCBs have been blamed in miscarriage and fetal-growth retardation.

How could I be exposed to PCBs?

We are exposed to PCBs through some of the foods we eat, such as fish.

How can pesticides harm a developing baby?

Pesticides have been held responsible for an increase in miscarriage and fetal-growth retardation.

How could I be exposed to pesticides?

Pesticides include a large number of agents used to control unwanted plants and animals. Human exposure is common because of the extensive use of pesticides. Those of most concern include DDT, chlordane, heptachlor and lindane.

How can I protect myself against these agents?

The safest course is to avoid exposure, whether by oral ingestion or through the air you breathe. Thoroughly wash all fruits and vegetables before eating. It may not be possible to eliminate all contact. If you know you will be around certain chemicals, be sure to wash your hands thoroughly after exposure.

Discomforts of Pregnancy

I've had a lot of problems with heartburn during my pregnancy. What causes it?

Discomfort from heartburn is one of the most common complaints during pregnancy. It may begin early in pregnancy, although it generally becomes more severe as pregnancy progresses. Heartburn is caused by reflux (regurgitation) of stomach contents into the esophagus.

I don't usually have heartburn when I'm not pregnant. Why does it occur so much during pregnancy?

It occurs more frequently during pregnancy because of two factors—decreased gastrointestinal function or movement (motility) and compression of the stomach by the uterus as it grows larger and moves up into the abdomen.

Is there anything I can do about heartburn?

Antacids may provide considerable relief. Follow the directions relating to pregnancy on the package or your health-care provider's instructions. Don't overdo it and take too much in an effort to find relief. You can use some antacids, such as Amphojel®, Gelusil®, milk of magnesia and Maalox®, without much concern. Avoid sodium bicarbonate because of the possibility it may cause you to retain water. In addition to antacids, the following tips may provide some relief.

 ❖ Eat smaller, more-frequent meals.
 ❖ Avoid eating before bedtime.
 ❖ When lying down, elevate your head and shoulders.

Can the foods I eat affect my heartburn?

Some foods can affect your heartburn. Try to find foods (and amounts) that don't give you heartburn. Eliminate foods that cause you problems. Add foods that benefit you and your growing baby.

What's the difference between heartburn and indigestion?

Indigestion refers to the inability to digest food or difficulty digesting food. *Heartburn* is a burning discomfort related to the lower end of the esophagus and is felt behind the lower part of the sternum (breastbone).

If I have indigestion, is there anything I can do about it?

Eat foods that "agree" with you; avoid spicy foods. Eat small meals frequently. If you need them, take antacids after meals, but don't overmedicate yourself with them.

I've never had hemorrhoids before, and now I do. Why?

Hemorrhoids are very common during pregnancy. They are caused by the increased, congested blood flow in the pelvis because of the increased weight and size of the uterus.

What exactly are hemorrhoids?

They are dilated blood vessels around the area of the anus or up inside the anus. They can itch, bleed and be painful.

What can I do about hemorrhoids?

Eat adequate amounts of fiber, and drink lots of fluid. Sitz baths help, and suppository medications, available without a prescription, can provide relief. You may need stool softeners. Apply ice packs or cotton balls soaked in witch hazel to the affected area. Discuss it with your health-care provider if hemorrhoids become a major problem for you.

I have headaches but don't want to take any medication I don't have to during pregnancy. What can I do about them?

It's a good idea to try to deal with your problem without medication. There are several things you can try that are medicine-free.

- ✧ Use deep-breathing exercises and relaxation techniques to help you relax.
- ✧ Close your eyes and rest in a quiet place.
- ✧ Eat regularly. Avoid foods or substances, such as caffeine, that might cause a headache.
- ✧ Apply an ice pack to the back of your head.
- ✧ Get enough sleep.

If my headaches won't go away using these techniques, is there any medicine I can take?

Acetaminophen (Tylenol) is recommended for headaches. You can take the regular or extra-strength version. If this doesn't help, call your health-care provider.

I suffer from migraine headaches. What can I do about them during pregnancy?

Migraine headaches during pregnancy are not unusual. Try the techniques described above. If they don't help, discuss the problem with your physician. Do *not* take any medications for a migraine headache without discussing it with your physician first.

I have problems with allergies. Will they cause me problems during pregnancy?

Your allergies may change with your pregnancy. Sometimes they get worse, or they may actually improve.

What can I do for my allergies while I'm pregnant?

Drink plenty of fluid, especially during hot weather. If there are foods you're sensitive to, be more careful what you eat. This also applies to other things you might be sensitive to, such as animals or cigarette smoke.

Can I take my regular allergy medications while I'm pregnant?

Ask your doctor or pharmacist before taking any medication; don't assume it's OK. Ask about the medication, whether it's a prescription or over-the-counter (OTC) medication. It's safer and easier to ask ahead of time rather than take a chance with a medication.

My nose has been stuffed up ever since I got pregnant. Is this normal?

Some women complain of nasal stuffiness or nosebleeds during pregnancy. We believe these occur because of circulation changes caused by hormonal changes in pregnancy that can cause mucous membranes of the nose and nasal passages to swell and to bleed more easily.

What can I do about my stuffed-up nose?

Do *not* use decongestants or nasal sprays to relieve stuffiness. Many are combinations of several medications that should not be used during pregnancy. Try a humidifier to relieve stuffiness. Increase your fluid intake, and use a gentle lubricant, such as petroleum jelly. Discuss it with your health-care provider if these remedies don't provide relief.

Special Concerns of Pregnancy

My mother told me to discuss my Rh-factor with my health-care provider. Why?

You may be Rh-negative, which requires some additional attention during pregnancy and after your baby is born.

What does it mean to be "Rh-negative"?

Your blood type, such as O, A, B, AB, contains a factor that determines if it is positive or negative. In the past, Rh-negative women who carried an Rh-positive child faced complicated pregnancies that could result in a very sick child. Today, most of these problems can be prevented. If you are Rh-negative, you need to know it.

Why is being Rh-negative a problem?

If you are Rh-negative and your baby is Rh-positive, if you have had a blood transfusion or if you received blood products of some kind, you could become Rh-sensitized or isoimmunized. This could affect the baby.

What does it mean to be "isoimmunized"?

If you are *isoimmunized*, you have antibodies that circulate inside your system. They won't harm you, but they can attack the blood of an Rh-positive fetus. Antibodies from you can cross the placenta and attack your baby's blood. This can make your baby anemic while it is still inside the uterus and can be very serious.

How does a woman become sensitized?

An Rh-negative woman becomes sensitized when Rh-positive blood gets into her bloodstream. This can happen with a blood transfusion with Rh-positive blood, the birth of an Rh-positive baby, a miscarriage or an ectopic pregnancy.

What can I do about this problem?

Many problems can be prevented with the use of RhoGAM®, which is Rh-immune globulin. If you are Rh-negative and pregnant, an injection of RhoGAM is given at 28 weeks of pregnancy to prevent sensitization before delivery.

When is it used after the birth?

Within 72 hours after delivery, you will be given a second injection of RhoGAM if your baby is Rh-positive.

Not all babies are Rh-positive, are they?

No. Some women who are Rh-negative carry a child who is also Rh-negative. In this case, no RhoGAM injection is given after delivery.

Are there other situations in which RhoGAM is used?

Yes. If you have an ectopic pregnancy and are Rh-negative, you should receive RhoGAM. This also applies to miscarriages and abortions. If you are Rh-negative and have amniocentesis, you will also receive RhoGAM.

A woman I met at my doctor's office told me she had an "incompetent cervix" with her last pregnancy. What is that?

An *incompetent cervix* is a condition in which a woman has painless dilatation (stretching) of the cervix that occurs prematurely. It is usually unnoticed by the woman. Membranes may rupture without any warning, and it usually results in premature delivery of the baby.

How will I know if this is happening to me?

The problem is not usually diagnosed until *after* one or more deliveries of a premature infant without any pain before delivery. If it's your first pregnancy, there is no way for you to know if you have an incompetent cervix.

What causes an incompetent cervix?

Some researchers believe it occurs because of previous trauma to the cervix, such as a D&C (dilatation and curettage) for an abortion or a miscarriage. It may also occur if surgery has been performed on the cervix.

If this problem occurs, is there any treatment for it?

Treatment is usually surgical. A weak cervix can be reinforced by sewing the cervix shut. When the woman goes into labor, the suture is opened and the baby can be born normally.

At my last appointment my doctor said my blood pressure was up. Should I be concerned?

It is normal for your blood pressure to change a little during pregnancy. It often decreases a little during the second trimester of pregnancy and increases toward the end of pregnancy.

What can I do about high blood pressure if it becomes a problem?

Resting in bed on your side can help. If your blood pressure is still too high, medications may be necessary to lower it.

I'm dizzy a lot. Should I worry?

Feeling dizzy while you're pregnant is a fairly common symptom. Anemia can cause dizziness any time during pregnancy and can be checked with a blood count. Another cause of dizziness is *hypotension* (low blood pressure). Hypotension in pregnancy usually occurs during the second trimester.

What causes hypotension in pregnancy?

There are two causes of hypotension during pregnancy. It can be caused by the enlarging uterus putting pressure on large blood vessels, such as your aorta and vena cava. This is called *supine hypotension* and may happen when you lie down.

It can be alleviated or prevented by not sleeping or lying on your back.

The second cause of hypotension is rising rapidly from a sitting, kneeling or squatting position; this is called *postural hypotension*. When you rise rapidly, gravity causes blood to leave your brain, which may result in a drop in blood pressure. This is avoided by rising slowly from a sitting or lying position.

Can problems with my blood sugar cause dizziness?

Yes. Pregnancy affects your blood sugar; either high blood sugar (*hyperglycemia*) or low blood sugar (*hypoglycemia*) can make you feel dizzy or faint. Many doctors routinely test pregnant women for problems with blood sugar.

If I have a problem with blood sugar, what can I do?

The problem can be avoided or improved by eating a balanced diet, not skipping meals and not going a long time without eating. If it is more serious, you may need to see a dietician. If blood tests show diabetes, see an internist.

My sister had pregnancy-induced hypertension. What is it?

Pregnancy-induced hypertension is high blood pressure that occurs only during pregnancy. It will disappear after the baby is born. It develops in about 3% of women under age 40, and in 10% of women over 40.

What can be done about pregnancy-induced hypertension?

It is treated with bed rest, drinking lots of fluid and avoiding salt and foods containing large amounts of sodium. Medications to lower blood pressure may be prescribed. For further information, see the discussion of *pre-eclampsia* in Chapter 15.

What is the difference between a urinary-tract infection (UTI) and a bladder infection?

UTI refers to an infection anywhere in the urinary tract, including the bladder, the urethra, the ureters and the kidneys. A *bladder infection* refers to an infection in the bladder only. The terms are often used interchangeably.

Why do I get more bladder infections now that I'm pregnant?

This happens because of changes in your urinary tract. The uterus sits directly on top of the bladder and on the tubes leading from the kidneys to the bladder, called *ureters*. As the uterus grows, its increased weight can block the drainage of urine from the bladder and cause an increase in bladder infections. From 5 to 10% of pregnant women will experience bladder infections.

How does my doctor check for bladder infections?

Usually your doctor will do a urinalysis and a urine culture at your first visit. He or she may may also check your urine for infections on subsequent visits.

What are the symptoms of a bladder infection?

Symptoms of a bladder infection include:
- frequent urination
- burning urination
- feeling as though you need to urinate and nothing will come out
- blood in your urine (with severe infection)

I've heard about a more-serious urinary-tract infection called "pyelonephritis." What is it?

Pyelonephritis is an infection of the urinary tract that also involves the kidneys. It occurs in 1 to 2% of all pregnant women.

What are the symptoms of pyelonephritis?

Symptoms of pyelonephritis include:

- ✧ frequent urination
- ✧ burning urination
- ✧ feeling as though you need to urinate and nothing will come out
- ✧ high fever
- ✧ chills
- ✧ back pain
- ✧ blood in the urine

How is pyelonephritis treated?

Pyelonephritis may require hospitalization and treatment with intravenous antibiotics.

How often do kidney stones occur during pregnancy?

Kidney stones, also called *urinary calculi,* occur about once in every 1500 pregnancies.

What are the symptoms of a kidney stone?

Symptoms usually include severe pain in the back and blood in the urine.

How is a kidney stone diagnosed?

In pregnancy, ultrasound is usually used to diagnose a kidney stone.

How is a kidney stone treated?

A kidney stone in pregnancy can usually be treated with pain medication and by drinking lots of fluid or receiving I.V.s.

I've read about a procedure called "lithotripsy" that is used to treat kidney stones. What is it?

Lithotripsy uses electrically generated shock waves to crush a kidney stone in the bladder or urethra. It is not usually used during pregnancy.

Anemia During Pregnancy

My doctor says I have anemia now that I'm pregnant. What is it?

Anemia is a common medical problem in many pregnant women. The number of red blood cells in your blood is low; the quantity of these cells is inadequate to provide the oxygen needed by your body.

Why does anemia occur so often in pregnancy?

Your blood volume increases by about 50% during pregnancy. Blood is made up of fluid and cells. The fluid usually increases faster than the cells. This may result in a drop in your *hematocrit* (the volume, amount or percent of red cells in the blood). The drop can result in anemia.

Why is it important to treat anemia during pregnancy?

If you suffer from anemia, you won't feel well during pregnancy, and you'll tire more easily. You may also experience dizziness. If you're anemic when you go into labor, you're also at a higher risk of needing a blood transfusion when your baby is born. Pregnancy anemia can cause an increased risk of preterm delivery, growth retardation in the baby and low birth weight. Your health-care provider will tell you if you are anemic and prescribe a course of treatment for you.

What is the most common type of anemia during pregnancy?

The most common type of anemia we see during pregnancy is *iron-deficiency anemia*. While you are pregnant, your baby uses some of your iron stores. With iron-deficiency anemia, your body does not make enough red blood cells to keep up with the increased demand.

What causes iron-deficiency anemia?

Several factors can cause this condition, including:

- ✧ bleeding during pregnancy
- ✧ multiple fetuses (twins, triplets)
- ✧ recent surgery on your stomach or small bowel
- ✧ frequent antacid use
- ✧ poor dietary habits

Is iron-deficiency anemia easy to control?

Yes, it usually is. Iron is contained in most prenatal vitamins. If you can't take a prenatal vitamin, you may be given iron supplementation. Eating certain foods, such as liver or spinach, also helps increase the amount of iron you take in.

I've heard about sickle-cell anemia. What is it?

Sickle-cell anemia occurs when a person's bone marrow makes abnormal red blood cells. It occurs most often in black people or those of mixed-black descent.

How do I know if I have sickle-cell anemia?

Your doctor can perform a blood test to see if you have this disease.

Doesn't sickle-cell anemia also cause pain?

Yes, it can cause pain in the abdomen or limbs of the mother-to-be if she has a *sickle crisis*. This can happen at any time in her lifetime, not just during pregnancy.

Are there any other problems with sickle-cell anemia?

In addition to a painful sickle crisis, the mother-to-be can suffer from more-frequent infections and even congestive heart failure. Risks to the fetus include a higher incidence of miscarriage and stillbirth.

I've heard there's a new treatment for sickle-cell disease that relieves severe pain. Can a pregnant woman take it?

You are probably referring to *hydroxyurea,* which has proved to be the first effective treatment of sickle-cell anemia. It reduces some of the excruciating pain, but its use carries some risk and is not for all sickle-cell sufferers. Because the drug is so new, no one yet knows the long-term effects, so women who are pregnant are advised *not* to use it.

What is thalassemia?

It is a type of anemia that occurs most often in people of Mediterranean descent. The body doesn't produce enough globulin that makes up the red blood cells, so anemia results. If you have a family history of thalassemia, discuss it with your health-care provider.

Your Pre-existing Medical Problems

I have diabetes. How does it affect my pregnancy?

Diabetes was once a very serious medical problem during pregnancy. It continues to be an important complication of pregnancy, but today a woman can go safely through a pregnancy if she has proper medical care, watches her diet and follows her doctor's instructions. Using a glucometer to measure your blood sugar is a good practice.

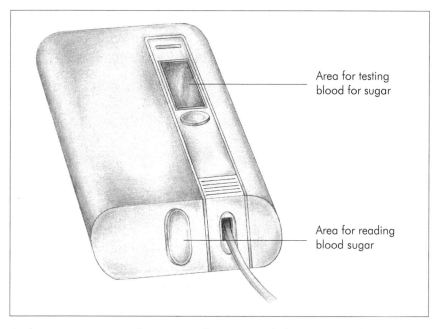

Area for testing
blood for sugar

Area for reading
blood sugar

A glucometer measures the amount of sugar in a diabetic woman's blood. Blood-sugar control is very important during pregnancy if you are diabetic.

What are the symptoms of diabetes?

The symptoms of diabetes include:

✧ an increase in urination
✧ blurred vision
✧ weight loss
✧ dizziness
✧ increased hunger

Why is diabetes serious in pregnancy?

Diabetes can cause several medical problems including kidney problems, eye problems, blood problems and heart problems, such as hardening of the arteries. Any of these can be very serious to you and your baby. If diabetes is not treated, you will expose your baby to a high concentration of sugar. This is called *hyperglycemia* and is not healthy for the baby.

Why is diabetes a problem for the baby?

If you have uncontrolled diabetes, you face a significant increase in the risk of miscarriage and of major abnormalities at the time of birth. The most common fetal problems are heart problems, genitourinary problems and gastrointestinal problems.

How is diabetes diagnosed?

Diabetes is diagnosed with a blood test called a *fasting blood sugar* or *glucose-tolerance test.*

If there is sugar in my urine, does it mean I have diabetes?

No, not necessarily. It is common for normal, pregnant, non-diabetic women to have a small amount of sugar in their urine, called *glucosuria.* This occurs because of changes in your sugar levels and the way sugar is handled in the kidneys during pregnancy.

I have epilepsy, and I just found out I'm pregnant. I'm very excited about the pregnancy, but I'm really concerned about the medicine I take. What should I do?

Call your physician *immediately;* tell him or her you are pregnant and you have epilepsy. Most medications to control seizures can be taken during pregnancy. However, some medications are safer than others.

What medications are OK to use?

During pregnancy, phenobarbital is often used to control seizures. Dilantin® is not good to use to control seizures because it can cause birth defects in a baby. Discuss this important issue with your health-care provider as soon as possible.

I suffer from asthma. Can I have a safe pregnancy even if I have problems with my asthma?

Most women who have asthma can have a safe pregnancy. If you have severe asthma attacks before pregnancy, you may have them during pregnancy. Usually the medications you use before pregnancy can be used while you are pregnant. Discuss medication use with your health-care provider.

Besides taking my medicine, is there anything else I can do for my asthma during pregnancy?

We've found that many women feel better and have fewer problems with their asthma if they increase their fluid intake during pregnancy. Try it—you should increase your fluid intake during pregnancy anyway.

An asthma attack can be frightening, especially during pregnancy. If you suffer from asthma, advise your health-care provider; some asthma medications are safe to use during pregnancy.

A pregnant woman I know just found out she has cancer.
Isn't this uncommon?

You're right; cancer during pregnancy is *not* common. Fortunately, many cancers in women occur after menopause, which lowers the likelihood of cancer in pregnancy. However, cancer does occur occasionally during pregnancy.

I hate to think about cancer during pregnancy. Should I be
concerned about it?

I agree with you—it's not a very pleasant subject to think about or to discuss, and most women do not need to be concerned about it. However, it's better to be aware that these problems do occur than not to know anything about them.

What is the most common type of cancer discovered during
pregnancy?

The most common cancer found is breast cancer. Gynecologic cancers, leukemia, lymphoma, melanoma and bone tumors are also found. (These cancers are listed in the order in which they most often occur.)

Is there any reason these cancers might appear during
pregnancy?

Researchers believe there are a couple of reasons cancers could appear during pregnancy.

  ✧ Some cancers arise from tissues or organs that are influenced by the increase in hormone levels caused by pregnancy.
  ✧ Increased blood flow and changes in the lymphatic system may contribute to the spread of cancer to other parts of the body.

I've heard it's harder to find breast cancer during pregnancy. Why?

Changes in the breasts, including breast tenderness, increased size and even lumpiness, may make it harder to discover this type of cancer. Of all women who have breast cancer, about 2% are pregnant when it is diagnosed.

How is breast cancer treated during pregnancy?

Treatment varies. It could be surgery, chemotherapy, radiation or a combination of treatments.

If a woman has breast cancer, can she breastfeed?

Most doctors recommend a woman not breastfeed if she has breast cancer.

Are treatments for cancer during pregnancy dangerous?

Cancer treatments can cause problems, including miscarriage, fetal death, fetal malformations and fetal growth retardation. The pregnant woman may also experience side effects from the treatment.

I've been having chemotherapy for 6 months and just found out I'm 8 weeks pregnant. What should I do?

It's very important with talk to your doctor immediately! What you will do depends on the medications you are taking.

Other Medical Concerns

I get awful leg cramps at night. What can I do about them?

Leg cramps, especially at night, can be very bothersome. The following may help you deal with leg cramps you experience at any time.

+ Wear support hose during the day.
+ Take warm baths.
+ Have your partner massage your legs at the end of the day or whenever you feel like it.
+ Wear comfortable clothing.
+ Take acetaminophen (Tylenol) for pain.
+ Rest on your side.
+ Use a heating pad for up to 15 minutes when you experience pain.

Can my activities affect my leg cramps?

Yes, they can. Avoid standing for long periods of time. Rest and lie on your side as often as possible. Make sure clothing is not restrictive.

Before pregnancy, I often visited a chiropractor for back pain. Can I go to a chiropractor if I have back pain during pregnancy?

Low-back pain is common during pregnancy—nearly half of all pregnant women suffer from it. If you have severe problems that you believe might be helped by chiropractic manipulation, discuss it with your regular physician *before* you do anything! Whatever you do, avoid X-rays of your pelvic and lower-back area.

I'm almost 36 and about 7 weeks pregnant. Is there anything I should worry about because of my age?

Today, more couples are waiting to start their families, so you're not alone. There are increased risks for the older mother-to-be and her baby, but it's still more likely you and your baby will be OK. The risks include Down's syndrome, high blood pressure, Cesarean delivery, multiple births, pre-eclampsia, placental abruption, bleeding and other complications.

I'm 35 and pregnant with my third child. I'm a lot more tired than I remember being before. What's wrong with me?

Putting it simply, it's harder to be pregnant when you're 35 than it is when you're 25. It doesn't necessarily mean anything is wrong; you just have more demands on your time and more to do.

I'm over 35. What are my chances of having a baby with Down's syndrome?

As you get older, the risk of delivering a baby with Down's syndrome increases. Look at the following statistics.

- ❖ at age 25 the risk is 1 in 1,300 births
- ❖ at 30 it is 1 in 965 births
- ❖ at 35 it is 1 in 365 births
- ❖ at 40 it is 1 in 109 births
- ❖ at 45 it is 1 in 32 births
- ❖ at 49 it is 1 in 12 births

But let's look at it in a more-positive light. If you're 45, you have a 97% chance of *not* having a baby born with Down's syndrome. If you're 49, you have a 92% chance of delivering a child without Down's syndrome.

⋄ 3 ⋄

Tests on You
&
Your Growing Baby

I am really anxious to be pregnant. How far along must I be for a pregnancy test to be positive?

Pregnancy tests have become increasingly sensitive and can be positive (pregnant) even before you miss a menstrual period. Most tests will be positive 7 to 10 days after you conceive; this includes blood, urine and home pregnancy tests. Most doctors recommend you wait until you miss your period before having a test. This will save you both money and emotional energy.

I did a home pregnancy test last night, and it was positive. How soon should I see my doctor?

Once you know you're pregnant, call and make an appointment. Most doctors will want to see you within a few weeks unless you are having problems and need to be seen right away. Good prenatal care is an important part of having a healthy baby. Don't wait for weeks or months to see your doctor; starting early is important for your health and the health of your baby.

My friend had a pregnancy test called a "quantitative HCG test" because she was having problems; the result was a number. What kind of test is it?

A *quantitative HCG (human chorionic gonadotropin)* test is a blood test done in the first trimester when there is concern about miscarriage or ectopic pregnancy. The test measures the hormone HCG, which is made early in pregnancy and increases rapidly. Two or more tests done a few days apart are more useful than one test because it is the *change* in the amount of the hormone that is significant. An ultrasound is also often done when a quantitative HCG test is ordered.

My doctor said I'm going to have to have a lot of tests done when I go in next time. What kind of tests will I need?

Your health-care provider will probably order several tests during the first or second visit. These may include:

- ✧ complete blood count (CBC)
- ✧ urinalysis and urine culture
- ✧ test for syphilis
- ✧ cervical cultures, as indicated
- ✧ rubella titers (for immunity against rubella)
- ✧ blood type
- ✧ Rh-factor
- ✧ test for hepatitis-B antibodies
- ✧ alphafetoprotein test
- ✧ ultrasound
- ✧ Pap smear
- ✧ mammogram (if woman is over 35 and a mammogram has not been done before)

See the chart on page 94 for a description of some common tests done during pregnancy.

Why do I need to have all these tests?

The results of these tests give your health-care provider information he or she needs to provide the best care for you. For example, if testing shows you have never had rubella or rubella vaccine (German measles), you will know you need to avoid exposure and receive the vaccine before your next pregnancy. Rubella can be responsible for miscarriage or fetal malformations if a woman contracts the disease during pregnancy.

I'm 28 weeks pregnant, and my doctor says I need some more tests. Why?

Many doctors repeat some tests or perform new tests at this time. For example, the 28th week of pregnancy is the best time to discover any abnormalities in glucose tolerance. It is at this point in your pregnancy that RhoGAM is given to an Rh-negative woman to protect her from becoming sensitized.

I'm pregnant for the first time and want everything to be all right. Do I need genetic counseling?

Probably not. Individuals who need genetic counseling are usually those who have had a malformed infant, those with a family history of inherited diseases, women who have had recurrent miscarriages (usually three or more) and women who will be 35 or older at the time of birth.

What happens when a couple goes for genetic counseling?

You and your husband will participate in this counseling together. Detailed questions will be asked about your medical history, other pregnancies, medication usage and the medical history of your family and your partner's family. If it is necessary to do chromosome tests, blood samples will be taken from both of you.

Ultrasound

All my friends have had ultrasounds during pregnancy. Will I have one?

Many doctors routinely perform ultrasounds on their patients, but not every doctor does them with every patient. Some doctors perform them only when there is a problem or a definite reason for doing one.

I'm confused about ultrasound and sonograms. What's the difference?

Ultrasound, sonogram and *sonography* refer to the same test. Ultrasound is a valuable medical tool, especially in pregnancy.

What exactly is an ultrasound?

Ultrasound is a test that gives a 2-dimensional picture of the developing embryo or fetus. It involves the use of high-frequency sound waves made by applying an alternating current to a transducer. This transducer is placed on the abdomen or

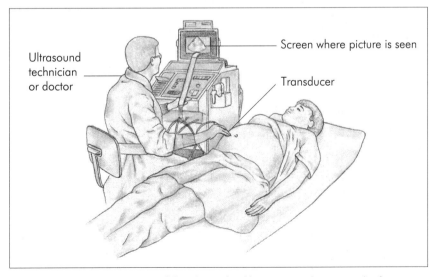

Ultrasound examination is a useful tool your health-care provider may order for you.

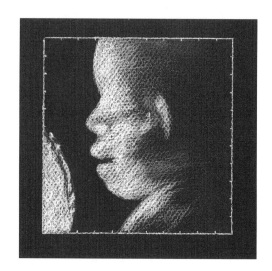

This ultrasound picture shows a baby's profile inside the uterus.

in the vagina. Sound waves projected from the transducer travel through the abdomen or vagina, bounce off tissues and bounce back to the transducer. The reflected sound waves are translated into a rough picture.

Is ultrasound safe?

Yes, it is. Most medical researchers agree ultrasound exams pose no threat to you or your baby. The possibility of ultrasound having adverse effects has been studied many times without evidence that the test causes any problems.

Why do doctors do ultrasounds?

There are three main reasons that your doctor will have you get an ultrasound:

  ✧ to help confirm or determine your due date
  ✧ to determine whether there is more than one baby (twins, triplets or more)
  ✧ to see if major physical characteristics of the fetus are normal

Will I automatically have an ultrasound?

No. Whether you have an ultrasound during your pregnancy depends on several factors. These factors include:

✧ problems during pregnancy, such as bleeding

✧ previous problem pregnancies

✧ your health-care provider

✧ your insurance company

Most doctors like to do at least one ultrasound during a pregnancy, but not all agree on this. If your pregnancy is "high risk," you may have several ultrasounds.

Are there other reasons for doing an ultrasound?

Some other reasons for doing an ultrasound are:

✧ identifying an early pregnancy

✧ showing the size and growth of the embryo or fetus

✧ measuring the fetal head, abdomen or thighbone to determine the duration of pregnancy

✧ identifying some fetuses with Down's syndrome

✧ identifying fetal abnormalities, such as hydrocephalus

✧ measuring the amount of amniotic fluid

✧ identifying the location, the size and the maturity of the placenta

✧ identifying abnormalities of the placenta

✧ detecting an IUD

✧ differentiating between miscarriage, ectopic pregnancy and normal pregnancy

✧ helping to find a safe location to perform an amniocentesis

How early in pregnancy can I have an ultrasound?

That depends on your health-care provider. If you're having problems, your doctor may want to do an ultrasound of you fairly early in pregnancy.

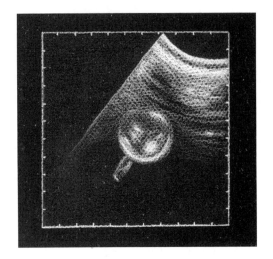

*Ultrasound of male scrotum
and penis at 33 weeks.*

Can an ultrasound help determine when I'm due?

Yes. Measurements can be taken of the baby with an ultrasound. Your doctor can compare these measurements with charts that have averages to help approximate your due date.

Will I be able to find out if I am having a boy or girl when I have my ultrasound?

If you are 18 weeks or more when you have an ultrasound, you *may* be able to determine the sex of your baby, but don't count on it. It isn't always possible to tell the sex if the baby has its legs crossed or is in a breech presentation.

Even if your doctor makes a prediction as to the sex of your baby, keep in mind that ultrasound is a test, and tests can sometimes be wrong. Most doctors recommend you not start buying for one sex or the other based on an ultrasound. If you do buy anything, save the receipts!

I've heard that sometimes the ultrasound instrument is put in the vagina. Is that dangerous; could it make me bleed or miscarry?

This type of ultrasound is called *vaginal ultrasound* and can be very helpful in evaluating problems early in pregnancy, such as possible miscarriage or an ectopic pregnancy. The instrument (probe or transducer) is put just inside the opening of the vagina, so it does not touch the cervix and will not cause bleeding or miscarriage. This type of ultrasound can sometimes give better information earlier in pregnancy than an abdominal ultrasound.

I'm supposed to have an ultrasound next week, and they told me to drink 32 ounces (960ml) of water before I come and not to empty my bladder. Why?

Your bladder is in front of your uterus. When your bladder is full, your uterus rises out of the pelvis and can be seen more easily. When your bladder is empty, your uterus is farther down in your pelvis, and it's harder to see it. The full bladder acts as a window from the outside of your abdomen into your uterus. With a vaginal ultrasound, your bladder doesn't have to be full.

Where are most ultrasounds done?

There are three locations where ultrasounds are usually done.

- ❖ Some doctors have an ultrasound machine in their office and have ultrasound training.
- ❖ Some doctors prefer to have you go to the hospital to have the ultrasound done and read by a radiologist.
- ❖ In certain high-risk situations, your doctor may send you to an ultrasound specialist to perform your ultrasound.

Each situation must considered individually; ask your doctor about where your ultrasound will be done.

My friend has a videotape of her ultrasound. Can I get one of mine?

Ask about it when your ultrasound is scheduled. Not all ultrasound machines are capable of making a video recording. Ask ahead of time to find out if you need to bring a videotape.

Can I get pictures from my ultrasound?

Most ultrasounds include black-and-white photos. Baby pictures before you have a baby!

How much does an ultrasound cost?

It varies depending on where the test is done and where you live. An average cost is about $150, but it can range from $100 to $300. With most insurance plans, ultrasound is an "extra" and not part of the normal fee for prenatal care. Ask about cost and coverage *before* having an ultrasound. Some insurance plans require "pre-approval" before an ultrasound is done.

I'm having an ultrasound next week. Can my partner come with me?

Yes. This is something your partner will probably want to see, so arrange to have the ultrasound when he can come. You may want to have others, such as your mother or older children, come when possible. Ask about this when your ultrasound is scheduled.

Amniocentesis

I heard some women talking about amniocentesis. Is this test for everyone?

No, amniocentesis does not need to be performed on every pregnant woman. It is usually performed on women:

- ❖ who will deliver after their 35th birthday
- ❖ who have had a previous baby with a birth defect
- ❖ with a family history of birth defects
- ❖ who have a birth defect themselves
- ❖ whose partners have a birth defect

When is the test done?

Amniocentesis is usually performed for prenatal evaluation between 16 and 18 weeks of pregnancy.

How is amniocentesis performed?

Ultrasound is used to locate a pocket of fluid where the fetus and placenta are not in the way. Skin over the abdomen is cleaned and numbed with a local anesthetic. A needle is passed through the abdomen into the uterus, and fluid is withdrawn from the amniotic cavity with a syringe.

How much fluid is withdrawn?

Only about 1 ounce (30ml) of amniotic fluid is needed to perform the tests.

What do they do with the amniotic fluid?

Fetal cells that float in the amniotic fluid can be grown in cultures. These cells can then be used to identify fetal abnormalities or to reassure you that your baby is healthy.

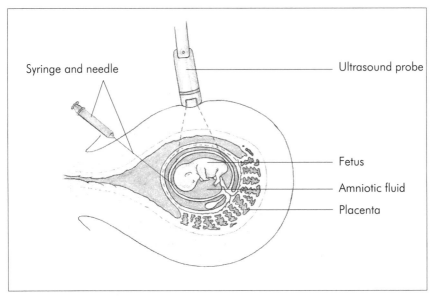

Amniocentesis is usually performed between the 16th and 20th weeks of pregnancy.

How many abnormalities can amniocentesis identify?

We know there are over 400 abnormalities a child can be born with. Amniocentesis can identify about 10% of them, or 40 problems.

What kind of abnormalities can be found with amniocentesis?

The problems a physician can identify include the following:

  ✧ chromosomal problems, particularly Down's syndrome
  ✧ skeletal diseases, such as osteogenesis imperfecta
  ✧ fetal infections, such as herpes or rubella
  ✧ central-nervous-system disease, such as anencephaly
  ✧ blood diseases, such as erythroblastosis fetalis
  ✧ chemical problems or deficiencies, such as cystinuria or maple-syrup-urine disease

Can't amniocentesis also determine the baby's sex?

Yes it can. However, the test is not used for this purpose, except in cases in which the sex of the baby could predict a problem, such as hemophilia.

What are the risks of this test?

Risks are relatively small, but there could be trauma to the fetus, placenta or umbilical cord, infection, miscarriage or premature labor. Fetal loss from complications is estimated to be between 0.5 and 3%. Discuss it with your doctor before you have the test.

Who performs amniocentesis?

The test should be performed *only* by someone who has experience doing it, such as a physician at a medical center. Your health-care provider will be able to give you more information if the test is to be performed on you.

I keep hearing about Down's syndrome. What is it exactly?

Down's syndrome is a condition caused by a defect in the baby's chromosomes. The baby will be mentally retarded and may have a somewhat dwarfed appearance, with a sloping forehead, short, broad hands, a flat nose and low-set ears. He or she may also have heart problems, gastrointestinal defects or leukemia. Down's syndrome can be diagnosed during pregnancy by amniocentesis.

Is there a way to diagnose Down's syndrome without doing amniocentesis?

Yes. Studies are now being done with other tests that can diagnose Down's syndrome. These tests include alphafetoprotein, chorionic villus sampling and ultrasound (in some cases).

The Alphafetoprotein Test

A friend told me about a blood test she had that can detect problems with the baby. What is it?

You probably mean the *alphafetoprotein (AFP)* test. It is a blood test done on *you* to determine an abnormality in your *baby*! Measurement of the amount of alphafetoprotein in your blood can help your health-care provider predict problems.

Is the AFP test done on all pregnant women?

At this time, it is not performed on all pregnant women. However it is required in some states, such as California and New York. If the test is not offered to you, discuss it with your health-care provider.

When is the test done?

It is usually performed between 16 and 20 weeks of pregnancy, and test results must be correlated with the mother-to-be's age and weight and the gestational age of the fetus. If AFP detects some problem, additional, more-definitive testing is usually ordered.

What kind of abnormalities can AFP detect?

The test is designed to detect babies with:

- neural-tube defects
- severe kidney disease
- severe liver disease
- esophageal or intestinal blockage
- Down's syndrome
- urinary obstruction
- osteogenesis imperfecta (fragility of the baby's bones)

I've heard that if I have an alphafetoprotein test, chances are rather high that it will be abnormal, even if there are no problems. Is this true?

Yes, this is true. The problem with the test is that it is not specific enough. For example, if 1,000 women are tested, 40 tests will come back abnormal. Of those 40 tests, only one or two actually have a problem. So if you have AFP and your test result is abnormal, don't panic. Another AFP test will be done to correlate results, and an ultrasound will be performed.

What is a neural-tube defect?

A *neural-tube defect* is an abnormality in the bone surrounding the spinal cord, in the brain stem or in the brain itself. One of the most common neural-tube defects is *spina bifida*— an absence of vertebral arches, which allows the spinal membrane to protrude. Another abnormality is *anencephaly;* the brain develops only a rudimentary brain stem and only traces of basal ganglia.

Chorionic Villus Sampling

I've heard about a test called "chorionic villus sampling." What is it?

Chorionic villus sampling (CVS) is a test that is done to detect genetic abnormalities. Sampling is done early in pregnancy, usually between the ninth and eleventh weeks.

How is the test done?

A small piece of tissue is removed from the placental area with an instrument placed through the cervix or with a needle inserted through the abdoman.

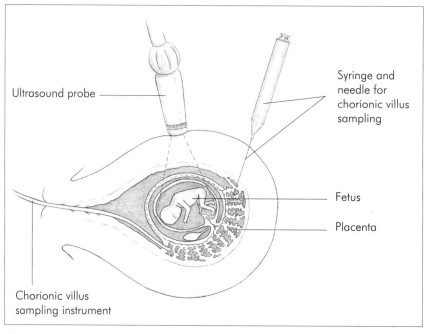

Chorionic villus sampling can be done earlier in pregnancy than other tests and is a valuable tool for your health-care provider.

Are there risks in having CVS done?

There is a small risk of miscarriage with this procedure. The test should be performed *only* by someone who is experienced in doing it.

Why is this test ordered?

The advantage of CVS is an earlier diagnosis of a problem, if one exists. The test can determine various fetal problems, such as Down's syndrome, Tay-Sachs disease and cystic fibrosis. Some women choose to have this test because they want results earlier so they can make decisions about the pregnancy.

Is CVS better than amniocentesis?

CVS does offer an advantage over amniocentesis because it can be done much earlier in pregnancy. Results are available in about a week. If the woman decides to terminate the pregnancy after learning results of the test, the procedure can be performed earlier in pregnancy and may carry fewer risks.

Should I have this test done?

Each woman's pregnancy is different. This test should be discussed with your health-care provider. He or she will be able to determine if your particular case requires it.

Fetoscopy

What's the test that uses some kind of scope to look at the baby?

You are probably referring to *fetoscopy*. It is performed on the fetus and placenta while both are still inside your uterus. It provides a view of the baby and placenta.

What is fetoscopy used for?

The doctor can actually see the baby through the fetoscope, and some abnormalities and problems can be detected. This very specialized test is not performed very often.

How is the procedure done?

A small incision is made in the mother's abdomen, and a scope similar to the one used in laparoscopy is placed through the abdomen. The doctor uses the fetoscope to examine the fetus and placenta.

Should I have fetoscopy?

If your doctor suggests fetoscopy to you, discuss it with him or her. This test is *not* done very often, but is used when it is necessary to look directly at the fetus or placenta.

Are there risks to fetoscopy?

Risk of miscarriage is 3 to 4% with this procedure. The test should be done *only* by someone experienced in this technique.

Other Tests for the Mother-to-be

My friend told me about a special stethoscope that my doctor will use to let me hear my baby's heart beat. What is it?

You're probably referring to a special listening machine called a *doppler*. It is not actually a stethoscope. It magnifies the sound of the baby's heartbeat enough so you can hear it.

When will I be able to hear the baby's heartbeat?

Around the 12-week visit this will be possible. If your health-care provider doesn't offer it to you, ask about it.

I'm concerned about having tests that use radiation during my pregnancy. Can they hurt my baby?

Avoid exposure to X-rays during pregnancy, unless it is an emergency. There is no known safe amount of radiation for a developing fetus. Dangers to the baby include an increased risk of mutations and an increased risk of cancer later in life.

I have to go to the dentist next week. Should I let them X-ray my teeth?

If possible, avoid dental X-rays while you are pregnant. However, if you *must* have a dental X-ray, be sure your abdomen and pelvis are completely shielded by a lead apron.

What should I do if I break my leg and need an X-ray while I'm pregnant?

There *are* medical reasons for X-rays, but the need for the X-ray must be weighed against the risk to your pregnancy. If you have an injury to your foot or hand, it is fairly easy to

Be careful with X-rays, whether a test requires them or whether your job exposes you to them. This test could be harmful to your developing baby.

shield the uterus with a lead apron while the area is X-rayed. However, if your injury is in your back or any place near the pelvic area, the risks increase. Discuss it with your physician before any X-ray is taken when you are pregnant.

Are there any other reasons to do an X-ray during pregnancy?

Some problems, other than broken bones, may occur that require X-rays. Pneumonia and appendicitis are two possibilities. Again, discuss the situation with your doctor.

What about CT scans—are they the same as X-rays?

Computerized tomographic scans, also called *CT scans* and *CAT scans,* are a form of very specialized X-ray. The technique involves the use of X-ray with computer analysis. Many researchers believe the amount of radiation received from a CT scan is much lower than a regular X-ray. However, it is probably wise to avoid even this amount of exposure, if possible.

When is the fetus most susceptible to the harmful effects of radiation from X-rays?

Risk to a fetus appears to the greatest between 8 and 15 weeks of pregnancy (between the fetal age of 6 weeks and 13 weeks). Some believe the only safe amount of radiation exposure for a fetus is no exposure.

I've heard about a test called "MRI." Is it the same as an X-ray?

No. *Magnetic resonance imaging*, also called *MRI*, is a diagnostic tool widely used today. At this time, no harmful effects in pregnancy have been reported from its use, but pregnant women are advised to avoid an MRI during the first trimester of pregnancy for the safety of the fetus.

I'm going for my first visit, and they told me that the doctor will want to do a Pap smear. What is a Pap smear?

A Pap smear is the removal of some cells from your vagina or cervix. It is done to look for abnormal cells, called *precancerous, dysplastic* or *cancerous cells*, in the cervical area.

Why does the doctor do a Pap smear at this time?

If you have had a normal Pap smear in the last few months, you won't need it. If it has been a year or more since you had the test, you should have a Pap smear. The goal of a Pap smear is to find problems early so they can be more easily dealt with.

I saw my doctor a week ago, and they just called to tell me my Pap smear wasn't normal. Will I need a biopsy?

It depends on how serious the problem might be. Usually a biopsy is not done while you're pregnant. Your doctor will probably wait until after your pregnancy for further testing. Instead of removing tissue for a biopsy, he or she may do a *colposcopy* (a very careful look at the cervix) during pregnancy.

An abnormal Pap smear during pregnancy is a very individual situation and must be handled carefully.

What is home uterine monitoring?

With *home uterine monitoring,* contractions of a pregnant woman's uterus are monitored in her home. This type of testing or monitoring is used when the doctor believes there could be a problem with premature labor. If necessary, labor would be stopped to prevent delivery of a premature baby.

How does home uterine monitoring work?

A recording of uterine contractions is transmitted from the woman's home, via telephone, to a center where contractions can be evaluated. With the use of a personal computer, your doctor may be able to view the recordings at his or her own home or office.

Who needs home uterine monitoring?

Conditions that require home uterine monitoring include:
 ❖ previous preterm delivery
 ❖ infections in the mother-to-be
 ❖ premature rupture of membranes
 ❖ pregnancy-induced hypertension
 ❖ multiple fetuses, such as twins or triplets

What does home monitoring cost?

Costs vary, but run between $80 and $100 a day.

My doctor wants me to have a non-stress test. What is that?

A *non-stress test* is a non-invasive procedure done in the doctor's office, in the labor room or in the delivery room. While you are lying down, a fetal monitor is attached to your abdomen. Every time you feel the baby move, you push a button to make a mark on the monitor paper. At the same time, the fetal monitor records the baby's heartbeat on the same paper.

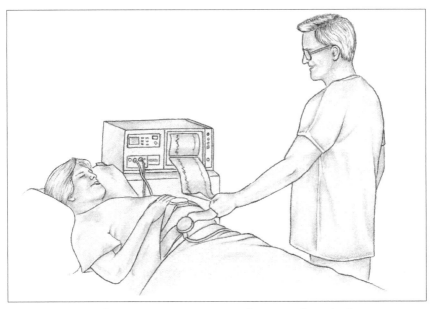

A non-stress test and a contraction stress test are done to evaluate the fetus.

What will a non-stress test show?

The information gained from a non-stress test gives reassurance that your baby is doing OK.

If my non-stress test isn't OK, what happens next?

Additional tests will be done, including a *biophysical profile* or a *contraction stress test.*

I'm close to delivery, and my doctor said I will have a pelvic exam the next time I come to the office. Why now, when I haven't had one for so long?

A pelvic exam is needed late in pregnancy because it tells us a lot of things, including:

- ❖ presentation of the baby—whether the baby is head first or breech
- ❖ dilatation of the cervix—how much the cervix has opened (if at all)

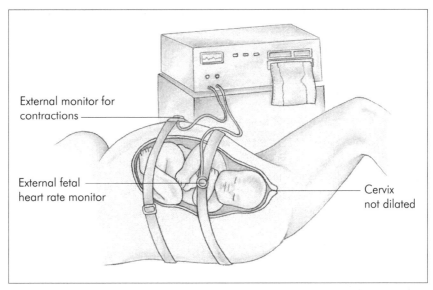

External monitor for contractions

External fetal heart rate monitor

Cervix not dilated

External fetal monitoring, with membranes intact (bag of waters has not broken).

❖ effacement—how much the cervix has thinned
❖ shape and size of your birth canal or pelvic bones
❖ station—how low the baby is in your birth canal

After my pelvic exam, my doctor said I was "2 and 50%." Why did she tell me this?

This information is important for two reasons. First, it tells you your cervix is open 2cm and thinned out 50% or halfway. (This is not an indication of when your baby will be born.) Second, this information is helpful if you go to the hospital thinking you're in labor. At the hospital, you'll be checked again. Knowing what you were at your last pelvic exam can help determine if you are in labor.

My health-care provider did a pelvic exam today and told me I was not dilated and my cervix had not thinned out. Does that mean I have a lot longer to go?

No. The pelvic exam tells you where you were at *that* time. Labor may begin at any time.

When my doctor does a pelvic exam, does that tell him when I will go into labor?

No. At this point in your pregnancy, labor might start at any time, no matter what the condition of your cervix.

My health-care provider was mentioning fetal monitoring during labor and delivery. What is it?

In many hospitals, a baby's heartbeat is monitored throughout labor to detect any problems early so they can be resolved.

What kind of monitoring do they do?

There are two types of fetal monitoring during labor—*external fetal monitoring* and *internal fetal monitoring*. See the illustration on the opposite page and the illustration below.

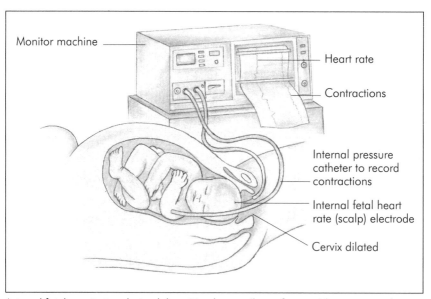

Internal fetal monitoring during labor. Membranes (bag of waters) have ruptured.

What is external fetal monitoring?

A belt with a receiver is strapped to your abdomen, and it records the baby's heartbeat. This type of monitoring can be done before your membranes rupture.

What is internal fetal monitoring?

Internal fetal monitoring is a more-precise method of monitoring the baby. An electrode is placed on the fetal scalp to give a more-exact reading of the fetal heart rate than external monitoring.

Tests for Your Developing Baby

My doctor mentioned doing a biophysical profile on my baby. What is it?

It is a comprehensive test that examines the fetus while it is still in your uterus. It helps determine the baby's health.

Why is a biophysical profile done?

The test is useful in evaluating an infant with intrauterine-growth retardation, when the mother-to-be is diabetic, with a pregnancy in which the baby doesn't move very much, in high-risk pregnancies and in overdue pregnancies.

What does a biophysical profile measure?

It measures and records:
 ✧ fetal breathing movements
 ✧ body movements
 ✧ fetal tone (tightening or contractability of muscles)
 ✧ reactive fetal heart rate (increase in heart rate when baby moves)
 ✧ amount of amniotic fluid

How is the test performed?

The test is done with various instruments. Ultrasound, external monitors and observation are used to make the different measurements.

How is the test scored?

Each area is given a score of 0, 1 or 2. A total is obtained by adding all five scores together. The higher the score, the better the baby's condition. A low score may indicate problems in the fetus.

If a baby has a low score, what can be done?

The situation will be evaluated—the baby may need to be delivered immediately. If the score is reassuring, the test may be repeated at intervals. It may be necessary to repeat the test the following day. Your doctor will evaluate the scores, your health and the entire pregnancy before any decisions are made.

I've heard about a contraction stress test for the baby. What is that?

A *contraction stress test (CST)*, also called a *stress test,* is another test that is used to evaluate the well-being of the baby.

How is a contraction stress test done?

A monitor is placed on the woman's abdomen to record the fetal heart rate. Sometimes nipple stimulation is used to make the woman's uterus contract, or an I.V. is started and oxytocin is given in small amounts to make the uterus contract. Results indicate how well a baby will tolerate contractions and labor.

What can a contraction stress test indicate?

If the baby doesn't respond well to the contractions, it can be a sign of fetal distress.

When is a contraction stress test done?

If a woman has had problem pregnancies in the past or experiences medical problems during this pregnancy, her doctor may have her tested the last few weeks of pregnancy. This is done when the non-stress test is not reassuring.

I recently read about fetal blood sampling during labor. What is this test?

It is another way of evaluating how well a baby is tolerating the stress of labor.

How is fetal blood sampling during labor done?

The membranes must have ruptured, and the cervix must be dilated at least 2cm. An instrument is placed inside the mother to make a small nick in the baby's scalp. The baby's blood is collected in a small tube, and its pH (acidity) is checked.

What can the doctor learn from fetal blood sampling?

The pH level can help determine whether the baby is having trouble during labor and is under stress. The test helps the physician decide whether labor can continue or if a C-section needs to be done.

I've heard about some test they can do to see if a baby is ready to be born; it has something to do with the baby's lungs. Why is it done?

You are probably referring to a couple of tests that are done to evaluate the maturity of fetal lungs. When a baby is born prematurely, a common problem is immaturity of the lungs, which can lead to development of respiratory-distress syndrome in the baby. Lungs are not completely mature, and the baby cannot breathe on its own without assistance.

Why is it important for a baby to be able to breathe on its own?

It's not just being able to breathe on its own. The last fetal system that matures is the respiratory system. If your doctor knows the baby's lungs are mature, it aids him or her in making a decision about early delivery.

What are the tests that can be done to check fetal lung maturity?

One called an *L/S ratio* measures the ratio of lecithin to sphingomyelin. Results give the doctor an index of the maturity of the baby's lungs. The other is the *phosphatidyl glycerol (PG) test,* which gives either a positive or negative result. Both tests are performed by amniocentesis. If the result shows phosphatidyl glycerol is present, there is greater assurance that the baby will not develop respiratory-distress syndrome.

If the baby's lungs have not developed enough, what can be done?

The first course of action is to avoid premature delivery of the baby, if possible. If this cannot be done, tests are done immediately after birth to determine if the baby has surfactant in its lungs. *Surfactant* is a chemical essential for respiration immediately after birth. If it is not present, the baby's doctor may introduce surfactant directly into the lungs of the newborn, preventing respiratory-distress syndrome. The baby will not have to be put on a respirator—it can breathe on its own!

Some Common Tests at a Glance

Test	How It's Done	What You and Your Doctor Can Learn
Ultrasound	Sound waves produce picture of uterus, placenta and fetus on the screen	Age of fetal growth, fetal position, heart rate, movement, number of fetuses, some birth defects, fetal sex (sometimes)
Alphafeto-protein	Blood sample drawn from mother	May indicate neural-tube defect (spina bifida) or risk of Down's syndrome
Amniocentesis	Sample of amniotic fluid drawn by needle from uterus	Early in pregnancy indicates chromosomal problems (Down's syndrome), neural-tube defects (spina bifida), genetic disorders (cystic fibrosis), sex of fetus; late in pregnancy indicates whether baby's lungs are developed
Chorionic villus sampling	Sample of placental tissue drawn from placenta through abdomen or vagina	Used to determine many inherited diseases, such as Down's syndrome, and some biochemical diseases, such as Tay-Sachs disease, and other fetal conditions such as cystic fibrosis
Stress/non-stress test	Fetal activity is monitored by mother-to-be and fetal monitor	Used to show fetal well-being or to look for fetal stress
Biophysical profile	Variety of tests, including ultrasound monitoring and observation	Used to show fetal well-being or to look for fetal stress

✦ 4 ✦

Medications &
Treatments for You

When should I discuss with my health-care provider the different medications that I must take for medical conditions I have?

Ideally, you will have had this discussion with your health-care provider *before* you got pregnant. If you were unable to do this, discuss all medications (prescription and over-the-counter) you take on a regular basis at your first visit with your health-care provider. Dosages may need to be adjusted, or you may have to stop taking a particular substance.

Can't I just stop taking the medicine I take before I visit the doctor? I'm not that sick.

Never stop taking any medication that you take for a chronic problem without first consulting your health-care provider! Some medication cannot and should not be stopped during pregnancy. Consult your health-care provider before making any decisions about medication use.

Medication usage is very important during pregnancy. Check with your health-care provider before you take any medications.

I've read that some of the medications I take can affect my growing baby. What are they and what are the effects?

Various substances you ingest affect the developing baby in many ways. See the chart on page 94, which lists some of these substances and their effects.

Vitamin Usage During Pregnancy
(Also see the discussion of vitamin usage in Chapter 5)

How important is it for me to take prenatal vitamins?

It's very important to take your prenatal vitamins for your entire pregnancy. Sometimes late in pregnancy a woman stops taking them—she gets tired of taking them or she decides they aren't necessary. The vitamins and iron in prenatal vitamins are essential to the well-being of your baby, so be sure you take your prenatal vitamins until your baby is born.

I usually take a lot of vitamins, but my doctor advised me to take only a prenatal vitamin during pregnancy. Why?

Too much of a good thing can be harmful. Some vitamins accumulate in your body's tissues when taken in megadoses and can have an adverse effect on you and your baby. Researchers believe that megadoses of vitamin A can cause birth defects when taken during pregnancy. In addition, we believe vitamins D, E and K in megadoses can also be harmful. Follow your doctor's advice, and eat nutritious, well-balanced meals to get the vitamins and minerals you and your baby need.

My friend is pregnant, and she's taking folic acid in addition to her prenatal vitamins. Is that something I need to do?

Most women don't need to take extra folic acid during pregnancy. (Folic acid is found naturally in green leafy vegetables.) A deficiency in folate (term used interchangeably with folic acid) can result in a type of anemia called *megaloblastic anemia*. Additional folate may be necessary in situations in which requirements are unusually high, such as twins, triplets, alcoholism or Crohn's disease. Prenatal vitamins have 0.8mg to 1mg of folic acid in each pill, which should be sufficient for a woman who has a normal pregnancy.

I've read that if a woman has a baby with spina bifida, she needs extra folic acid in subsequent pregnancies. Is that true?

Some studies indicate a women who has had a baby with a neural-tube defect, such as spina bifida, may be able to reduce her chances of having another baby with the same problems if extra folic acid is taken before pregnancy and through early pregnancy.

Prescription Medications During Pregnancy

Why should I discuss the prescription medications I take with my health-care provider?

This is a very important aspect of your prenatal care. Discuss *all* medications (prescription and over-the-counter) you take on a regular basis at your first visit with your health-care provider. You may need to have your dosage adjusted, you may have to stop taking a particular substance or certain conditions may require additional medication.

I take thyroid medication. Is it necessary during pregnancy?

Yes, it is very important to continue taking your thyroid medication throughout your pregnancy. Be sure your doctor knows what you take.

Why is thyroid medication important in pregnancy?

Thyroid hormone is made in the thyroid gland, which is found in your neck over the area of your windpipe. This hormone affects your entire body and is important in your metabolism. Thyroid hormone is also important in your ability to get pregnant.

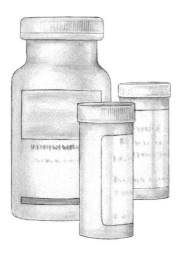

Be sure to consult with your health-care provider about all medications you are now taking.

Possible Effects of Some Medications on the Fetus

Medication	Possible Effects
Androgens (male hormones)	Ambiguous genital development (depends on dose given and time when given)
Anti-coagulants (warfarin)	Bone and hand abnormalities, intrauterine-growth retardation, central-nervous-system abnormalities, eye abnormalities
Anti-thyroid drugs (propylthiouracil, iodide, methimazole)	Hypothyroidism, fetal goiter
Chemotherapeutic drugs (methotrexate, aminopterin)	Increased risk of miscarriage
Diethylstilbestrol (DES)	Abnormalities of female-reproductive organs, female and male infertility
Isotretinoin (Accutane®)	Increased miscarriage rate, nervous-system defects, facial defects, cleft palate
Lithium	Congenital heart disease
Phenytoin (Dilantin®)	Growth retardation, mental retardation, microcephaly
Streptomycin	Hearing loss, cranial-nerve damage
Tetracycline	Hypoplasia of tooth enamel, discoloration of permanent teeth
Thalidomide	Severe limb defects
Trimethadione	Cleft lip, cleft palate, growth retardation, miscarriage
Valproic acid	Neural-tube defects

Chart modified from ACOG Technical Bulletin #84, Teratology, 2/85, American College of Obstetricians and Gynecologists

Can medications for thyroid problems be taken safely during pregnancy?

Thyroxin (medication for low thyroid or hypothyroid) can be taken. Propylthiouracil (high-thyroid or hyperthyroid medication) passes to the baby; you will probably be given the lowest amount possible during your pregnancy.

I have lupus, and I take pills every day. Can this affect my pregnancy?

The medication used to treat lupus is steroids; the primary steroid given is prednisone. Many studies have been done on the safety of prednisone during pregnancy, and it has been found to be safe.

Before pregnancy, I was taking Prozac® for depression. Can I continue taking it?

With this medication, there is little information about its use or safety. Discuss taking Prozac with your physician as soon as you discover you are pregnant.

I asked my doctor for a prescription for Accutane® to treat my acne, but she told me she couldn't prescribe it because I'm pregnant. Why?

Accutane (retinoic acid isotretinoin) is a common treatment for acne. However, it must not be taken by any woman who is pregnant! There is a higher frequency of miscarriage and malformation of the fetus if a woman takes Accutane during the first trimester of pregnancy.

I use Retin-A® for my skin. Should I discontinue using it now that I'm pregnant?

This medication is too new for us to know whether it is safe to use during pregnancy. We do know that any type of medication you use can get into your bloodstream, which could be passed to your baby. It's best to avoid Retin-A during pregnancy because we do not know its effects on the fetus at this time.

I often take tetracycline for a skin problem, but my brother warned me it can harm my baby. How?
None of the tetracyclines, a family of antibiotics, should be taken during pregnancy. They can cause discoloration of your baby's permanent teeth later in life. For that reason, tetracyclines should *not* be prescribed for any child under age 8.

I occasionally use a steroid cream for a skin condition I have. Can I use it during pregnancy?
It's best to discuss this with your health-care provider. There may be another preparation you can use that is considered safer during pregnancy.

Non-Prescription or Over-the-Counter Medications

Is it OK for a pregnant woman to take medicines that don't require a prescription?
Over-the-counter (OTC) medications should be taken with care during pregnancy. Ask your doctor about any medication *before* you take it, whether it is prescription or non-prescription. Many OTCs contain aspirin, caffeine or phenacetin—all should be avoided during pregnancy. Limit your use of cough syrups, which may contain as much as 25% alcohol. Be careful with medications containing ibuprofen, such as Advil®, Motrin® and Rufen®. Avoid new medicines, such as Aleve®, until we know more about them and their safety in pregnancy. Read package labels and ask your health-care provider or pharmacist before taking anything.

What are some safe OTC medications?

OTCs that are safe include acetaminophen (Tylenol), some antacids (Amphojel, Gelusil, Maalox, milk of magnesia), throat lozenges (Sucrets®), some decongestants (Sudafed®) and some cough medicines (Robitussin®).

Is it OK for me to take aspirin during my pregnancy?

Almost any medication you take when you are pregnant passes to your baby or has some effect on your pregnancy. This is true for aspirin. Most doctors recommend you avoid aspirin during pregnancy because aspirin can cause an increase in bleeding. Even with an over-the-counter medication like aspirin, it's best to consult your doctor before taking it.

Won't my doctor or the nurses get mad if I call them about every medication I'm thinking of taking?

No. They would rather answer a question about medication use before you take something than worry about its effect on your baby after you have taken it.

Can Birth-Control Methods Affect Pregnancy?

I just found out I'm pregnant, and I'm taking birth-control pills. What should I do?

Stop taking the pills, and notify your doctor. Any method of contraception can fail; the chance of failure with birth-control pills is less than 1%. There is a small increase in problems for the fetus if you take birth-control pills while you're pregnant. It is not cause for great alarm, but discuss it with your doctor.

I have an IUD and just found out I'm pregnant. What should I do?

Notify your doctor immediately. You will need to discuss with him or her whether the IUD should be removed. Usually most doctors will attempt to remove the IUD, if possible. The risk for miscarriage is higher if your IUD is left in place. The risk for ectopic pregnancy is also higher if you get pregnant with an IUD.

My partner uses condoms and spermicides, and I just found out I'm pregnant. Will the fact that we have been using spermicides hurt our baby?

Spermicides have not been shown to be harmful to a developing fetus.

Immunizations & Vaccinations in Pregnancy

I've heard I should be careful about immunizations and vaccinations during pregnancy. Why?

Some immunizations contain substances that may harm the developing fetus and should not be received by a pregnant woman. The risk of exposure to various diseases is an important consideration, however, and not all vaccines will cause harm to the fetus. That's why it is very important to discuss this concern with your doctor.

If I do need an immunization, what will my doctor do?

Once your doctor determines you have been exposed to a disease, or exposure is possible, he or she will weigh the risk of the disease against the potential harmful effects of the immunization. As I've already stated, some vaccines *are not harmful* to a fetus and may be used without problems.

Are there some vaccines that I should never receive if I know I'm pregnant?

Yes. Live-virus vaccines should *never* be given to a pregnant woman. Live-virus vaccines include those for measles, mumps and rubella (MMR), poliomyelitis and yellow fever. You should receive primary vaccine against polio *only* if your risk of exposure is high, such as if you are traveling to a high-risk area.

What types of vaccines are given to people?

The categories of vaccines are:
- live virus (mumps vaccine)
- inactivated virus (influenza, hepatitis B)
- inactivated bacterial (cholera, plague)
- toxoids (tetanus, diphtheria)
- specific immune globulins (rabies)
- standard immune globulins (hepatitis A)

Are any vaccines regarded as safe for a pregnant woman?

The only vaccines generally regarded as safe during pregnancy are tetanus and diphtheria. Others may be safe, but we are unsure about them at this time, so avoid them.

How can I know if I should receive a vaccine?

If you are pregnant, ask your health-care provider. If you don't think you are pregnant, it would still be wise to have a pregnancy test and to be using reliable contraception before receiving a vaccine.

There are so many different kinds of medicine. How can I remember which are safe to take?

You don't have to remember them all. Ask your health-care provider about those that pertain to your own special care. Much of the information in this chapter probably won't apply to you, but it's good information to have at hand. The important thing is to call your doctor about any over-the-counter medication before you take it. And remember to read labels!

⋄5⋄

Nutrition, Exercise & Weight Management

I've heard that during pregnancy I'm "eating for two."
Is this true?

What the old adage "a pregnant woman is eating for two" actually means is that you must be concerned about nutrition for yourself and for your growing baby. However, many women take this to mean they can eat *twice as much*, which is incorrect! Be smart about your food choices—you must eat wisely for both of you.

Can't I eat all I want during pregnancy?

Only a very few lucky women can eat all they want at any time. Some women have the false idea they can eat all they want during pregnancy. Don't fall into this trap. You don't want to gain more weight than your doctor recommends during your pregnancy—it can make you uncomfortable and it will be harder to lose the extra pounds after your baby is born.

Keeping track of your weight is one way your health-care provider measures your progress through pregnancy.

Why is it important for me to eat well during pregnancy?

In one study, it was shown that 95% of the women who had good-to-excellent diets had babies in good-to-excellent health. Of women who ate poor diets (lots of junk food), only 8% had babies in good-to-excellent health. One of your main goals in pregnancy is to have the healthiest baby you can. Your nutrition during pregnancy has a great impact on your baby's health.

Do I need to increase the number of calories I consume now that I'm pregnant?

Yes. Most experts say a normal-weight pregnant woman needs to increase her caloric intake by 300 to 800 calories a day. These extra calories are important for tissue growth in you and your baby. Your baby is using the energy from your calories to create and store protein, fat and carbohydrates and to provide energy for its own body processes. Expect to gain some weight during your pregnancy—it's natural and normal.

What foods should I eat every day?

A variety of foods should be included to supply you with the nutrients you need. You'll want to eat dairy products, protein foods, fruits and vegetables, and breads and cereals.

I don't think I eat very many foods with protein in them. Why should I eat foods containing protein?

During pregnancy, you need protein for growth and repair of the embryo/fetus, placenta, uterus and breasts. The recommended amount of protein in pregnancy is 6 to 7 ounces (168 to 196g) a day.

How many grams of carbohydrate should I eat daily during pregnancy?

There is no recommended dietary allowance (RDA) for carbohydrate intake during pregnancy. Most physicians believe carbohydrates should make up about 60% of the total number of calories in your diet. If you are eating 2,000 calories a day, you would consume about 1,200 calories as carbohydrate calories.

Do I need to worry about getting enough fat in my diet during pregnancy?

There is rarely concern about inadequate fat intake; usually fat intake is excessive. There is no recommended daily amount for fat intake during pregnancy.

I read that everyone has to have fat in their diet. I shouldn't avoid all fats, should I?

That's a good point. No, you shouldn't avoid all fats, but you should include them only in small amounts. Measure how much you use of each, and use them sparingly!

I'm confused about what I should eat every day. Can you recommend a healthy eating plan?

It's a good idea to eat a variety of foods throughout your pregnancy. Below is a list of daily servings from six food groups.

- ✧ Dairy products—4 to 5 servings a day
- ✧ Protein sources—3 to 4 servings a day
- ✧ Vegetables—at least 4 servings a day
- ✧ Fruits—2 to 4 servings a day
- ✧ Breads, cereal, pasta and rice—6 to 11 servings a day
- ✧ Fats/flavorings—3 to 5 servings a day

What kinds of foods are dairy products, and how much should I eat of each?

Some foods you might choose from this group, and their serving sizes, include:

- ✧ 3/4 cup (336g) cottage cheese
- ✧ 2 ounces (56g) of processed cheese (such as American cheese)
- ✧ 1-1/2 ounces (42g) natural cheese (such as Cheddar)
- ✧ 1 ounce (28g) hard cheese (such as Parmesan or Romano)
- ✧ 1 cup (240ml) of pudding or custard
- ✧ 1 8-ounce (240ml) glass of milk
- ✧ 1 cup (240ml) yogurt

To keep the fat content low, choose skim milk, lowfat yogurt and lowfat cheese instead of whole milk and ice cream.

What kinds of foods are good sources of protein, and how much should I eat of each?

Some foods you might choose from this group, and their serving sizes, include:

- ✧ 2 tablespoons (30ml) peanut butter
- ✧ 1/2 cup (120ml) cooked dried beans

❖ 2 to 3 ounces (56 to 84g) cooked meat

❖ 1 egg

Aim for a total of 6 to 7 ounces daily. Poultry, fish, lean cuts of red meat, dry beans, eggs, nuts and seeds are all good sources of protein.

What kinds of foods are in the vegetable group, and how much should I eat of each?

Some foods you might choose from this group, and their serving sizes, include:

❖ 3/4 cup (180ml) vegetable juice

❖ 1/2 cup (120ml) broccoli, carrots or other vegetable, cooked or raw

❖ 1 medium baked potato

❖ 1 cup (240ml) raw, leafy vegetables (salad greens)

Eating a variety of vegetables gives you a good nutritional balance. Eat at least one vegetable a day that is high in folic acid, such as green leafy vegetables.

*Make healthy food choices
for yourself and your baby.*

What kinds of foods are in the fruit group, and how much should I eat of each?

Some foods you might choose from this group, and their serving sizes, include:

- ✧ 1/2 cup (120ml) canned or cooked fruit
- ✧ 3/4 cup (180ml) grapes
- ✧ 1/2 cup (120ml) fruit juice
- ✧ 1 medium banana, orange or apple
- ✧ 1/4 cup (60ml) dried fruit

Include one or two servings of a fruit rich in vitamin C, such as orange juice or orange slices. Fresh fruits are also a good source of fiber, which is important during your pregnancy if you suffer from constipation.

What kinds of foods are in the bread-pasta-cereal-rice group, and how much should I eat of each?

Some foods you might choose from this group, and their serving sizes, include:

- ✧ 1 large tortilla
- ✧ 1/2 cup (120ml) cooked pasta, cereal or rice

✧ 1 ounce (28g) of ready-to-eat cereal
✧ 1/2 bagel
✧ 1 slice of bread
✧ 1 medium roll

What kinds of foods are in the fat/flavorings group, and how much should I eat of each?

Some foods you might choose from this group, and their serving sizes, include:

✧ 1 tablespoon (15ml) sugar or honey
✧ 1 tablespoon (15ml) olive oil or other type of oil
✧ 1 pat of margarine or butter
✧ 1 tablespoon (15ml) jelly or jam
✧ 1 tablespoon (15ml) prepared salad dressing

Be a little more careful in your use of these foods because they can be troublesome when you are trying to control your weight.

I have a hard time avoiding foods that are high in sugar and fat. What can I do?

Foods such as cookies, chocolate, candy and ice cream have a lot of empty calories. Fill up instead on foods that are high in fiber and low in sugar and fat. Choose fruits and vegetables, legumes and whole-grain crackers and breads.

I really love protein foods that have a lot of fat, like bacon and cheeses. What can I substitute for them?

Choose foods that are high in protein but low in fat, such as skinless chicken and turkey, tuna packed in water, cod, ground turkey and lowfat (1%) or skim milk.

I love junk food. Do I have to give it up completely?

You may have to forgo most junk food while you're pregnant. The foods we consider "junk food" are usually high-calorie, high-fat foods that contain little nutrition for you or your baby. It's probably OK to eat junk food once in a while, but don't make it a regular part of your diet.

I've been craving certain foods now that I'm pregnant. Is this normal?

For many women, cravings during pregnancy are normal. Cravings for particular foods during pregnancy can be both good and bad. If you crave foods that are nutritious and healthy, eat them in moderate amounts. If you crave foods that are high in sugar and fat, and loaded with empty calories, be very careful about eating them.

Why do I have these cravings now, especially for foods that I might not normally eat?

No one knows for sure, but many believe it is because of the hormonal changes and emotional changes that occur during pregnancy.

Some foods I normally love make me sick to my stomach now. Why?

This is normal and very common during pregnancy. The hormones of pregnancy have a significant impact on the gastrointestinal tract, which can affect your reaction to certain foods.

I've heard bad things about artificial sweeteners and pregnancy. Are they really something to worry about?

Studies to date have not shown any harm to pregnancy from aspartame (Equal®, Nutrasweet®). However, women who suffer from phenylketonuria need to follow a low-phenylalanine diet, or their babies may suffer from delayed development or even mental retardation. The phenylalanine in aspartame contributes to phenylalanine in your diet.

Saccharin is another artificial sweetener found in foods and beverages. It is still being tested for its effect on pregnancy. My advice with artificial sweeteners is to avoid them or use them in moderation during pregnancy.

I've found that I want to eat late at night, even though I've never felt hungry at night before. Should I eat late at night?

Late-night nutritious snacks are beneficial for some women, especially if they must eat many small meals a day. However, many women should not snack at night because they don't need the extra calories. Food in the stomach late at night may also cause more distress if heartburn or nausea and vomiting are problems.

I'm 11 weeks pregnant and had my cholesterol checked at the supermarket last week. It was higher than the last time I had it checked. Is that normal?

Yes. Cholesterol levels usually increase during pregnancy and nursing because of hormonal changes, so it's rather useless to have them tested at this time.

I feel so nauseous that I can't eat anything. Is this dangerous?

Nausea, also called *morning sickness*, is usually not dangerous because it doesn't last too long. It becomes dangerous when you are unable to eat an adequate amount of food or to drink enough fluid. You should be able to eat nutritious foods even if you have morning sickness.

Nausea is typically the worst during the beginning of pregnancy. It usually lessens and disappears after the first trimester, and you will feel better for the rest of your pregnancy.

See Chapter 2 for further information about nausea and morning sickness.

My doctor told me to drink lots of water every day, but I hate it. Do I really need it?

Water is necessary for your body to process nutrients, develop new cells and sustain blood volume. You may also feel better if you drink more fluid than you normally do. Your blood volume increases during pregnancy; drinking extra fluids helps you keep up with this change.

How can drinking fluid help me?

Many women who suffer from headaches, uterine cramping and other problems during pregnancy find increasing their fluid intake helps resolve some of their symptoms. It also helps avoid bladder infections.

How much water do I need to drink?

Drink 6 to 8 glasses (64 ounces; 1.9 liters) of liquid every day. Water is the best liquid to choose. When your urine is light yellow to clear, you're getting enough water. Dark-yellow urine is a sign that you need to add more fluid to your diet.

If I drink beverages that normally act as diuretics, will it counteract the increase in fluids?

No, it will not.

Drinking water is important throughout pregnancy, especially during and after exercise.

How can I possibly drink this much extra fluid?

It's really not that hard. Some women drink water, one glass at a time, throughout the day. (Decrease your intake later in the day so you don't have to go to the bathroom all night long.)

My husband and I eat out a lot because we're tired after work. Are there any foods I should avoid at restaurants?

It's OK to eat out at restaurants; you just need to be a little more careful about what you eat. Avoid any raw meats or raw seafood such as sushi. You may also find that certain foods do not agree with you, so avoid those foods.

What foods should I choose at a restaurant?

Fish, fresh vegetables and salads are usually your best bets, but be careful with calorie-loaded salad dressings if excessive weight gain is a concern. Avoid highly spicy foods or foods that contain a lot of sodium, such as some Chinese food. You may experience water retention after eating these foods.

I drink a few cups of coffee and several glasses of diet cola every day. Do I need to worry about caffeine?

Drinking as few as 4 cups of coffee a day (800mg of caffeine) by a pregnant woman has been associated with decreased birth weight and a smaller head size in newborns.

Although an exact "toxic" amount for caffeine has not been determined, it makes sense to limit your caffeine intake.

What foods contain caffeine?

Caffeine is found in many beverages and foods, including coffee, tea, cola drinks and chocolate. Some medications, such as cough medicines and headache medicines, also contain a lot of caffeine. It's important to read labels.

Why is caffeine a problem?

Caffeine is a central-nervous-system stimulant. There are no known benefits for you or your unborn fetus from caffeine. Caffeine can also affect calcium metabolism in both you and your baby.

What do you suggest about caffeine intake in pregnancy?

Limit your caffeine intake during pregnancy and if you breastfeed. Read labels on foods, beverages and over-the-counter medications to find out about caffeine. Eliminate caffeine from your diet as much as possible.

Is there any place I can get more information on nutrition while I'm pregnant?

There is an excellent resource that can provide you with information on all aspects of nutrition, whether or not you are pregnant. The National Center for Nutrition and Dietetics' Consumer Nutrition Hotline is a toll-free number that you can call to talk directly with a registered dietician. The number is 1-800-366-1655.

Vitamins & Minerals

Do I really need to take prenatal vitamins?

Yes. Prenatal vitamins contain the recommended daily amounts of vitamins and minerals you need during pregnancy. They are taken to ensure your health and your baby's health. However, they aren't a substitute for food or a good diet.

How are prenatal vitamins different from other vitamins?

The main difference between prenatal vitamins and regular vitamins is that prenatal vitamins also contain iron and folic-acid supplements.

Do I need mineral supplements during my pregnancy?

The only mineral that needs to be supplemented during pregnancy is iron. The average woman's diet seldom contains enough iron to meet the increased demands of pregnancy. Your blood volume increases by 50% in a normal pregnancy, and iron is an important part of blood production in your body.

I've heard I might have to take iron supplements during pregnancy. Does it really make a difference if I don't take an iron supplement?

Prenatal vitamins contain some iron but you may need to take extra iron. One of the first tests your health-care provider does is one for anemia. If she determines that you need an iron supplement, you must take it for your health and that of your baby.

How much iron is in prenatal vitamins?

Most prenatal vitamins contain 60mg of elemental iron.

Won't iron make me constipated?

Constipation can be a side effect of taking iron. Work with your doctor to find the correct amount of iron to avoid side effects.

Will my baby have healthier teeth (when he or she gets them!) if I take extra fluoride during my pregnancy?

The use of fluoride and fluoride supplementation during pregnancy is controversial. Some researchers believe fluoride supplementation during pregnancy results in improved teeth in your child, but not everyone agrees. However, no harm to the baby has been shown from fluoride supplementation in a pregnant woman. Some prenatal vitamins contain fluoride.

I've heard I should avoid sodium during pregnancy. What is it?

Sodium is a chemical that works to maintain the proper amount of fluid in your body. During pregnancy, it can also affect your baby's system. Sodium is found in salty foods (such as potato chips and dill pickles) and in processed foods, from soups to meats. You need *some* sodium; you just don't need too much of it. Read food labels to discover just how much you are getting!

How much sodium should I take in each day?

During pregnancy, keep your consumption of sodium under 3g (3000mg) a day.

How can too much sodium hurt me or my baby?

Too much sodium causes water retention, swelling and high blood pressure. Any of these can be a problem for you.

I don't know what foods contain sodium. What should I avoid?

You can't avoid something unless you know where to find it. With sodium, that can be tricky. It's in the salt shaker and in salty-tasting foods, such as pretzels, chips and salted nuts. You may be surprised by the amount of sodium in foods that *don't* taste salty.

Sodium is found in canned and processed products, fast foods, cereals, desserts and even soft drinks and some medications! See the chart on the opposite page for a listing of the sodium content in a variety of foods. Read the labels!

Sodium Content of Some Foods

Fresh or Minimally Prepared Foods

1 cup apple juice	2mg
3 apricots (fresh)	1mg
1 medium banana	1mg
8 ounces of bluefish	170mg
1 head Boston lettuce	15mg
1 medium carrot	35mg
1 large egg	70mg
1 cup green beans (frozen)	2mg
3 ounces ground beef	60mg
1 lemon	1mg
1 cup whole milk	120mg
1 cup oatmeal (long-cooked)	10mg
1 cup orange juice	2mg
1 peach	1mg
3 ounces pork	65mg

Prepared Foods

3 ounces bacon	1400mg
1 cup baked beans	100mg
1 slice white bread	100mg
1 frozen chicken dinner	1400mg
1 cup chicken-noodle soup	1050mg
1 cinnamon roll	630mg
1 tablespoon cooking oil	0mg
3 ounces corned beef	1500mg
1 cup corn flakes	305mg
1 cup green beans (canned)	320mg
1 cup all-purpose flour	2mg
1 cup self-rising flour	1565mg
1 tablespoon Italian dressing	250mg
1 tablespoon catsup	155mg
1 olive	165mg
1 dill pickle	1930mg
1 cup pudding, instant	335mg
1 cup puffed rice	1mg
1 cup tomato juice	640mg

Fast Foods

1 Arby's turkey sandwich	1060mg
1 Burger King Whopper	675mg
1 Dairy Queen hotdog	990mg
1 KFC dinner (3 pcs chicken)	2285mg
1 Taco Bell enchirito	1175mg
1 McDonald's Big Mac	1010mg

Exercise

I love to exercise and don't want to stop while I'm pregnant. Do I have to?

Experts agree that exercise during pregnancy is safe and beneficial for most pregnant women, if it is done properly. This is definitely an area to discuss with your health-care provider at the beginning of your pregnancy!

I don't really like to exercise, but I do it. Are there benefits to continuing my exercise program during my pregnancy?

Regular, moderate exercise during pregnancy can be beneficial for you in many ways. It can help:

❖ relieve backache

❖ prevent constipation and varicose veins

❖ strengthen muscles needed for delivery

❖ leave you in better shape after delivery

❖ help you feel better about yourself

Exercise is beneficial during pregnancy and can be more enjoyable if you do it with a friend.

What should my exercise goals be during pregnancy?

The goal of exercising during pregnancy is overall good health. It will make you feel better physically, and it can give you an emotional boost.

My mother told me I shouldn't exercise during pregnancy; she was warned not to when she was pregnant with me. Why the change now?

Exercise was not always approved for a pregnant woman. In the past, doctors were concerned about the redirection of blood flow from the fetus to the mother-to-be's muscles during exercise. We now know this occurs to a small degree, but it is not harmful to the fetus.

I've never exercised before, but I'd like to begin now. Can I?

Some women become interested in exercising during pregnancy to help them feel better. If you've never exercised before, you *must* discuss it with your health-care provider before you begin. Pregnancy is *not* the time to begin a vigorous exercise program.

What kind of exercises will my health-care provider recommend?

If you've never exercised before, walking and swimming are excellent forms of exercise. Riding a stationary bike can also be enjoyable.

I want to exercise, and it scares me that I might do something to hurt my pregnancy. Should I be scared?

It's a good idea to be fit and to exercise when you're pregnant. If you're fit, you'll do better with weight gain during pregnancy, be able to do the work of labor and delivery better, and feel better after the birth. Exercise during pregnancy isn't without risks, including increased body temperature, decreased blood flow to the uterus and possible injury to you.

Most experts recommend reducing your exercise to 70 to 80 percent of your prepregnancy level. If you have problems with bleeding or cramping or have had problem pregnancies before, you will need to modify your exercise with your doctor's advice.

Someone told me exercising can cause early labor. Should I believe her?

It was once believed that exercise could cause preterm labor because there is a temporary increase in uterine activity following exercise. However, in a normal pregnancy, this does not cause a problem.

I read that my baby's heart rate increases when mine does during exercise. Can this cause a problem?

The fetal heart rate increases somewhat during and immediately after exercise, but it stays within the normal fetal range of 120 to 160 beats a minute. This should not cause any problems for you or the baby.

My aerobics instructor said my heart rate changes during pregnancy. Why?

During pregnancy, your heart rate is higher so you don't have to exercise as vigorously to reach your target-heart-rate range. Be careful not to stress your cardiovascular system.

What if my heart rate is too high?

If it's too high, slow down but don't stop exercising completely. Continue exercising but at a more-moderate rate.

What if my pulse rate is too low?

If you don't feel too winded, pick up the pace a bit, but don't overdo it. Check your pulse rate again in a few minutes to make sure you aren't overexerting yourself.

How often should I check my pulse rate?

During pregnancy, you should do this fairly often. It will surprise you how fast your pulse can increase during a pregnancy workout.

I'm not sure how I figure out my heart rate. Can you explain it?

While you are pregnant, your pulse rate should not exceed 140 beats per minute for more than 15 minutes during a workout. Check your pulse with the following steps.

- ✧ Have a clock with a second hand in view.
- ✧ Place the index and middle fingers of one hand on the side of your neck where you can feel your pulse.
- ✧ After finding your pulse, watch the second hand until it reaches the 12.
- ✧ Begin counting the pulse beats until the second hand reaches the 2 (10 seconds).
- ✧ Multiply that number by 6 to find your heart rate.

When should I consult my doctor about exercising during pregnancy?

Discuss it with him or her at your *first* prenatal visit. If you decide later to start or to change your exercise program, be sure to consult your physician before you begin. Some women should *not* exercise during pregnancy. If you experience any of the following symptoms, do *not* exercise during your pregnancy:

- ✧ a history of an incompetent cervix, preterm labor or repeated miscarriages
- ✧ high blood pressure early in pregnancy
- ✧ multiple fetuses (twins, triplets or more)
- ✧ diagnosed heart disease
- ✧ pre-eclampsia
- ✧ vaginal bleeding

Will I have to change my exercise program during pregnancy?

Changes in your body due to pregnancy will cause you to change the way you exercise. Your center of gravity changes, so you will need to adjust your exercise for that. As your abdomen grows larger, you will find you can't do some activities very comfortably and you may have to stop other activities all together.

I feel out of breath more quickly when I exercise now that I'm pregnant. Is something wrong with me?

Your growing abdomen can put a strain on your respiratory system, causing you to feel out of breath sooner than normal. When you exercise, don't work to the point that you cannot talk and have trouble breathing. This indicates that you are working too strenuously; cut back on your workout.

I feel a lot hotter when I exercise during pregnancy. Is this normal?

When you're pregnant, you normally feel warmer than usual. You'll feel warmer, too, when you exercise, so try to avoid becoming overheated during workouts. Work out in a well-ventilated room, and drink lots of water while you exercise.

I'm 9 weeks pregnant and haven't exercised in years. Can I start now?

It is possible to start exercising now, but begin gradually. It's best to discuss your desire to exercise with your health-care provider *before* you begin any program. If you don't have any problems with your pregnancy, you should be able to exercise as long as you are comfortable. The key is not to try to do too much too fast. The best exercises for you are walking and swimming.

Can I play competitive sports during pregnancy?

If you are used to playing a competitive sport, such as tennis, you should be able to continue, but expect to reduce the level of competition. The point to remember is not to get carried away or to overwork yourself.

What are some good sports to do while I'm pregnant?

Some of the less-strenuous sports are listed below. Most are generally considered safe for a normal, low-risk pregnancy.

- walking
- swimming
- low-impact aerobics designed especially for pregnancy
- water aerobics
- stationary bicycling
- regular cycling (if you're experienced)
- jogging (if you jogged before pregnancy)
- tennis (played moderately)

Swimming is an excellent way to exercise when you are pregnant. You feel a lot lighter in the water, too.

What sports should I avoid during pregnancy?

The sports listed below should be avoided during pregnancy because of the potential problems associated with each.

* scuba diving
* water skiing
* surfing
* horseback riding
* downhill skiing or cross-country skiing
* any contact sport

My health club offers aerobics classes for pregnant women. Are these better than the regular aerobics classes?

Aerobics classes specifically designed for pregnant women are a good choice. They concentrate on the unique needs of the pregnant woman, such as strengthening abdominal muscles and improving posture. When choosing a class, be sure the instructor has proper training and the class meets the exercise guidelines developed by the American College of Obstetricians and Gynecologists. To obtain the guidelines write to:

ACOG Exercise Program
4021 Rosewood Ave.
Los Angeles, CA 90004
1-213-383-2862

If I exercise, do I need to eat more?

Your nutrition needs increase during pregnancy, and you do burn extra calories during exercise, so you should consume enough calories to ensure a balanced diet. As I've already discussed, a woman of normal weight before pregnancy needs to eat between 300 and 800 extra calories a day during pregnancy. Exercising may require you to eat more.

Will exercise during pregnancy make labor and delivery easier?

Exercise during pregnancy should help you have an easier time with your labor and delivery.

Will exercise help me recover more quickly after my baby is born?

Many believe that women who exercise during pregnancy have a shorter recovery time after birth. Exercise keeps you fit so you can get back in shape more quickly.

Can you give me some guidelines about exercising during pregnancy?

As I've stated, be sure you consult with your health-care provider before you begin any exercise program. Follow the tips below to keep you healthy and in good shape.

- ❖ Try to exercise at least 3 times a week for 20 to 30 minutes each time.
- ❖ Start your exercise routine with 5 minutes of warmup and end with a 5-minute cool-down period.
- ❖ Wear comfortable clothes that offer support. Wear a support bra and good athletic shoes.
- ❖ Drink plenty of water during exercise.
- ❖ Don't exercise strenuously for more than 15 to 20 minutes.
- ❖ Check your pulse rate; keep it below 140 beats a minute.
- ❖ Don't exercise in hot, humid weather.
- ❖ After the fourth month of pregnancy, avoid exercises that require you to lie on your back.
- ❖ Never allow your body temperature to rise above 100.4F (38C).
- ❖ Stop immediately and consult your physician if you experience any problems.

What kind of problems should I watch out for while I'm exercising?

Be aware of any unusual occurrences, and report them to your doctor immediately. Be careful about the following:

- ❖ pain
- ❖ bleeding

✧ dizziness

✧ extreme shortness of breath

✧ heart palpitations

✧ faintness

✧ abnormally rapid heart rate

✧ back pain

✧ pubic pain

✧ difficulty walking

Weight Management

I'm in good shape; I exercise regularly and my weight is about where it should be. How much weight should I gain during my pregnancy?

Normal weight gain during pregnancy is 25 to 35 pounds (11.25 to 15kg). This may sound like a lot, but if you add up weight for the baby, placenta, amniotic fluid and changes in you, it really isn't that much. See the chart on the opposite page for general guidelines to weight gain during pregnancy.

How am I supposed to watch my weight gain and still eat 300 to 800 calories more a day?

Not every woman needs to increase her food intake by 300 to 800 calories; that's just a general guideline. You must look at your individual case. If you are underweight when you begin pregnancy, you may have to eat *more* than 800 extra calories each day. If you're overweight when you get pregnant, you may have less need for extra calories.

I believe the key to good nutrition and weight management is to eat a balanced diet throughout your entire pregnancy. Eat the foods you need to help your baby grow and develop, but choose wisely. For example, if you're overweight, avoid peanut butter and other nuts as a protein source; choose water-packed tuna or low-fat cheeses instead. If you're underweight, select ice cream and milkshakes as sources of dairy foods.

I have such a fear of getting fat during pregnancy, I know it's going to cause me a lot of problems. What can I do about it?

You must be prepared to gain weight while you're pregnant. It is a normal part of pregnancy, and it is necessary for your baby's health! Getting on the scale and seeing your weight increase can be hard for some women, especially those who have to watch their weight closely. You must decide at the beginning of your pregnancy that it is all right to gain weight—it's for the health of your baby. You can control your weight gain by eating carefully and nutritiously; you don't have to gain an extra 50 pounds (22.5kg). But you must gain enough weight to meet the needs of pregnancy.

When my mother was pregnant with me, she was allowed to gain just 13 pounds (5.85kg) for her entire pregnancy. Was that normal 35 years ago?

Yes, it was fairly normal then. We have learned a lot about pregnancy because of advances in technology and information from research and other sources. We realize today that it is

General Weight-Gain Guidelines for Pregnancy

Current Weight	*Acceptable Gain*
Underweight	28 to 40 pounds 12.6 to 18 kg
Normal weight	25 to 35 pounds 11.25 to 15.75 kg
Overweight	15 to 25 pounds 6.75 to 11.25 kg

permissible and advisable for a woman to gain a sufficient amount of weight during pregnancy; today the normal weight gain during pregnancy is 25 to 35 pounds (11.25 to 15.75kg)—quite a change from 13 pounds (5.85kg)!

I'm pregnant, and know I'm underweight. How much should I gain during my pregnancy?

If you start your pregnancy underweight, the normal weight gain is 28 to 40 pounds (12.6 to 18kg). It is important for you to eat regularly and to eat nutritiously, even if you are not used to doing this.

I'm overweight, and I just found out I'm pregnant. How much weight should I gain while I'm pregnant?

If you're overweight before pregnancy, you probably should not gain as much as other women during your pregnancy.

As much as you may dislike it, keeping track of your weight is important during pregnancy.

Acceptable weight gain is 15 to 25 pounds (6.75 to 11.25kg). This is an individual problem that you should discuss with your doctor. It is important for you to eat nutritious, well-balanced meals during your pregnancy. Do *not* diet!

How much should I gain each week during pregnancy?

As an average for a normal-weight woman, many health-care providers suggest 2/3 of a pound (10 ounces; 300g) a week until 20 weeks, then 1 pound (0.45kg) a week from 20 to 40 weeks. However, this varies for each woman. If you're concerned, talk with your doctor about it.

I'm 7 weeks pregnant and haven't gained any weight; I think I may even have lost 2 or 3 pounds (0.9 or 1.35kg). Is that OK?

It isn't unusual not to gain weight or even to lose a little weight early in pregnancy. Your health-care provider will keep track of the change in your weight during your pregnancy.

My doctor said I must get weighed each time I come in. Can't I just weigh myself at home before I come in and tell the doctor or nurse my weight?

It's best to be weighed at the office. It is one way your doctor can tell that everything is progressing normally with your pregnancy. Although you may be shy about being weighed, it's an important part of your visit to the doctor. Your health-care team is doing it to make sure everything is OK with your pregnancy.

My friend told me I should gain about 25 to 30 pounds (11.25 to 13.5 kg) with my pregnancy. That sounds like a lot to me when the baby only weighs about 7 pounds (3.15kg). Where does all that weight go?

Your friend is right. The weight that you gain is distributed as shown in the chart below. As you can see, some weight will be lost during the birth process. More weight is often lost as your body readjusts to its non-pregnant state.

Distribution of Weight Gained During Pregnancy

Weight	Location
7-1/2 pounds (3.38kg)	Baby
7 to 10 pounds (3.15 to 4.5kg)	Maternal stores (fat, protein and other nutrients)
4 pounds (1.8kg)	Increased fluid volume
2 pounds (0.9kg)	Uterus
2 pounds (0.9kg)	Amniotic fluid
2 pounds (0.9kg)	Breast enlargement
1-1/2 pounds (0.68kg)	Placenta

♦ 6 ♦

Fatigue, Work & Pregnancy

I just found out I'm pregnant. I'm so tired all the time. Is it normal for a pregnant woman to feel so exhausted?

Pregnancy can cause you to feel extremely tired. Fatigue is normal and common, and may continue during your entire pregnancy. For most women, it is the worst early in pregnancy, then gets better. Eating right, taking vitamins and getting plenty of rest will help. We know pregnant women need more sleep than they normally would. In most cases, 8 to 10 hours of sleep at night will help you feel better. When you see your doctor, one of the first tests he or she will do is a hematocrit to check for anemia, which can also be a reason for feeling tired.

My sister said it's not good for me to lie on my back during pregnancy. Does she know what she's talking about?

It *is* best for you not to lie on your back when you sleep or rest. As your uterus grows, lying on your back can place the uterus on top of important blood vessels (*inferior vena cava*

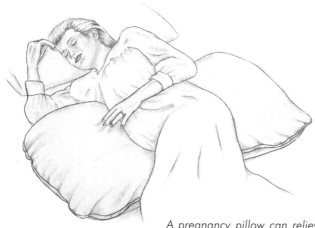

A pregnancy pillow can relieve stress points and help you feel more comfortable resting or sleeping.

and *aorta*) that run down the back of your abdomen. This can decrease circulation to your baby and to parts of your body. It may also be harder for you to breathe when you lie on your back.

I usually lie on my stomach when I sleep. Will I be able to do this as I get bigger?

Lying on your stomach when you sleep or rest isn't a good idea. It puts a lot of pressure on your growing uterus, which will become a comfort problem later. The bigger you get, the harder it is to lie on your stomach.

What is the best position for sleeping?

Learn to sleep on your side—you'll be glad you did as you get bigger. Use some extra pillows to support your back so you don't lie flat. Rest your top leg on another pillow. A "pregnancy pillow" that provides support for your entire body may help. See the illustration above.

I've been under a lot of stress during my pregnancy. Is there anything I can do to help me better manage the stress?

The following breathing exercise can help you relax when you feel stressed:

- ✧ Inhale slowly as you count to 4. Push your abdomen out as you breathe in.
- ✧ Let your shoulders and neck relax as you slowly exhale while counting to 6.
- ✧ Repeat as often as you need to.

Hint: Play gentle, soothing music as background music as you practice this exercise.

I've heard that there are exercises to do to help relieve stress. Can you tell me about them?

One exercise I recommend to my patients is to relax each muscle group with each deep breath. Start with the feet and work up through the legs, hands, arms, torso, shoulders, neck and face. Continue for 10 to 20 minutes. This exercise also works when you're lying in bed and are having trouble getting to sleep.

As my pregnancy progresses, I find that I'm having trouble getting comfortable. What should I do?

If you're having trouble sleeping, experiment with different positions when you rest. Lie on your side, with a pillow under your abdomen. Elevate your feet to help keep blood moving throughout your body, especially your legs. Or you might feel better if you elevate your head and shoulders.

I can't sleep enough at night to make me feel better. How do I get the rest I need?

Try taking naps during the day. If you can't nap, sit down and relax—listen to music or read, if that helps. When you relax, prop your feet above your chest, if possible, to help with swelling and to ease discomfort in your legs.

Working During Pregnancy

My mother told me I shouldn't work during pregnancy. Is this true?

In the past, women were encouraged or even forced to stop working when they were pregnant. Today, many women work until they deliver their baby. Whether you work your entire pregnancy depends on your particular circumstances. If you are concerned about it, discuss it with your physician.

My husband is concerned about my working during my pregnancy. Should he be?

More than half of all women work outside the home; many pregnant women work and do well. If you are concerned about whether your job is safe for your pregnancy, discuss your particular situation with your health-care provider. It may be difficult to know the specific risk of a particular job—the goal is to minimize the risk to you and your baby while still enabling you to work. A normal, healthy woman should be able to work at most jobs throughout her pregnancy.

Can my work be hazardous to my pregnancy?

Certain factors may increase your risk of working during your pregnancy. If your job includes two or more of the following, discuss it with your health-care provider. He or she may want to monitor your pregnancy more closely.

- ✧ prolonged standing (more than 3 hours a day)
- ✧ work on an industrial machine, especially if it vibrates a great deal or requires strenuous effort to operate it
- ✧ strenuous physical tasks, such as heavy lifting or heavy cleaning
- ✧ repetitious, tedious work, such as assembly-line jobs
- ✧ environmental factors, such as high noise levels or extreme temperatures
- ✧ long working hours
- ✧ shift changes

I don't want to stop working while I'm pregnant. What precautions should I take?

You will probably have to slow down if you continue to work. You may also have to take it a little easier; you may not be able to do some of the things you do when you are not pregnant. It may also be necessary to ask for help in some of the tasks you are required to perform.

Should I try to rest during my work day?

If possible, try to lie down during breaks or on your lunch hour. Even sitting down in a quiet place can be beneficial. Ten or 15 minutes of rest can make you feel better and restore your energy.

A co-worker who just had a baby said her doctor told her she should exercise her legs and feet often during the day while she was pregnant. Should I do the same?

Yes. Try to do some leg-stretching foot exercises several times each hour. Remove your shoes before doing the following exercise. Extend your legs in front, then point your toes and flex your feet. Repeat this four or five times. It helps circulation in your feet and may prevent some swelling in your legs.

I've heard I should wear maternity stockings to work. Why?

Whether you sit or stand at work, maternity stockings provide support for your legs. They can be helpful, even if you don't work. Maternity stockings may be preferable to regular support stockings because they don't constrict your waist or abdomen. If you are concerned, discuss it with your health-care provider.

My job requires me to stand all day. Will that be a problem?

Studies show that women who stand all day have smaller babies. If you stand all day, you may have problems at the end of your pregnancy with swelling of your feet and ankles. It may be necessary for you to modify your work or to be able to lie down a couple of times during the day or to work fewer hours.

I have to climb a lot in my job. Should I talk to my supervisor about it?

It's probably best to avoid activities that involve climbing and balance in your job, especially during the third trimester. Talk with your supervisor about eliminating these activities.

I seem to have terrible mood swings while I'm at the office. Is this normal?

Elevated hormones can trigger mood swings in you. You may also find you're more tired; it's normal. Take a break if any situation becomes more than you can bear.

It's important to lift boxes, cartons and packages correctly. Always bend your knees, squat and lift. Don't bend over and lift!

I know my center of gravity is changing. What's the best way for me to lift an object?

Do most of your lifting with your legs. Bend your knees to lift; don't bend at the waist. As your abdomen grows larger, don't lift anything over 30 pounds (13.6kg).

I work at a computer terminal all day long, and I've heard some bad things about the terminals. Can this harm my baby?

To date, we have no evidence that working at a computer terminal can harm a growing baby. However, if you work at a computer terminal, you should be aware of how long you sit and the way you sit. See the next question.

I have a job that keeps me sitting behind a desk all day. Is there anything I need to be concerned about?

If you have a "sit-down" job, it's probably best to get up and move around regularly to stimulate your circulation. Take short walks frequently. Sit in a chair that offers good support for your back and legs. Don't slouch or cross your legs while sitting. Make sure you get up and walk around every 15 minutes.

I read that some substances or conditions in the workplace can harm a developing baby. What are they?

According to Maureen Paul, M.D., M.P.H., director of the Occupational Reproductive Hazards Center at the University of Massachusetts, some substances can cause harm to a developing fetus. The chart on the opposite page describes various agents, their sources and the possible effects they may have on a growing baby.

Is there a danger that my partner or I could bring home traces of substances we are exposed to at work?

Yes. Substances may be brought into your home on your work clothes or the work clothes of someone else in your family. If you think you may be exposed to hazardous substances, be sure to discuss it with your physician.

Research has been done on pregnant women working at computer terminals; very few problems have been reported.

Workplace Hazards and Possible Effects on the Fetus

Agent	Sources	Possible Effects
Cytomegalovirus	Hospitals, day-care centers	Congenital malformation
Cytotoxic drugs	Hospital or pharmacy preparation of chemotherapeutic drugs	Miscarriage
Ethylene oxide	Surgical-instrument sterilization	Miscarriage
Ionizing radiation	X-rays and radiation treatments, radioactive implants, nuclear power plants	In very high doses, congenital malformation; lower doses may increase childhood cancer risk
Lead	House, automotive and art paints made before 1980; battery manufacturing plants and radiator repair shops; ceramics and glass manufacturers; toll booths on heavily traveled roads	Preterm birth, delayed cognitive development
Organic solvents	Paint thinners, lacquers, adhesives; electronics and printing plants	Congenital malformation
PCBs	Electronic capacitors and transformers; hazardous waste industry	Delayed cognitive development
Rubella virus	Day-care centers, schools	Congenital malformation
Toxoplasmosis	Veterinary clinics, animal shelters, meat-packing operations	Congenital malformation

I work full time and worry about how people at my job will treat me if I have problems or need time off during my pregnancy. Is there anything I can do?

The U.S. Pregnancy Discrimination Act of 1978 prohibits job discrimination on the basis of pregnancy, childbirth or related disability. It guarantees equal treatment of all disabilities, including pregnancy, birth or related medical conditions, by companies that employ 15 or more people. If you have problems, ask your health-care provider for help. Most doctors will encourage you to work, if working isn't harmful to you or your baby.

How does the law affect me as a pregnant woman?

Under the law, several areas may apply to you.

❖ You must be granted the same health, disability and sick-leave benefits as any other employee for any other medical condition.

❖ You must be given modified tasks, alternate assignments, disability leave or leave without pay (depending on your company's policy).

❖ You are allowed to work as long as you can perform your job.

❖ You are guaranteed job security on leave.

❖ You continue to accrue seniority and vacation, and to remain eligible for pay increases and benefits.

Wasn't another law passed more recently that affects pregnant women?

The Family and Medical Leave Act was passed in 1993. It allows you or your husband to take up to 12 weeks of unpaid leave in any 12-month period for the birth of your baby. Leave may be taken intermittently or all at the same time. You must be restored to an equivalent position with equal benefits when you return.

It's important to keep working during pregnacy, if you want to. As a working pregnant woman, you have many rights. Ask your personnel director for further information.

However, the act applies only to companies that employ 50 or more people within a 75-mile radius. States may allow an employer to deny job restoration to those in the top 10% compensation bracket. Check with your state's labor office.

What about my state's employment laws; do they affect me as a pregnant woman?

State laws differ, so check with your state's labor office. You may also receive a summary of state laws on family leave from:

> The Women's Bureau Publications
> U.S. Department of Labor
> Box EX
> 200 Constitution Avenue, NW
> Washington, DC 20210

∗ 7 ∗

More than
One Baby!

How does a multiple pregnancy occur?

The babies may come from a single egg that divides after fertilization, or more than one egg may be fertilized.

How frequent are twins?

Twins from one egg occur about once in every 250 births around the world. Twins from two eggs occur in 1 out of every 100 births in white women and in 1 out of 79 births in black women. In certain areas in Africa, twins occur once in every 20 births! The occurrence of twins in Oriental populations is less common—about 1 in every 150 births.

Is it true that Hispanics also have a higher incidence of multiple births?

Some studies have shown that this is true.

My doctor told me she thinks I may be carrying triplets. How common are they?

Triplets are not very common; they occur only once in every 8,000 deliveries. Many doctors never deliver a set of triplets in their entire career!

I heard the incidence of twins is on the increase. Why is that?

Researchers believe two factors are responsible for this increase. One is the wider use of fertility drugs, which can result in multiple births. The second is the growing number of women who are having babies at an older age. We know the chance of twins increases as a woman gets older.

How do fertility drugs cause an increase in the rate of twins?

Fertility drugs can stimulate the ovaries to release more than one egg, increasing the chance of a multiple pregnancy.

Why do older women have a greater chance of having twins?

The incidence of twins is highest among women between ages 35 and 39. This increase has been attributed to higher levels of *gonadotropin,* the hormone that stimulates the ovaries to develop and release eggs. As a woman gets older, the level of gonadotropin increases, and she is more likely to produce two eggs during one menstrual cycle.

What is the difference between identical and fraternal twins?

Identical (or *monozygotic*) *twins* develop from a single egg that divides after being fertilized. Babies are always the same sex, and they look alike. When two eggs are fertilized, the babies will be as different in appearance as any other brothers and sisters. They are called *fraternal* or *dizygotic twins.*

Dealing with twins can be challenging and very rewarding.

Are most twins born to older women fraternal twins?

Usually that is the case. Because babies are born from two different eggs, they are fraternal (not identical).

I've heard that twin births can run in families. Is this true?

Yes, on the *mother's* side. One study showed that if a woman was a twin, the chance of her giving birth to twins was about 1 in 58! If a woman is the daughter of a twin, she also has a higher chance of having twins. Another study reported that 1 out of 24 twins' mothers (4%) was also a twin, but only 1 out of 60 (1.7%) of the fathers was a twin.

I read that the more children a woman has, the more likely she is to have twins. Does this really happen?

Yes, it does. Research has proved that a woman has a greater chance of having twins the more pregnancies she has. I know of one lady who had three single births, then twins, then triplets!

A friend told me about her sister-in-law, who was told early in pregnancy she was going to have twins. Then sometime later, one of the twins disappeared. Is she making this up?

No, this has happened. Early ultrasound exams have revealed two babies; later ultrasounds of the same woman show one baby disappeared, but the other baby was OK. We believe one of the fetuses may die, then be absorbed in the mother's body. This is one reason many health-care providers prefer not to predict a twin birth before 10 weeks of pregnancy.

Someone said twins are more common with in vitro fertilization. Why?

This may be due to the frequent use of fertility drugs to increase the chance of pregnancy. It's also interesting to note that more girls are born to women who undergo in vitro fertilization (fertilization outside the body).

When is a twin pregnancy most often discovered?

A twin pregnancy is usually found during the second trimester because the woman is larger than expected and growth seems to be too fast.

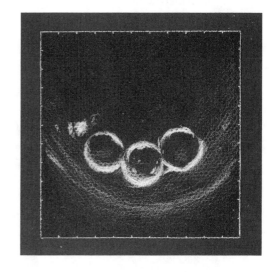

Ultrasound of three fetuses (triplets) early in pregnancy.

What's the best way to diagnose a multiple pregnancy?

Ultrasound is the best way to see if a woman is carrying more than one baby.

If a woman is pregnant with more than one baby, is she likely to have more problems during pregnancy?

The possibility of problems does increase slightly when a woman is carrying more than one baby. Possible problems include:

   ✦ increased miscarriage
   ✦ fetal death or mortality
   ✦ fetal malformations
   ✦ low birth weight or growth retardation
   ✦ pre-eclampsia
   ✦ maternal anemia
   ✦ problems with the placenta
   ✦ maternal bleeding or hemorrhage
   ✦ problems with the umbilical cords
   ✦ hydramnios or polyhydramnios (too much fluid in the bag of waters)
   ✦ labor complicated by breech or transverse presentation
   ✦ premature labor

If I'm expecting more than one baby, what do I have to keep in mind during my pregnancy?

One of the most important things you must remember with a multiple pregnancy is to take things more slowly, from the beginning of your pregnancy until delivery. Taking care of yourself is the best way to take care of your developing babies.

Is it true that a woman who is carrying more than one baby needs to eat more?

It is necessary for a woman who is carrying more than one baby to eat more—at least 300 more calories *per baby* each day than in a single pregnancy! A woman needs more protein, minerals, vitamins and essential fatty acids. Iron supplementation is also necessary.

I recently read an article about "conjoined twins." What are they?

Conjoined twins, until recently also called *Siamese twins,* are twins whose bodies are connected at some point. It is a very serious complication of pregnancy because these babies may share important internal organs, such as the heart, lungs or liver. Sometimes they can be separated; often they cannot.

How are conjoined twins delivered?

It is usually necessary to deliver conjoined twins by Cesarean section.

Does the birth of conjoined twins occur very often?

No, it is very rare.

Will I have a greater chance of having iron-deficiency anemia if I have twins?

Often women who are pregnant with more than one baby do have iron-deficiency anemia. A multiple pregnancy is more stressful for your body than a single pregnancy, and your needs increase in many areas.

Can I exercise during pregnancy if I'm expecting twins?

As a general rule, we advise women who are carrying more than one baby *not* to exercise during pregnancy because of the extra stress their bodies will be dealing with.

I'd like to try to keep in shape during pregnancy. What exercises can I do?

Walking and swimming *may* be permissible for you while you're pregnant with multiple fetuses. Be sure to check out any exercise program with your health-care provider before you do anything. However, do not do anything that is strenuous—and stop immediately if you feel overexerted. As much as you want to stay in shape, you may have to forgo all exercise until after your babies are safely delivered.

Is it true I'll put on a lot more weight with twins or triplets?

You are more likely to put on extra weight with multiple fetuses. For a normal-weight woman, a weight gain of 35 to 45 pounds (15.75 to 20.25kg) for a twin birth is recommended. However, some women do not gain as much weight because of the added stress on their bodies.

Is it true that a woman expecting more than one baby has more heartburn than other pregnant women?

This is often the case. It is caused by the larger uterus encroaching on the space the stomach usually enjoys by itself.

I've heard that most complications in a multiple-fetus pregnancy arise in the last trimester. Is this true?

Yes, this is true. As the babies grow larger, the mother-to-be may experience more problems. The biggest problem with twins is premature labor and premature delivery. When you are carrying twins, you get "big" earlier and you get larger than with a single pregnancy. This can cause problems earlier, such as difficulty breathing, back pain, hemorrhoids, varicose veins, pelvic pressure and pelvic pain.

I heard a mother of twins talking at my doctor's office. She said she waited too long to buy the things she needed for her babies. What did she mean?

Many expectant mothers wait until they are close to the delivery date of their baby to buy nursery items they will need. However, the expectant mother of twins, triplets and more shouldn't wait this long—your second trimester is not too early to buy the things you will need. It may be better to choose these things while you can get around easily than to have to wait until after your babies are born!

A friend who had twins told me her doctor advised her to begin her maternity leave from work early. Is this true?

Often a physician will advise a woman expecting twins to stop working at least 8 weeks before her due date. Ideally, a woman should stop working at 28 weeks with a twin pregnancy—24 weeks if her job requires standing or physical exertion.

My husband and I want to take childbirth-education classes. Can we when we're expecting twins?

It's a very good idea to take these classes for any pregnancy, even twins, triplets or more. However, be realistic and schedule your classes to begin at least *3 months* before your due date. If you have time, a brief course in Cesarean birth might also be worthwhile, if you can find one in your area.

I've heard that multiple fetuses are usually delivered early. What is the average length of pregnancy with more than one baby?

We try to delay delivery of twins until about the 37th week of pregnancy, and triplets until about the 35th week.

How are multiple fetuses usually delivered?

This is somewhat controversial and often depends on how the babies are lying in the uterus. All possible combinations of fetal positions can occur. Some doctors believe two or more babies should always be delivered by Cesarean section. When twins are both head first, a vaginal delivery may be attempted. One baby may be delivered vaginally, with the second requiring a C-section if it turns, if the cord comes out first or if the second baby is distressed after the first baby is born.

I'm expecting twins, and I want to breastfeed. Can I?

Yes, you can. It may be more difficult and more demanding, but many women successfully breastfeed twins.

I've heard breast milk and breastfeeding are good for twins. Why?

We know that breast milk is especially valuable for small or premature infants; often twins are both. For this reason, if you want to breastfeed, go ahead and try it.

We're going to have triplets. Is it possible to breastfeed triplets?

If you're going to try to breastfeed triplets, you'll find it will be more challenging than breastfeeding twins. But it's important to try, if you really want to. One way you may be able to do it is to let each baby breastfeed for a bit at a feeding, then supplement with formula. You can also express your milk, and divide it between the three of them. Because triplets are usually small and premature, your breast milk is very valuable to them.

I have a friend who had triplets born 10 weeks early. Her breast milk never came in. Is this common?

No, this is not common. Usually a mother produces breast milk without complications.

What kind of familial support would you recommend when my twins are born?

Your time of greatest need will be immediately after your babies are born. Ask for help from family, neighbors and friends for the first 4 to 6 weeks after you bring your babies home. You may be fairly exhausted yourself, so it's very helpful to have extra pairs of hands available until you all settle into a routine.

I've heard there are some special groups for families with twins, triplets or more. What are they?

There are some wonderful resource groups for parents and families of multiples. Contact them for information and assistance. See the box on the following page for listings.

Resources for Parents of Multiples

National Organization of Mothers of Twins Clubs, Inc.
P.O. Box 23188
Albuquerque, NM 87192-1188
505-275-0955
> Offers free information to expectant parents or new parents of
> multiples. Will also refer you to local Twins Clubs.

Twin Services
P.O. Box 10066
Berkeley, CA 94709
510-524-0863
> Offers publications and information to parents. Will also refer to local
> groups.

Center for Study of Multiple Births
333 E. Superior St., Rm. 464
Chicago, IL 60611
312-266-9093
> Will supply list of current resources and references for parents of
> multiples.

Twins magazine
5350 S. Roslyn St., Suite 400
Englewood, CO 80111
800-328-3211
1-303-290-8500
customer.service@businessword.com
> Bimonthly magazine for the parents of twins, triplets and more.
> Contact for information about subscribing.

✧ 8 ✧

Changes in Your Growing Baby

I'm confused about how my doctor determines when my baby is due. Can you explain it so I can understand it?

Most women don't know the exact date their baby was conceived, but they usually know the day their last menstrual period began. Because ovulation occurs near the middle of their cycle, or about 2 weeks before the beginning of their next period, the doctor uses the date of the last period and adds 2 weeks as an estimate of when conception occurred. Your estimated due date is 38 weeks after the date of conception.

Is there any other way to determine when my baby is due?

Yes. Add 7 days to the date of the beginning of your last menstrual period, then subtract 3 months. This gives you the *approximate* date of delivery. For example, if your last period began on January 20, your estimated due date is October 27.

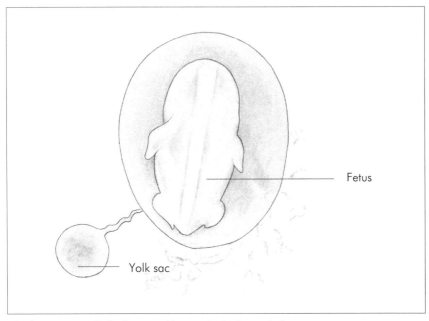

The fetus at 6 weeks looks more like a tadpole than a baby.

I've heard my health-care provider talk about the "gestational age" of my growing baby. What is it?

Gestational age, also called *menstrual age,* dates a pregnancy from the first day of the last menstrual period. It is two weeks longer than the fertilization age.

Then what is the "fertilization age" that I heard my doctor's nurse mention?

Fertilization age, also called *ovulatory age,* is 2 weeks shorter than gestational age and dates from the *actual date of conception.* This is the actual age of the fetus.

These dating techniques are confusing. When my doctor says I'm 12 weeks pregnant, how old is my baby?

Most health-care providers count the time during pregnancy in weeks. If your doctor says you're 12 weeks pregnant, he's referring to the *gestational age*. Your last menstrual period began 12 weeks ago, but you actually conceived *10 weeks ago*, so the fetus is *10 weeks old*.

What is the difference between an embryo and a fetus?

The designation between "embryo" and "fetus" is somewhat arbitrary. During the first 8 weeks of development (10 weeks of gestation), the developing baby is called an *embryo*. From 8 weeks of development until delivery, it is called a *fetus*.

I know my developing baby is going through lots of changes. Can you explain some of them to me?

Your baby grows and changes a great deal during your pregnancy, from a small group of cells to a fully developed baby ready to begin life. Changes are more easily discussed if we look at them in each trimester.

What is a trimester?

The length of your pregnancy is divided into three trimesters, each about 13 weeks long.

How does my baby change during the first trimester?

This trimester is the one of greatest change for any developing fetus. In the first 13 weeks of development, your baby grows from a collection of cells the size of the head of a pin to a fetus the size of a softball. Organs begin developing, and your baby begins to look more normal.

How does my baby change during the second trimester?

At the beginning of the second trimester (14th week), your baby weighs less than 1 ounce (28g) and is only about 4 inches (10cm) long. By the end of this trimester, he or she is almost 9 inches (22cm) long and weighs close to 1-1/2 pounds (700g).

How does my baby change during the third trimester?

Your baby weighs about 1-1/2 pounds (0.7kg) at the beginning of this trimester (27th week) and its crown-to-rump length is under 9 inches (22cm). When it is delivered, your baby will weigh close to 7-1/2 pounds (3.4kg) and be about 21 inches (53cm) long.

I read recently that the baby doesn't change very much after about the twelfth week of pregnancy. What does this mean?

Very few, if any, structures in the fetus are formed after the twelfth week of your pregnancy. This means your baby forms all of its major organ systems by the end of the first trimester. However, these structures continue to grow and to develop until your baby is born.

What is a full-term infant?

A fetus born between the 38th and 42nd week of pregnancy is called a *term baby* or a *full-term infant*.

What is a preterm baby?

If a baby is born before the 38th week of pregnancy, it is called a *preterm baby*.

What is a post-term baby?

A baby delivered at 42 weeks or more of pregnancy is called a *post-term baby*.

How big are most babies when they are born?

The weight varies greatly from baby to baby. However the average weight of a baby at term is 7 to 7-1/2 pounds (3.3 to 3.4kg).

Is there any way to estimate from my size how big my baby will be?

It's very hard to estimate the weight of any baby before birth. Many doctors will take a guess and give a range of a couple of pounds. Some of my estimates have really been off! It's not uncommon to estimate a baby will weigh 8-1/2 (3.8kg) pounds and find it's only a 7-pound (3.15kg) baby when it's born.

My doctor said that ultrasound can sometimes be used to gauge a baby's weight. Is that true?

Ultrasound is sometimes used to estimate fetal weight, but errors do occur. However, the accuracy of predicting fetal weight with ultrasound is improving.

How does ultrasound measure a baby's weight?

A formula has been established to help estimate fetal weight with ultrasound. Several measurements are used, including the diameter of the baby's head, circumference of the baby's abdomen and length of the femur (thighbone) of the baby's leg. Occasionally other fetal measurements are taken.

How accurate is ultrasound in measuring a baby's weight before birth?

It is the test of choice to estimate fetal weight. However, estimates may vary as much as half a pound (225g) in either direction.

I'm 13 weeks pregnant and read that my baby's head is about half or 50% of its body length. Can this be true?

Yes, at this point the head is about half the crown-to-rump length. In 2 months, when you are 21 weeks pregnant, the head will be about one-third of the fetal body. At birth, your baby's head will be one-fourth the size of its body.

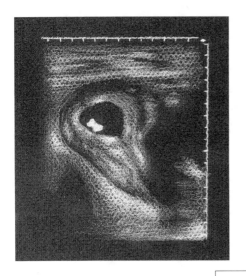

Early ultrasound done at 6 weeks.

Illustration of what ultrasound at 6 weeks shows.

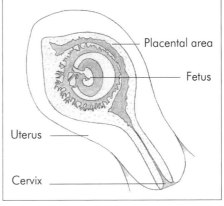

My doctor told me that my baby's heart starts beating very early. When does this happen?

By the sixth week of pregnancy (age of fetus is 4 weeks), the heart tubes fuse and contractions of the heart begin. This can be seen on ultrasound.

When will I be able to hear my baby's heart beat?

It may be possible to hear your baby's heart beat with a stethoscope at around 20 weeks of pregnancy. If you can't hear your baby's heartbeat with the stethoscope, don't worry. It's not always easy, even for a doctor who does this on a regular basis.

With doppler ultrasound, it is possible to hear the heartbeat as early as 12 weeks.

While I was listening to my baby's heart beat the other day at my doctor's office, I heard it skip a beat. Is this serious?

An irregular heartbeat is called an *arrhythmia*. Arrhythmias in a fetus are not unusual, so don't be overly concerned about it. Also, the equipment could be faulty or there may be some other problem transmitting the sound. Your health-care provider will be on the watch for these kinds of problems; if he or she believes there is a problem with the baby, you may be referred to a perinatologist for further evaluation.

If my baby does have an arrhythmia, what can be done about it?

Arrhythmias are not usually serious in a baby before birth; many disappear after the baby is born. If an arrhythmia is discovered before labor and delivery, you may require fetal heart-rate monitoring during pregnancy. When an arrhythmia is discovered during labor, it may be desirable to have a pediatrician present when the baby is born.

How it is decided whether I will have a boy or a girl. Is it very complicated?

The sex of the baby is determined at the time of fertilization. If a sperm carrying a Y chromosome fertilizes the egg, it results in a male child; a sperm carrying an X chromosome results in a female child. It's all determined at the time the sperm fertilizes your egg.

When I had my ultrasound last week it looked like my baby had its mouth open. Is that possible?

Yes, it is. In addition to opening and closing its mouth, the fetus may also suck its thumb or finger.

I've heard a developing baby swallows amniotic fluid.
Is that true?

By 21 weeks, the fetal digestive system has developed enough to allow the fetus to swallow amniotic fluid. The fetus absorbs much of the water in the swallowed fluid. Hydrochloric acid and adult digestive enzymes are present in small amounts in the fetal digestive system at 21 weeks.

Why does my baby swallow the amniotic fluid?

Researchers believe swallowing amniotic fluid may help growth and development of the fetal digestive system. It may also condition the digestive system to function after birth.

How much fluid does my baby swallow?

By the time a baby is born, he or she may swallow large amounts of amniotic fluid, as much as 17 ounces (500ml) of amniotic fluid in a 24-hour period.

Does my baby open its eyes inside my uterus?

Eyelids cover the eyes and are fused or connected around 11 to 12 weeks. They remain fused until about 27 to 28 weeks, when they open.

A friend told me a baby can hear inside the womb, before it's born. Is this true?

Yes. Life inside the womb may be like living near a busy airport. The developing baby hears a constant background of digestive noises and the maternal heartbeat. The mother-to-be's voice is also heard, although the fetus may not hear higher-pitched tones.

Does my growing baby respond to sounds?

There is evidence that by the third trimester the fetus responds to sounds it hears. Researchers have noted fetal heart-rate increases in response to tones it hears through the mother's abdomen.

Will my baby know my voice after she is born?

Newborns have been found to prefer their mother's voice to a stranger's, which suggests they recognize the mother's voice. They have also been found to prefer their mother's native language, and they respond strongly to a recording of an intrauterine heartbeat.

Problems for the Developing Fetus

An article I read said early pregnancy is the time the fetus is most susceptible to malformations. What did it mean?

The first 10 weeks of pregnancy (8 weeks of fetal development) are called the *embryonic period* and is a time of extremely important development in the baby. At this time, the embryo is *most susceptible* to factors that can interfere with its development. Most malformations originate during this period.

What is the chance of my baby having a major birth defect?

Every pregnant couple worries about birth defects. The risk of a major birth defect is about 3%.

I was reading a book that mentioned "teratology." What is that?

Teratology is the study of abnormal fetal development. When a birth defect occurs, we want to know why it happened. This can be frustrating because in most instances we are unable to determine a cause. A substance that causes birth defects is called a *teratogen* or is said to be *teratogenic*. Some things may have a bad effect (be teratogenic) at one point in pregnancy, then be safe at others.

The most critical time appears to be early in pregnancy, during the first trimester or first 13 weeks. An example of this is rubella (German measles). If the fetus is infected during the first trimester, abnormalities such as heart defects can occur. If infection happens later, problems may be less serious.

Do all medications I take affect my baby? I thought some were safe.

Medications can be grouped into three main groups—safe, unsafe and unsure. It's best to avoid medications during pregnancy unless you discuss them with your doctor. Some medications, such as thyroid medication, are necessary and important during pregnancy.

It's easier and safer to discuss this with your physician ahead of time rather than after you have taken the medicine and want to know if it is safe or if it has harmed your baby. For a chart on how some medications can affect the developing fetus, see page 99.

I read about a baby born with cataracts. I thought that only happened to older people—is it possible?

Congenital (present-at-birth) cataracts rarely happen and are usually genetic. With cataracts, the lens of the eye is not transparent. Children born to mothers who had German measles (rubella) around the 6th or 7th week of pregnancy may be born with cataracts.

What is microphthalmia?

Microphthalmia is an abnormal congenital condition of the eye in which the overall size of the eyeball is too small. This occurs more often with other problems of the eyes. The cause is generally thought to be from infections, such as cytomegalovirus (CMV) or toxoplasmosis.

We live in an area with lots of air pollution. Can my exposure to smog and bad air affect my baby?

This is very rarely a problem and would be very hard to prove. Your lungs and airways filter the air you breathe, and that protects your baby.

Premature Birth

I'm 25 weeks pregnant. If my baby was born now, would it be OK?

It is hard to believe, but many babies born at 25 weeks survive. Some of the greatest advances in medicine have been in the care of premature babies. However, don't start wishing for delivery now; babies born this early are in the hospital a long time and often have serious problems.

Why is it risky for the baby to be born early?

Premature birth increases the risk of physical and/or mental impairment in the baby. It also increases the risk of fetal death.

How early is "too early"?

It depends on your particular situation. In many cases, 1 or 2 weeks is not going to make much difference in your baby— the baby may only be slightly smaller. However, the earlier the baby is born, the greater the risks.

I've heard that more premature babies are surviving today. Is that true?

Yes, it is. Because of advances in technology, today fewer than 10 deaths per 1,000 are reported in premature births.

Is it true that premature babies have long hospital stays?

The average hospital stay for a premature baby in 1995 ranges from 50 days to more than 100 days.

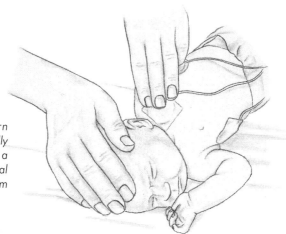

When a baby is born prematurely, it is usually very small and needs a great deal more hospital care than a full-term infant.

How are these premature babies affected?

In babies born extremely early, there is an increased rate of physical and mental handicaps, some of them severe. This is the reason your health-care provider will attempt to prolong your pregnancy as long as possible.

Hydrocephalus

I read an article that talked about hydrocephalus. What is it?

Hydrocephalus is a problem with the development of the baby that causes an enlargement of the head. It occurs in about 1 in 1,000 babies in the U.S. and is responsible for about 12% of all severe fetal malformations found at birth.

How does hydrocephalus happen?

The organization and development of the brain and central nervous system of the baby begin early. Cerebral spinal fluid circulates around the brain and spinal cord, and must be able to flow without restriction. If openings are blocked and the flow of fluid is restricted, it can cause hydrocephalus (sometimes called *water on the brain)*. The fluid accumulates and causes the baby's head to enlarge.

If my baby has hydrocephalus, can anything be done?

Hydrocephalus is a symptom and can have several causes, including spina bifida, meningomyelocele and omphalocele. Sometimes intrauterine therapy—while the fetus is still in the uterus—can be performed.

How is hydrocephalus treated in utero?

There are two ways of treating hydrocephalus in utero (inside the uterus). In one method, a needle is passed through the mother's abdomen into the affected area of the baby's brain to remove fluid. In the other method, a small plastic tube is placed into the area of fluid in the fetal brain. This tube is left in place to drain fluid continuously from the baby's brain.

The Presence of Meconium

A couple of friends of mine who've had babies were discussing meconium. What is it?

The term *meconium* refers to undigested debris from swallowed amniotic fluid in the fetal digestive system. It is a greenish-black to light-brown substance that your baby may pass from its bowels into the amniotic fluid. This may happen before or at the time of delivery.

Is meconium important?

The presence of meconium can be important at the time of delivery. If a baby has a bowel movement and meconium is in the amniotic fluid, the infant may swallow the fluid before birth or at the time of birth. If meconium is inhaled into the lungs, it may cause pneumonia or pneumonitis.

Is there any way to know about meconium ahead of time?

Meconium is detected when your water breaks. Before this time, the only way to know about it is by amniocentesis.

If there is meconium present when I am in labor, what can be done?

If meconium is present at the time of delivery, an attempt is made to remove it from the baby's mouth and throat with a small suction tube so the baby won't swallow it.

What causes meconium in the amniotic fluid?

Passage of meconium into the amniotic fluid may be caused by distress in the fetus. When meconium is present, it doesn't always mean distress, but it must be considered.

Intrauterine-Growth Retardation

A friend of mine was telling me her doctor was concerned about intrauterine-growth retardation. It sounds very serious; what is it?

Intrauterine-growth retardation (IUGR) means a newborn baby is small for its age. By medical definition, the baby's weight is below the 10th percentile for the baby's gestational age. This means that 9 out of 10 babies of the same gestational age are larger. The condition is also called *fetal-growth retardation.*

If my baby has IUGR, does it mean he will be mentally retarded?

No, not usually. The word "retardation" may cause a mother-to-be some concern. Retardation in this sense does not apply to the development or function of the baby's brain. It does not mean the baby will be mentally retarded. It means the growth and size of the fetus are inappropriately small; *growth* and *size* are considered to be retarded or slowed.

Why is IUGR serious?

When the baby's weight is low, the risk of fetal death increases significantly.

What causes intrauterine-growth retardation?

There are many conditions that increase the chance of IUGR. These include the following situations:

- ❖ small size of mother-to-be (probably not a cause for alarm)
- ❖ maternal anemia
- ❖ smoking by the mother-to-be during pregnancy
- ❖ poor weight gain by the mother-to-be
- ❖ vascular disease in the mother-to-be, including high blood pressure

❖ kidney disease in the mother-to-be
❖ alcoholism or drug abuse by the pregnant woman
❖ multiple fetuses
❖ infections in the fetus
❖ abnormalities in the umbilical cord or the placenta

If a woman has one baby with IUGR, will her next baby be affected?

Research has shown that a previous delivery of a growth-retarded infant indicates it might happen again in subsequent pregnancies.

How will my doctor know if my baby is too small?

The problem is usually found by watching the growth of your uterus for a period of time and finding no change. If you measure 10.8 inches (27.4cm) at 27 weeks of pregnancy and at 31 weeks you measure only 11 inches (28cm), your doctor might become concerned about IUGR. This is one of the important reasons for you to keep all your prenatal appointments.

If IUGR is diagnosed, can anything be done for the baby?

Your health-care provider will advise you to avoid anything that can make it worse. Stop smoking. Stop using drugs or alcohol. Eat nutritiously. Bed rest may also be prescribed. This allows your baby to receive the best blood flow from you and thus to receive as much nutrition as possible.

What is the most serious risk to a baby with IUGR?

The greatest risk is stillbirth (death of the baby before delivery). To avoid this, it may be necessary to deliver the baby before full term.

If I have a baby with IUGR, is it more likely I will have a C-section?

Because infants with IUGR may not tolerate labor well, the possibility of a C-section increases due to fetal distress. The baby may be safer outside the uterus than inside, where there is some problem.

Umbilical-Cord Problems

I heard about a baby born recently that had knots in its umbilical cord. What causes this?

We believe knots in the umbilical cord form as the baby moves around early in pregnancy. A loop forms in the umbilical cord, and when the baby moves through the loop, a knot forms.

I've heard that the baby can get tangled up in the umbilical cord. Is this true?

In some cases this is true, but it usually isn't a problem. There is nothing you can do to prevent this from happening.

Could a tangled cord hurt my baby?

It isn't necessarily a problem. It only becomes a problem if the cord is stretched tightly around the neck or in a tight knot.

Is there anything I can do to keep my baby from getting a knot in its umbilical cord?

No, there is nothing you can do to prevent it. Be reassured to know these knots do not occur often.

∗9∗

Changes in You

I know the baby grows and changes a great deal during pregnancy. What can I expect for me?

The time of pregnancy is an exciting time for you and may be a little frightening, too. You will see yourself change in many ways—your abdomen will grow much larger, your breasts will enlarge, you may experience some swelling in hands and feet, and you may experience many other changes. By being aware of these changes, you should be more comfortable with them.

What changes will I see during the first trimester?

You will see very little change in yourself, although your baby is growing and changing quite rapidly. You may not even realize you are pregnant until the middle or close to the end of this trimester! You will experience very little weight gain during this time—probably no more than 5 pounds (2.25kg) for the entire 13 weeks. Your abdomen will grow a little—you may be able to feel your uterus about 3 inches (7.6cm) below your bellybutton. You won't feel the fetus move during this time.

What changes will I see during the second trimester?

You will begin showing to others you are pregnant during this trimester. You will be able to feel your uterus about 3 inches (7.6cm) *below* your bellybutton at the beginning of this trimester. By the end, you will feel your uterus about 3 inches (7.6 cm) *above* your bellybutton.

Average weight gain for this trimester is a total (including weight from the first trimester) of 17 to 24 pounds (7.65 to 10.8kg). You will begin to feel your baby move during this time.

A pregnant woman's uterus takes up a great deal of space in the abdominal cavity. Other organs are pushed out of the way, which can make the woman feel very uncomfortable.

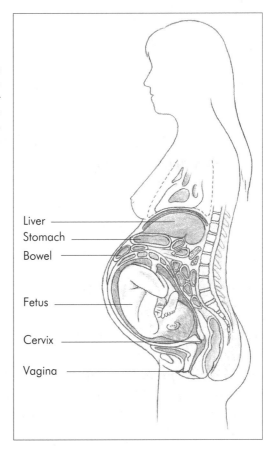

Liver
Stomach
Bowel

Fetus

Cervix

Vagina

What changes will I see during the third trimester?

You will experience a great deal of change in you during this time because your baby will be growing so much. You will be able to feel your uterus about 3 inches (7.6cm) above your bellybutton at the beginning of this trimester. By delivery, you will feel your uterus 6-1/2 to 8 inches (16.5 to 20.3cm) above your bellybutton.

Your baby will be gaining a great deal of weight during this time, even though you may not. Total weight gain by delivery is 25 to 35 pounds (11.25 to 15.75kg) for the average woman.

What can I do about the changes I go through during pregnancy?

The most important thing you can do for yourself is to get good prenatal care. Follow your doctor's recommendations about nutrition, medication and exercise. Keep all your appointments. Establish good communication with your health-care provider. Ask any question that bothers you.

My cousin said that with her second and third pregnancies, her body started to change much earlier than with her first pregnancy. Why?

The way a woman's body responds to pregnancy is influenced by her previous pregnancies. Skin and muscles stretch to accommodate the enlarged uterus, placenta and baby. Stretched muscles and stretched skin are never exactly the same again. They may give way faster to accommodate the growing uterus and baby with subsequent pregnancies, which causes a woman to show sooner and feel bigger.

I'm 11 weeks pregnant and know I'm almost done with the first trimester, but I don't even show yet. Should I be concerned?

No. A lot has been happening with the development of your

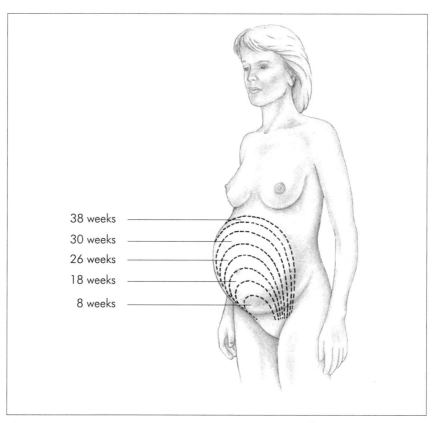

38 weeks
30 weeks
26 weeks
18 weeks
8 weeks

This illustration shows how a woman's uterus grows during pregnancy. The dotted lines represent growth from about 8 weeks through the end of the third trimester (about 38 weeks).

baby's organs and organ systems. However, friends are probably not yet able to tell you're pregnant. You may be able to feel your uterus down by your pubic bone or your clothes may be getting a little snug.

If this is your first pregnancy, it often takes longer to see a change in your "tummy." If you have had other pregnancies, you will probably show sooner. Don't despair—you'll be getting larger soon, then everyone will know you're pregnant!

I'm not very far along and feel a lot bigger than with my last pregnancy. Is this OK?

It isn't unusual to show sooner or feel bigger if you have had other pregnancies. You can blame the other pregnancies for stretching your skin and muscles so you show sooner. Another couple of possibilities are that you are farther along than you think or you are carrying twins! Discuss it with your health-care provider if you are concerned.

Everyone tells me I'm too big. What's wrong?

Before you become overly concerned, discuss it with your health-care provider. Friends may tell you you are too big or too small; probably nothing is wrong. Women and babies are different sizes and grow at different rates. What is of greatest importance is the continual change and continual growth of the fetus.

Changes in Your Skin

I've noticed a dark line has appeared on my abdomen. What is it?

The vertical line that appears down the midline of your abdomen is called the *linea nigra*. It appears on many women during pregnancy.

Will this line disappear after pregnancy?

The linea nigra often fades markedly after pregnancy, but it may never fully disappear.

I've got brown patches on my face that I never had before. What are they?

Occasionally irregular brown patches appear on the face and neck of a pregnant woman. Patches are called *chloasma* or *mask of pregnancy* and are believed to be caused by the hormonal changes brought about during pregnancy. Usually these dark patches disappear completely or get lighter after your baby is born. (Oral contraceptives often cause similar pigmentation changes.)

Since I got pregnant, I've noticed some small red elevations on the skin of my neck and upper chest. What causes this?

During pregnancy, you may experience vascular changes to your skin. These small red elevations, with branches extending outward, are called *vascular spiders, telangiectasias* or *angiomas*. They usually occur on the face, neck, upper chest and arms, and will disappear after delivery.

My sister-in-law had red palms all during her pregnancy. Is this common?

The condition you're referring to, called *palmar erythema,* is not uncommon. It occurs in 65% of pregnant white women and 35% of pregnant black women. It is probably caused by increased estrogen in the system and is usually symptomless. It's OK to use lotions but the redness of your palms may not disappear until after you deliver.

Can vascular spiders and red palms occur together?

Yes, they often occur together. Symptoms are temporary and disappear shortly after delivery. Researchers believe the occurrence of these conditions is caused by high levels of estrogen during pregnancy.

I've noticed that I have a mole that seems to be getting larger. Is this something I should be concerned about?

Pregnancy can cause many changes in your skin. Moles may appear for the first time, or existing moles may grow larger and darken during pregnancy. If you have a mole that changes, be sure to have your health-care provider check it.

I have little tags of skin that seemed to have grown since I became pregnant. What are they?

Skin tags are small lumps or bumps of skin that may appear for the first time during pregnancy. If you already have them, they may grow larger while you are pregnant. Don't worry too much about them. If they are in an area that is rubbed frequently, you may want to talk to your doctor about removing them.

I've noticed since I've been pregnant that my skin feels itchy, and I scratch a lot. Does this indicate a problem?

Itching, also called *pruritis gravidarum*, is a common symptom during pregnancy. It usually occurs later in pregnancy, and about 20% of all pregnant women suffer from it. Itching does not indicate any problem in your pregnancy.

The skin over my abdomen itches the worst. What causes this?

As your uterus grows and fills your pelvis, abdominal skin and muscles must stretch to accommodate it. Stretching of the skin causes abdominal itching in many women.

What can I do about this itching?

If you scratch the skin, it can make it worse, so try not to scratch. There are lotions available to help reduce the itching. Occasionally cortisone creams are used. Ask your health-care provider about relief.

I've noticed I've had flareups of pimples lately. Is this related to my pregnancy?

Most women experience some changes in their skin while

pregnant. Some women find their skin breaks out more often. Some lucky women find their skin becomes less oily and softer. These changes are due to the hormones of pregnancy; your skin will probably return to normal after your baby is born.

My dermatologist just told me I have a couple of precancerous spots on my face. I've had them before and usually get them removed. Can I do this during pregnancy, or should I wait until after the baby is born?

Yes, you can have these spots removed. This is usually done in the doctor's office and is not a problem.

What are stretch marks?

Stretch marks, also called *striae distensae,* are areas of stretched skin that may be discolored. They usually occur on the abdomen as your growing uterus stretches the skin. They can also occur on the breasts, hips or buttocks.

Will my stretch marks go away after my pregnancy?

Stretch marks usually fade and won't be as noticeable after your pregnancy, but they won't go away completely.

Is there anything I can do to avoid getting stretch marks?

No one has found a reliable way of avoiding stretch marks. Women have tried many kinds of lotions with little success. There is no harm in trying lotion products, but they probably won't help.

Varicose Veins

My mother had varicose veins during her pregnancies. Will I?

Varicose veins, also called *varicosities* or *varices,* occur to some degree in most pregnant women. There seems to be an inherited predisposition to varicose veins that can become more severe during pregnancy. If your mother had varicose veins, you have a greater chance of having them.

What causes varicose veins?

Varicose veins (varices) are dilated blood vessels that fill up with blood. They usually occur in the legs but also may be seen as hemorrhoids or appear in the birth canal and in the vulva. The pressure from the uterus and the change in blood flow make varices worse.

What do varicose veins look like?

Symptoms vary. For some women varicose veins are only a blemish or purple-blue spot on the legs. These cause little or no discomfort, except in the evening. For other women, varices are bulging veins that require elevation of the legs at the end of the day.

Will varicose veins get worse during pregnancy?

They may. In most cases, they become more noticeable and more painful as pregnancy progresses. Increasing weight (from your growing baby), clothing that constricts at the waist or legs, and standing a great deal will cause them to worsen.

If I have varicose veins, what can I do?

Many women wear maternity support hose; there are various types available. Clothes that don't restrict circulation at the knee or groin may also help. Spend as little time as possible on your feet. Elevate your feet above the level of your heart or lie on your side when possible to allow drainage of the veins. Wear flat shoes. Don't cross your legs when you sit down. If you continue to have problems after your pregnancy, surgery may be required.

Friends who have varicose veins say the maternity support hose really do work, but they are almost impossible to get on. Do you have any suggestions?

Support hose can be very difficult to put on, but there are a couple of tricks that can help you get them on more easily. First, turn stockings inside out. Starting at the toe, unroll the stockings up your legs. Second, put your support hose on *before* you get out of bed in the morning—your legs may tend to swell as soon as you get up.

Is there anything I can do during pregnancy to decrease my chances of getting varicose veins?

There are some things you can do to help decrease your chances of developing varicose veins. Some of these practices are the same ones you would use if you suffer from varicose veins.

- ✧ Exercise.
- ✧ Don't cross your legs at the knee.
- ✧ Don't stand for long periods of time.
- ✧ If you must stand, bounce gently on the balls of your feet every few minutes.
- ✧ Elevate your legs above the level of your heart or lie on your side several times a day.
- ✧ Keep your total pregnancy weight gain in the normal range—from 25 to 35 pounds (11.25 to 15.75kg) for a normal-weight woman.

Emotional Changes During Pregnancy

I seem to cry at the least little thing. Why does this happen?

Crying easily, mood swings, energy lows and fatigue are all normal aspects of pregnancy. During the first trimester of pregnancy, your body experiences an increase in hormones that are needed to support a pregnancy. Some women are more sensitive to these changes, especially those who are sensitive to a similar hormonal shift before menstruation. If you become weepy or edgy around your menstrual period, you may experience similar emotions as your body adjusts to pregnancy.

I am experiencing conflicting feelings about my pregnancy. Is this normal?

It is very normal. Your conflicting feelings arise from your adjustment to your pregnancy—you are taking the first steps toward an incredible role change that will involve many aspects of your life. Your feelings of conflict come from your attempts to deal with all the questions and concerns you have.

I've been very depressed during my pregnancy. Should I ask my doctor for an anti-depressant?

Anti-depressant medication is not usually prescribed during pregnancy because it is not considered safe. However, if it is necessary, most physicians prefer to use tricyclic anti-depressants, such as amitriptyline and desipramine. Treatment must be done on an individualized basis. Your doctor and possibly a psychiatrist or psychologist will discuss the situation with you.

I'm in my third trimester and seem to be more emotional than ever. Is there anything wrong with me?

No, you're normal. You may be getting a little more anxious about the upcoming labor and delivery. You may find mood swings occur more frequently, and you may be more irritable. Try to relax and not focus on your feelings. Talk to your partner about how you are feeling and what you are experiencing.

Some Discomforts of Pregnancy

I have terrible morning sickness. When will it end?

By the end of the first trimester, most women experience an improvement in morning sickness. For more information on morning sickness, see Chapter 2.

Is it true that it's not unusual to experience pain in my uterus during pregnancy?

As your uterus grows during pregnancy, you may feel slight cramping or even pain in your lower abdominal area on your sides. Your uterus will tighten or contract throughout your pregnancy. If you don't feel this, don't worry. However, if contractions are accompanied by bleeding from the vagina, call your health-care provider immediately!

A friend mentioned Braxton-Hicks contractions. What are they?

Braxton-Hicks contractions during pregnancy are painless, non-rhythmical contractions you may be able to feel when you place your hands on your abdomen. You may also feel them in the uterus itself. These contractions may begin early in your pregnancy and are felt at irregular intervals. They are not signs of true labor.

I've had a weird feeling in my pelvic area—sort of a "pins and needles" feeling. Is there something wrong?

Not usually. This is another feeling associated with increased pressure as the baby moves lower in the birth canal. Tingling, pressure and numbness are common at this time and shouldn't concern you.

Can I do anything to alleviate any of this pressure?

Lie on your side to help decrease pressure in your pelvis and on the nerves, veins and arteries in your pelvic area.

When I move or get up, it hurts on my sides. Should I worry?

Probably not. What you are describing is usually called *round-ligament pain.* The round ligaments are on either side of the uterus; as your uterus gets bigger, these ligaments stretch and get longer and thicker. Quick movements can stretch these ligaments and hurt. This is not harmful to you or your baby, but it can be uncomfortable.

What can I do for round-ligament pain?

Be careful about quick movements. It may feel better to lie down and rest. Most doctors recommend acetaminophen (Tylenol) if the pain bothers you. Tell your doctor if it gets worse.

Feeling Your Baby Move

My friend was talking about "quickening." What is it?

Quickening is feeling your baby move. It usually occurs between 16 and 20 weeks of pregnancy.

I'm 15 weeks pregnant and felt my baby move already. Is there something wrong?

The time at which you first feel your baby move is different for every woman. It can also be different from one pregnancy to another. One baby may be more active than another, so movement is felt sooner.

I thought I felt my baby move when I was 11 weeks pregnant, but my doctor said it probably was gas. How will I know that what I feel is my baby moving?

Many women describe the first feelings of movement from their baby as a gas bubble or fluttering in their abdomen. It may be something you notice for a few days before you realize what it is. Movements will be more common and occur fairly frequently—that's how you'll know that what you're feeling is your baby moving. The movement will be below your belly-button. If it's your first baby, it may be 19 or 20 weeks before you are sure you feel movement.

I'm in the early part of my second trimester, and I haven't felt my baby move yet. Is that OK?

Yes, it's all right. The normal time to feel movement is between 16 and 20 weeks.

I just felt my baby move for the first time last week but haven't felt it for a couple of days. What's wrong?

Probably nothing. It is normal not to feel it every day at first. As your baby grows, you'll feel movements become stronger and probably more regular.

Taking care of yourself is very important during pregnancy. Be sure you get enough rest, eat healthy meals and exercise. Plan some quiet time for yourself every day.

My friend, who is also pregnant, complains that her baby moves all the time. My baby doesn't move that much. Should I be worried?

This is a hard question to answer. Your sensation of your baby moving is different from your friend's, and the movement of every baby is different. It isn't unusual for one baby to move less than another. If your baby has been very active then is very quiet for a while, you may want to discuss it with your doctor. He or she will determine if there is any concern.

My baby is extremely active during the night, and it keeps me awake. Is there anything I can do about it?

There really isn't much you can do about this. You might try changing your position in bed. Avoid exercising just before bed—it may cause your baby to move more. If these tips don't work, you may have to be patient and just endure it until your baby is born.

My baby kicks a lot, and it hurts. Is there anything I can do to make her stop?

Try changing your position and lying on either side. It still may be uncomfortable. Taking acetaminophen or relaxing in a warm (not hot) bath may also help.

I get a sort of pain under my ribs sometimes when my baby is active. Can I do anything about it?

There isn't very much you can do about the pain or the pressure you feel when your baby moves. You might try lying on your side and resting for a while. For example, if you feel pressure under your right ribs, lie on your left side.

A friend of mine is 26 weeks pregnant. Her doctor wants her to keep track of her baby's movements. Why?

A doctor may have a mother-to-be monitor her baby's movements around this time if she has had a difficult pregnancy, if she had a previous stillbirth or if she has a medical condition, such as diabetes. Recording the movements at certain times each day may provide the doctor with additional information about the status of the fetus.

Between 20 and 32 weeks of pregnancy, the fetus can move between 200 and 500 times a day, including kicking, rolling or wiggling.

My health-care provider said my baby is "floating." What did she mean?

This means the baby can be felt at the beginning of the birth canal, but it has not dropped into the birth canal. That is, the baby is not engaged (fixed) in the birth canal at this time. The baby may even move away from your health-care provider's fingers when you are examined.

I feel as though my baby is going to fall out. This can't happen, can it?

No, it can't. What you are probably experiencing is the pressure of your baby as it moves lower in the birth canal. If this occurs, bring it to your doctor's attention. He or she may want to do a pelvic exam to check how low the baby's head is.

Constipation

I've never had problems with constipation before. Why do I have it now?

It is common during pregnancy for bowel habits to change. Most women notice an increase in constipation, often accompanied by irregular bowel habits and an increase in the occurrence of hemorrhoids. These problems are usually the result of a slowdown in the movement of food through the gastrointestinal system and iron supplements or iron in prenatal vitamins.

What can I do to relieve constipation?

There are some things you can do to help relieve the problem. Increase your fluid intake, and exercise three or four times a week. Many doctors suggest prune juice or a mild laxative, such as milk of magnesia. Certain foods that are high in fiber, such as bran and prunes, increase the bulk in your diet and may help relieve constipation.

Can I take laxatives to relieve the constipation?

Do *not* use laxatives, other than those mentioned above, without consulting your health-care provider. If your constipation is a continuing problem, discuss it with your health-care provider.

Taking Care of Your Teeth

I've always heard that a woman should avoid any dental treatment when she is pregnant. Is this true?

No! As a matter of fact, you should have regular dental checkups during your pregnancy. They are very important.

My gums seem to be bleeding more now that I'm pregnant. Should I be concerned?

Pregnancy can cause sore, bleeding, swollen gums because of the hormonal changes your body goes through. Your gums are more susceptible to irritation and may bleed more often when you floss or brush your teeth.

Will my gums get better after pregnancy?

Yes. The condition usually clears up by itself after the baby is born. Talk to your dentist if the problem becomes too uncomfortable.

Should I tell my dentist I'm pregnant?

Yes. If you need any dental treatment, advise your dentist you are pregnant before anything is done. Some dental anesthetics might harm your baby. In most cases, a pregnant woman should not have a general anesthetic.

I have a small nodule on my gum that bleeds when I brush it. What is it?

This is called a *pyogenic granuloma* or *pregnancy tumor* and may bleed when you brush your teeth or eat. This condition usually clears up after pregnancy, but don't ignore it if it causes you problems.

I was scheduled to have cosmetic bonding done to my teeth then found out I was pregnant. Should I cancel my appointment?

I usually advise a pregnant woman to wait until after the baby is born to have any *elective* dental procedure. However, if you have a dental trauma, such as an abscess or a broken tooth, get it taken care of immediately!

I usually have X-rays at my dental checkups. Should I have them now?

Be sure you tell your dentist you are pregnant before you begin your exam. In most cases, avoid dental X-rays while you are pregnant. If there is a particular need for them, discuss the problem with your dentist *and* your health-care provider before proceeding any further. If you *must* have an X-ray, shield your pregnancy with a lead apron.

I had to have a root canal done last year and had to take antibiotics before the procedure. If I have the same kind of problem while I'm pregnant, should I take antibiotics?

You must discuss this situation with both your dentist and your doctor. They will be able to decide the best course of action. You must understand that taking care of this kind of problem is important—an infection in you might possibly harm the baby. Together, your dentist and doctor will plan the safest course of treatment for you and your baby.

Are there any ways I can help keep my teeth in good shape during pregnancy?

There are many things you can do yourself to keep your teeth and gums healthy while you are pregnant. Follow these tips.

- ✧ Brush your teeth after every meal.
- ✧ Floss teeth at least once a day.
- ✧ Have at least one checkup and dental cleaning during pregnancy, preferably after the first trimester.
- ✧ Watch your diet. Eat foods rich in vitamin C (good for gums) and calcium (to keep teeth healthy).
- ✧ If you have morning sickness, rinse teeth thoroughly after vomiting.

Miscellaneous Problems You May Experience

I just found out I'm 9 weeks pregnant, and I have to go to the bathroom all the time. Does this last all through pregnancy?

One of the first symptoms of early pregnancy is frequent urination. This problem continues off and on throughout pregnancy; you may have to get up to go to the bathroom at night when you never did before. It usually lessens during the second trimester, then returns during the third trimester, when the growing baby puts pressure on the bladder.

My friend, who is also pregnant, told me she has a urinary-tract infection. She said it's common in pregnancy. Is it?

It is more common to get urinary-tract infections during pregnancy. They are also called *bladder infections, cystitis* and *UTIs*.

How will I know if I have a urinary-tract infection?

Symptoms include painful urination, a burning during urination, the feeling of urgency to urinate, blood in the urine and frequent urination.

Can I do anything to avoid a urinary-tract infection?

You can do yourself a favor by not "holding" your urine. Empty your bladder as soon as you feel you need to. Drink plenty of fluids. Cranberry juice helps acidify your urine (kills bacteria) and may help you avoid infections. For some women, it helps to urinate after having intercourse.

Can a urinary-tract infection harm my baby?

A urinary-tract infection during pregnancy may be a cause of premature labor and low-birth-weight infants. If you think you have an infection, discuss it with your health-care provider. If you do have an infection, take the entire prescription of antibiotics prescribed for you.

Ever since I got pregnant, I've noticed I have more vaginal discharge. Is this a sign of a problem?

No. It's normal to have an increase in vaginal discharge or vaginal secretion during pregnancy. It is called *leukorrhea*. The discharge is usually white or yellow and fairly thick. It is not an infection.

What causes the increase in vaginal secretions?

We believe it is caused by the increased blood flow to the skin and muscles around the vagina, which also causes

Chadwick's sign in early pregnancy. This symptom is visible to your doctor as a violet or blue coloration of your vagina when he or she does a pelvic exam. (It's one of the reasons your doctor performs a pelvic exam on you in early pregnancy.)

How do I treat this vaginal discharge?

Do *not* douche if you have a heavy vaginal discharge during pregnancy. Wear sanitary pads for protection. Avoid wearing pantyhose and nylon underwear—choose cotton underwear or underwear with a cotton crotch.

What if the vaginal discharge is caused by an infection? How will I know?

The discharge that accompanies a vaginal infection is often foul-smelling, has a greenish or yellowish color, and causes itching or irritation around or inside the vagina. If you have any of these symptoms, notify your health-care provider. Treatment is often possible; there are many creams and ointments available that are safe to use during pregnancy.

Changes in Your Breasts

I'm 13 weeks pregnant, and my breasts are getting bigger. Isn't this a little early?

There are many changes in your breasts during pregnancy. After about 8 weeks, it's normal for your breasts to start getting larger. You may even notice they are lumpy or nodular. These are all normal changes in pregnancy.

My breasts are very tender and sore. Is this normal?

Tenderness, tingling or soreness of your breasts early in pregnancy is common.

I've noticed the area around my nipples is getting darker. Should I be concerned?

No, this is normal. The nipple is surrounded by the *areola*. Before pregnancy the areola is usually pink but turns brown or red-brown and may get larger during pregnancy and lactation (when you are producing milk).

I've noticed some fluid coming from my breasts, staining my clothes. I'm only about halfway through my pregnancy. Is this breast milk already?

No, it isn't. During the second trimester, a thin yellow fluid called *colostrum* is formed; it is the precursor to breast milk.

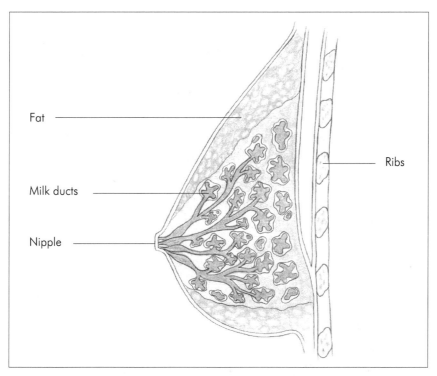

A pregnant woman's breasts change a great deal during pregnancy. One of the greatest changes is the increase in the number of milk ducts, which prepares the breast for nursing.

Sometimes it will leak from the breasts or can be expressed by squeezing the nipples. This is normal. It is usually best to leave your breasts alone; don't try to express the fluid. Wear breast pads if you have problems with leakage.

I've heard about "inverted nipples," but don't know what that means. Can you tell me more about them?

Some women have inverted nipples, which are nipples that are flat or that invert (retract) into the breast. Women with inverted nipples may find it more difficult to breastfeed. Ask your doctor about this. There are devices you can use to help prepare your breasts for nursing and make it possible for you to breastfeed your baby.

How can I tell if I have inverted nipples?

To determine if you have inverted nipples, place your thumb and index finger on the areola, the dark area surrounding the nipple. Gently compress the base of the nipple. If it flattens or retracts into the breast, you have inverted nipples.

Can I do anything about inverted nipples?

Yes. You can begin wearing breast shells during the last few weeks of pregnancy. These plastic shells are worn under your bra and create a slight pressure at the base of the nipple. This pressure helps draw the nipple out. Ask your health-care provider for further information.

I know it sounds silly, but I read in one of the supermarket tabloids about a woman who got pregnant, and her breasts went from a size 34B to a size 56H. Is this possible?

Your breasts will enlarge during your pregnancy. However an increase of this type would be extremely unlikely.

Other Changes You Experience

When will I have to start wearing maternity clothes?

By the beginning of the second trimester (around the 14th week of pregnancy), maternity clothes will probably be a necessity. If this is your first pregnancy, you may not need maternity clothes until a little later. Also see the discussion of maternity clothes in Chapter 16.

I'm 18 weeks pregnant, and I'm having trouble getting into my clothes. Is it time for me to get maternity clothes?

When your clothes don't fit well and you're uncomfortable, it's time for more comfortable clothes. You still may not "show" a lot, but it's important to wear clothes that you feel comfortable in. There are many choices for pregnant women, so you should be able to find clothes that are comfortable and will allow you to grow bigger.

I've noticed that my hair has been growing faster and feels thicker now that I'm pregnant. Is this common?

Changes in your hair are often triggered by the pregnancy hormones circulating through your body. You may also notice less hair loss than usual. Unfortunately, after your baby is born, the hair you have been retaining during pregnancy is lost. Don't worry about it if it happens to you—you're *not* going bald!

My nails, which have always been soft and hard to grow, are now long and grow very fast. Will they always be like this?

The same hormones that grow your hair also influence your nails. You may find during pregnancy that you have problems keeping your nails filed to a practical length. Enjoy them while you're pregnant. They probably won't last.

I seem to be getting more facial hair now that I'm pregnant. Is this normal?

Some women find they have an increase of facial hair during pregnancy. Usually it's not a problem, but check with your health-care provider if it worries you. Facial hair will probably disappear or decrease after the pregnancy, so wait before making any decisions about permanent hair removal.

I've been perspiring so much during my pregnancy. Why?

Pregnancy hormones can elevate your body temperature slightly, which may lead to greater perspiration. Use absorbent talc to help keep you dry. If you perspire heavily, make sure you keep your fluid intake up to avoid dehydration.

When I'm lying down and look at my stomach, there's a bulge there I didn't have before (not the baby). Is this the sign of a problem?

Abdominal muscles are stretched and pushed apart as your baby grows. Muscles that are attached to the lower portion of your ribs may separate in the midline, which is called a *diastasis recti*. It isn't painful, and it does not harm the baby.

Will this go away after pregnancy?

It may still be present after the birth of your baby, but the separation won't be as noticeable. Exercising can strengthen the muscles, but you may still have a small bulge or gap.

Every time I go to the doctor, she measures my stomach with a tape measure. Why?

As you progress in your pregnancy, your doctor needs a point of reference to measure how much your uterus is growing. Some measure from the bellybutton to the top of the uterus. Others measure from the *pubis symphysis,* the place where pubic bones meet in the middle-lower part of your abdomen, to the top of the uterus.

What kind of things can these measurements tell her?

These measurements can reveal a great deal. If at 20 weeks, you measure 11.2 inches (28cm), your doctor may be concerned about the possibility of twins or an incorrect due date. If you measure 6 inches (15cm) at this point, your due date may be wrong or there may a concern about intrauterine-growth retardation or some other problem. In either case, your doctor would probably have you further evaluated by ultrasound.

I'm due in a couple of weeks, and I've noticed a change in the shape of my abdomen—it seems lower. Should I be concerned about this?

Often a few weeks before labor begins or at the beginning of labor, the head of your baby begins to enter the birth canal, and your uterus seems to "drop" a bit. This is called *lightening*. Don't be concerned if this occurs.

A friend told me that when her baby dropped, she felt better. Why?

One benefit of your baby dropping is an increase in space in your upper abdomen, which gives you more room to breathe. However, as your baby descends, you may notice more pressure in your pelvis, bladder and rectum, which may make you uncomfortable.

Someone told me that my center of gravity changes during pregnancy. How does this affect me?

When your uterus grows, it grows out in front of you, and the center of gravity moves forward over your lower extremities (your legs). There is also an increased mobility of your joints. That is, the joints are looser and it may feel as if they are slipping. This can cause a change in posture, which may cause backaches.

I'm 19 weeks pregnant and have only gained 4 pounds (1.8kg). Should I be concerned?

Weight gain can vary a great deal. If you were sick a lot or had nausea during the first few months, you may have lost weight at first and may be a little behind in gaining weight. If you were overweight before you got pregnant, you may not have gained as much. At this point, you should be gaining weight regularly. Discuss it with your health-care provider if you are concerned.

⋄ *10* ⋄

Sex During Pregnancy

My husband and I are concerned about sexual activity during pregnancy. What should we do?

Discuss this question with your health-care provider. You need to rule out any complications and ask for individual advice. Most doctors agree sex can be a part of a normal pregnancy.

My partner is scared to have sex with me because he's afraid it will hurt the baby. What can I tell him?

Sexual activity doesn't usually harm a growing baby. Neither intercourse nor orgasm should be a problem if you have a healthy pregnancy. The baby is well protected by the amniotic sac and amniotic fluid. Uterine muscles are strong and protect the baby, and a thick mucus plug seals the cervix, which helps protect against infection. Often it's the man who asks about sex during pregnancy. You might want to discuss this with your health-care provider if your partner goes with you to your appointments. If he doesn't, assure him there should be no problems if the pregnancy is normal.

After my husband and I have sex, I feel the baby move a lot. Is this because we had sex?

Your baby moves a lot, no matter what you are doing. If you feel it move more after sexual intercourse, it doesn't mean it was disturbed, uncomfortable or in danger.

My partner and I enjoy sex a lot. Is this bad for me or the baby?

Frequent sexual activity should not be harmful to a healthy pregnancy. Usually a couple can continue the level of sexual activity they are used to. If you are concerned, discuss it with your health-care provider.

I read that some women have a greater desire for sex during pregnancy. Is this true?

It has been reported by researchers that pregnancy does enhance the sex drive for some women. Some women may experience orgasms or multiple orgasms for the first time during pregnancy. This is due to the heightened hormonal activity and increased blood flow to the pelvis.

Physically, I don't feel very much like having sex. Why?

During the first trimester, you may have experienced fatigue and nausea. During the third trimester, your weight gain, your enlarging abdomen, tender breasts and other problems may make you feel less desirous for sex. This is normal. Tell your partner how you are feeling, and try to work out a solution that is good for both of you.

I don't feel very sexy now that I'm pregnant. Is this normal?

You may feel less attractive now that you're pregnant, but many men find a pregnant woman *very* attractive. If you are experiencing these feelings, discuss them with your partner.

Isn't there some happy medium to my feelings about sex during pregnancy?

According to research, women generally experience one of two sex-drive patterns. One is a lessening of desire in the first and third trimesters, with an increase in the second trimester. The second is a gradual decrease in desire for sex as the pregnancy progresses. Sex is individual; you're not going to fit any pattern perfectly. Discuss your feelings with your partner. Tenderness and understanding can help you both.

I feel physically uncomfortable having sex the way my body is changing. What can we do about it?

You may find new positions for lovemaking are necessary as your pregnancy progresses. Your larger abdomen may make some positions more uncomfortable than others. In addition, physicians advise a woman not to lie flat on her back from the beginning of the third trimester until the birth. The weight of the uterus restricts circulation. Try lying on your side or with you on top.

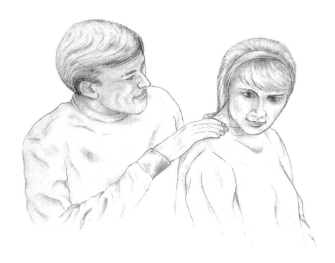

What should I do if I have problems or concerns?

As I stated before, discuss any complications and concerns with your health-care provider throughout your pregnancy. If you have any unusual symptoms during or following sexual activity, discuss them with your health-care provider *before* resuming sex.

What about sex and miscarriage?

If you have a history of miscarriage, your doctor may caution you against sex and orgasm. However, there is no data that actually links sex and miscarriage.

My friend told me that having sex can cause me to go into labor early. Is this true?

Orgasm causes mild uterine contractions, so if you have a history of early labor your health-care provider may warn against intercourse and orgasm. Chemicals in semen may also stimulate contractions, so it may not be advisable for the woman's partner to ejaculate inside her. However, in a normal pregnancy, even one near delivery, this is usually not a problem.

What should we avoid during sex now that I'm pregnant?

Some practices should be avoided during sex if you're pregnant. Don't insert any object into the vagina that could cause injury or infection. Blowing air into the vagina is dangerous because it can force a potentially fatal air bubble into the woman's bloodstream. Nipple stimulation releases *oxytocin*, which causes uterine contractions. You might want to discuss this with your doctor.

Are there times we should avoid sex during pregnancy?

Avoid sexual activity if you have any of the following problems or conditions:

 ❖ placenta previa or a low-lying placenta
 ❖ incompetent cervix
 ❖ premature labor
 ❖ multiple fetuses
 ❖ ruptured bag of waters
 ❖ pain
 ❖ unexplained vaginal bleeding or discharge
 ❖ you can't find a comfortable position
 ❖ either partner has an unhealed herpes lesion
 ❖ you believe labor has begun

·11·
Your Partner
& Your Pregnancy

How should I involve my partner before we try to conceive?

Getting pregnant and having a baby involves *both* of you. Talk about the decision to get pregnant, your health and your partner's health. Do this before you try to get pregnant.

How much should my husband be involved in my pregnancy?

Your partner can be a very important source of support for you. It's probably a good idea to involve him as much as he is willing to be involved. Make him feel he's a part of what's going on.

How can I involve my partner more in my pregnancy?

Because the pregnant woman is the focus during pregnancy, a man may feel left out. Educate him so he understands what you and the baby are going through. Share this book and other books and information you receive with him. Take him with you to see the doctor.

My husband seems to find me very sexy now that I'm beginning to show. Is sex OK during pregnancy?

In a normal pregnancy, sex can be a wonderful experience for you both. For a more-detailed discussion of sex during pregnancy, see Chapter 10.

My partner isn't as enthusiastic as I am about the upcoming birth of our first baby. Is this normal?

Few expectant fathers are as excited about the impending birth as the mother-to-be is. You are directly involved in the pregnancy because you are carrying the baby. Your partner is less involved, so you may have to adjust your expectations somewhat. You may need to take an active role in encouraging your partner to become more involved, such as asking him to accompany you to a prenatal visit. Discuss with him his feelings about the pregnancy. He may have fears and uncertainties he hasn't voiced to you. Be open and direct with each other about your feelings—it will help both of you.

Is it OK for my husband to go to my prenatal appointments with me?

It's actually a great idea for him to accompany you. It will help him realize what is happening to you and may help him feel more like he's a part of the pregnancy. It's also good for your husband and your health-care provider to meet before labor begins.

My partner seems very anxious about my pregnancy. Is this normal?

Your partner may feel increased anxiety as your pregnancy progresses. He may be concerned about your health, the health of the baby, sex, labor and delivery, and his abilities to be a good father. Share your own concerns with him. It may help him calm his anxieties.

My husband wants to know how he can make our pregnancy easier for me. What can I tell him?

A man can help his pregnant partner in many ways.

- ❖ Keep stress to a minimum.
- ❖ Communicate about everything.
- ❖ Be patient and supportive.
- ❖ Promote good nutrition.
- ❖ Encourage exercise.
- ❖ Help around the house when possible, and do the more-strenuous chores.
- ❖ Attend prenatal checkups when possible.
- ❖ Plan for the baby's arrival.
- ❖ Learn about the birth process.

***I've heard the baby's father can begin bonding with the baby
as soon as it is born. How can he do this?***

The baby's father can begin bonding with the baby *before*
birth and continue after the baby is born. Encourage your
partner to try the following suggestions.

- ✧ Have your partner talk to the baby while it is in the
  uterus.
- ✧ Encourage your partner to talk to the baby soon after
  birth. Babies bond to sound very quickly.
- ✧ Have your partner hold the baby close and make eye
  contact; a baby relates to people through sight and
  smell.
- ✧ Let your partner feed the baby. It's easy if you bottlefeed.
- ✧ If you breastfeed, let him give the baby a bottle of your
  expressed breast milk.

✧ Encourage him to help with daily chores, such as changing diapers, holding the baby when it is restless, dressing and bathing the baby.

This may sound weird, but I've heard that a man can suffer from morning sickness when his wife is pregnant. Is this true?

Many fathers-to-be experience some sort of physical problem during their wife's pregnancy. The condition is called *couvade,* from a Carib Indian tribe in which every expectant father engages in rituals that enable him to understand what his wife is experiencing. In our culture, a father-to-be may experience nausea, headache, back and muscle aches, insomnia, fatigue and depression.

I recently read that reproduction and fetal development may be affected if a man is exposed to various chemicals. Is this true?

Yes. Exposure by the father-to-be to alcohol, cigarettes, certain drugs and some environmental hazards could harm the unborn baby. This could also affect the man's ability to father a child.

What kind of problems can be caused by a man's exposure to these substances?

Problems include miscarriage, stillbirth, birth defects, low-birth-weight babies, a greater risk of childhood cancer and even subtle learning disabilities.

When is this exposure the most important?

Usually male exposure is harmful if it occurs before and around the time of conception. However, we also know that a father-to-be's smoking throughout pregnancy has been linked to various problems.

I've heard that my husband's use of alcohol before my pregnancy may have an effect on the baby. In what way?

Some researchers believe heavy alcohol consumption by the baby's father may produce *fetal alcohol syndrome (FAS)* in the baby. See Chapter 13 for further information on FAS. Alcohol intake by the father has also been linked to intrauterine-growth retardation.

My partner has used "recreational drugs" on and off. I think he was using them when I got pregnant. Is this going to cause any problems?

Your partner's drug habits may have an effect on your pregnancy. The best thing to do is to tell your doctor and see if there is anything that can be done to reassure you about the well-being of your baby.

Is it true I need to be concerned about substances my partner is exposed to at work?

Yes. Substances may be brought into your home on your partner's work clothes. If you think you may be exposed to hazardous substances in this manner, be sure to discuss it with your partner and your health-care provider.

I don't smoke, but my partner does. Should I try to get him to stop now that I'm pregnant?

When a non-smoking pregnant woman and her unborn baby are exposed to secondary smoke, both are exposed to chemicals that can harm them. It is a good idea to ask your husband to stop smoking during your pregnancy or at least not to smoke inside your home.

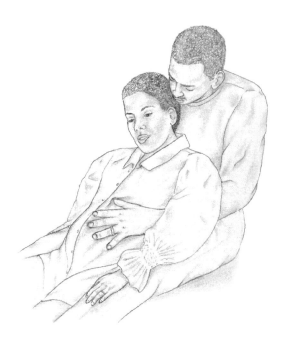

My partner is 53. Can his age cause problems for me or my baby?

We now have information indicating the age and health of the father of your baby *does* make a difference in the health of your baby. Some researchers believe there may be an increased risk of Down's syndrome if the baby's father is over 50.

My husband and I have talked about having him cut the umbilical cord after the baby is born. Will the doctor let him do this?

Cutting the cord is something many men enjoy doing. Talk to your doctor about your husband's participation in the delivery.

I'm afraid I'm going to feel exhausted dealing with the baby after we get home. How can I get my husband to help me?

It's better when both partners share the responsibilities and chores of parenthood. Form an equal-parenthood partnership with your husband, and encourage him to take equal responsibility for parenting your new baby. He'll enjoy being a father much more if he is actively involved in the care and decision-making for his new daughter or son.

My doctor said my husband can be very important to me during labor and delivery. How?

Your husband can help in many ways. He can help prepare you for labor and delivery and can support you as you labor. He can share in the joy of the delivery of your baby. He can also support you emotionally, which can be very important to you both.

⊹ *12* ⊹

Sexually
Transmitted
Diseases

I've heard sexually transmitted diseases can harm a growing baby. Is this true?

A *sexually transmitted disease (STD)* can harm a developing fetus. If you have an STD, you must be treated as soon as possible!

What exactly is a sexually transmitted disease?

A sexually transmitted disease is a disease that is contracted during sexual activity, whether it is sexual intercourse, oral intercourse or anal intercourse.

What are some of the STDs that I need to be aware of?

The most common sexually transmitted diseases include:

- ⊹ monilial vulvovaginitis
- ⊹ trichomonal vaginitis
- ⊹ condyloma acuminatum (venereal warts)
- ⊹ genital herpes simplex infection
- ⊹ chlamydia
- ⊹ gonorrhea
- ⊹ syphilis
- ⊹ AIDS

What is monilial vulvovaginitis?

Monilial vulvovaginitis is an infection caused by yeast, or monilia, and usually affects the vagina and vulva. Yeast infections are more common in pregnant women than in non-pregnant women.

What kind of problems can yeast infections cause during pregnancy?

This STD has no major negative effects on pregnancy, but it can cause discomfort and anxiety for you.

How are yeast infections treated during pregnancy?

Yeast infections are harder to control when you are pregnant. They may require frequent retreatment or longer treatment (10 to 14 days instead of 3 to 7 days). Creams or suppositories used for treatment are safe during pregnancy, although most physicians recommend avoiding treatment during the first trimester. Your partner does not have to be treated unless he has symptoms.

If you think you have a sexually transmitted disease, discuss it with your doctor and your partner.

I've heard of a new medication that I only have to take once, orally, to clear up a yeast infection. Can it be taken during pregnancy?

You're talking about Diflucan® (fluconazole), a new anti-fungal drug. You take it orally, just once, to treat a yeast infection. Unfortunately, we are not recommending it during pregnancy or lactation because it has not yet been proved safe for use in either situation.

What kind of problems can a yeast infection cause the baby?

A newborn infant can get *thrush* (a mouth infection) after passing through a birth canal infected with a yeast infection. Treatment of the newborn infant with nystatin is effective.

What is trichomonal vaginitis?

Trichomonal vaginitis is a venereal infection caused by parasites called *trichomonas*. Symptoms include persistent burning and itching of the vulva area accompanied by a frothy white or yellow discharge.

What kind of problems can trichomonal vaginitis cause during pregnancy?

This infection has no major effects on a pregnancy.

Why is treatment of trichomonal vaginitis a concern during pregnancy?

Metronidazole, the drug used to treat trichomonal vaginitis, should not be taken during the first trimester of pregnancy. It is prescribed after the first trimester.

What are condylomata acuminatum (venereal warts)?

Condylomata acuminatum are skin tags or warts that are transmitted by sexual contact.

What causes condylomata?

Condylomata are caused by a virus called the *human papilloma virus (HPV)*, which is passed during intercourse.

Why are veneral warts a problem during pregnancy?

Warty skin tags often become enlarged during pregnancy and have been known to block the vagina at the time of delivery. If a woman has extensive veneral warts, a Cesarean delivery may be necessary to avoid heavy bleeding and other complications.

How can veneral warts affect a baby?

Infants delivered through a birth canal infected with venereal warts have been known to get laryngeal papillomas (small benign tumors on the vocal cords) after delivery.

Can venereal warts be treated during pregnancy?

Often they can be. Doctors use several methods to treat them, including freezing the warts off, laser therapy and chemical

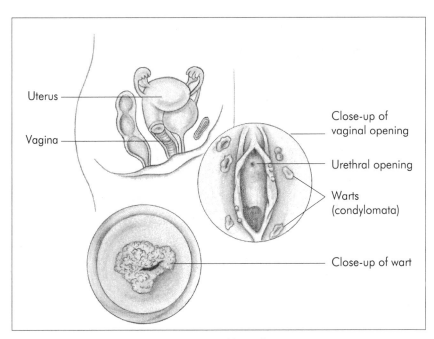

Condylomata (venereal warts) can cause problems during pregnancy.

removal. If warts become large enough to interfere with delivery, your physician may recommend removing them. With the exception of one chemical irritant, podophyllin, all three treatment methods have been safely used during pregnancy.

What is genital herpes simplex infection?

Genital herpes simplex infection is a herpes simplex infection involving the genital area. It can be significant during pregnancy because of the danger of infecting a newborn with the disease at the time of delivery.

What are the symptoms of genital herpes?

Usually clusters of small blisters appear in the genital area within a week after infection. At first the blisters are itchy, then they become painful and break, leaving painful ulcers. Symptoms can also include aches and pains, fatigue, fever and a vaginal discharge. These symptoms usually disappear within three weeks. Subsequent outbreaks can occur at any time, but are usually shorter and milder.

What kind of problems can herpes cause a mother-to-be?

Infection early in pregnancy may be associated with an increase in miscarriage or premature delivery.

What kind of problems can herpes cause the baby?

Infection in the mother is associated with low birth weight in the baby. We believe an infant can contract the infection from traveling through an infected birth canal. When membranes rupture, the infection may also travel upward to the uterus and infect the baby. This could result in fetal infections. Infected newborns have a mortality rate of 50%.

How can herpes simplex be treated during pregnancy?

There is no effective treatment. Acyclovir may decrease the symptoms, but the safety of acyclovir in pregnancy has not been established. When a woman has an active herpes infection late in pregnancy, a Cesarean section is performed to prevent the infant from traveling through the infected birth canal.

If I have herpes, can I prevent my baby from becoming infected?

If you have an outbreak at the time of delivery, a C-section is often done to protect the baby from exposure.

How can I avoid getting genital herpes?

You must know your partner is free from infection. If your partner suspects he has herpes, he should see a health-care provider for treatment. If your partner has herpes or could have been exposed to it, the best way to avoid the disease is through abstinence from sex during outbreaks and having him wear a condom during intercourse.

What is chlamydia?

Chlamydia is a common sexually transmitted disease. It is estimated that between 3- and 5-million people are infected each year. Symptoms include vaginal discharge and pelvic pain. However, it can be symptomless—you may not know you have been exposed. Between 20 and 40% of all sexually active women have been exposed at some time.

How can chlamydia affect pregnancy?

One of the most important complications of chlamydia is *pelvic inflammatory disease (PID)*, which is a severe infection of the female organs. If you have had PID, your chance of having an ectopic pregnancy is greater. During pregnancy, a mother-to-be can pass a chlamydial infection to her baby as it travels through the birth canal. The baby will have a 20 to 50% chance of getting chlamydia.

How does a chlamydial infection affect the baby?

A baby exposed to chlamydia may be born with an eye infection or pneumonia.

If chlamydia is often symptomless, how will I know I have it?

Tests that can be done for chlamydia include a pelvic exam and a swab of the discharge in the vagina.

How is chlamydia treated?

Treatment of chlamydia usually involves tetracycline, which should not be given to a pregnant woman. During pregnancy, erythromycin is the drug of choice.

What is gonorrhea?

Gonorrhea is a venereal infection transmitted primarily by sexual intercourse. In a woman, the urethra, vulva, vagina and Fallopian tubes may be involved. There may be no symptoms of the disease.

How can gonorrhea affect the baby?

The baby may be infected as it passes through the birth canal, resulting in severe conjunctivitis (eye inflammation). Eyedrops are routinely used in newborns to prevent this problem. Other infections in the baby may also occur.

How is gonorrhea treated during pregnancy?

Gonorrheal infections are easily treated with penicillin and other medications that are safe to use during pregnancy.

What is syphilis?

Syphilis is a sexually transmitted disease characterized by lesions that may involve any organ or tissue. The disease may be present for years without symptoms.

How can syphilis affect a pregnancy?

Syphilis increases the chance of stillbirth. It can also cause infection in the newborn's lungs, liver, spleen, pancreas or other organs. Any stage of syphilis during pregnancy can result in infection in an infant.

How can syphilis be treated during pregnancy?

Syphilis can be treated effectively during pregnancy with penicillin and other medications that are safe to use.

I know that AIDS affects more women today. In addition to the personal issue, why is this important to a pregnant woman?

Pregnancy may hide some of the symptoms of *AIDS (Acquired Immune Deficiency Syndrome),* which can make the disease harder to discover. Some possible treatments may not be used during pregnancy.

Can a woman infected with AIDS pass it to her baby?

It is possible for a woman to pass HIV, the virus that causes AIDS, to the baby before birth, during birth and, if she breast-feeds, after birth. The survival rate for children diagnosed with AIDS in the first 6 months of life is very low.

How can a woman find out if she has AIDS or is positive for HIV?

Two blood tests are used—the ELISA test and the Western Blot test. If the ELISA test is positive, it is confirmed by the Western Blot test. Both tests measure antibodies to the virus, not the virus itself. No test should be considered positive unless the Western Blot test is done—it is believed to be 99% sensitive and specific.

I just heard about a new treatment plan for pregnant women who have AIDS. If a woman is given AZT during her pregnancy, the baby almost always will be born without AIDS. Is this true?

The risk to a baby infected with the HIV virus is serious and significant, but advances continue to be made in AIDS research. Recent research has shown that AZT treatment can decrease the likelihood that an infected mother will pass the infection to her baby. If you are concerned about HIV and AIDS, discuss it with your physician.

⋄13⋄
Substance Use
& Abuse

Can my activities affect my developing baby?

Yes, they can and do. It's *never* too early to start thinking about how your actions affect the baby growing inside you. Some substances that you can use safely *may* have adverse effects on a developing fetus. Other substances are bad for both you and your baby.

What kind of activities can affect my baby?

Just about anything you do can affect your baby. Cigarette smoke, alcohol, drugs, tranquilizers, even caffeine can affect a fetus. (For a discussion of caffeine, see Chapter 5.)

How do researchers know that these substances affect a developing baby?

Information about the effects of specific substances on a human pregnancy often comes from cases of exposure before the pregnancy is discovered. These cases help researchers understand possible harmful effects, but they don't help us to understand the picture completely. For this reason, we cannot make exact statements about particular substances and their effects on the mother or developing baby.

Cigarette Smoking

I smoke cigarettes every day. Should I stop?

Yes! A pregnant woman who smokes one pack of cigarettes a day (20 cigarettes) inhales tobacco smoke more than 11,000 times during an average pregnancy! Tobacco smoke inhaled by the mother *can* affect a growing baby.

Why is cigarette smoking so harmful?

Tobacco smoke inhaled by the mother contains many harmful substances, including nicotine, carbon monoxide, hydrogen cyanide, tars, resins and some cancer-causing agents.

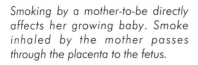

Smoking by a mother-to-be directly affects her growing baby. Smoke inhaled by the mother passes through the placenta to the fetus.

When a pregnant woman inhales cigarette smoke, these chemicals pass through the placenta to the developing baby.

What kind of effects will my cigarette smoking have on the baby?

Infants born to mothers who smoke weigh less than other babies. This can cause problems for the baby. Lower IQ scores and increased incidence of reading disorders have been noted in children born to mothers who smoked during pregnancy. Hyperactivity is also higher in babies born to women who smoked. Research has shown that smoking during pregnancy interferes with the body's absorption of vitamins B and C and folic acid, and increases the risk of pregnancy-related complications.

I've heard pregnancy complications can increase for the mother-to-be if she smokes. Is that true?

Yes. Smoking increases the incidence of serious complications for the pregnant woman. The risk of developing placental abruption increases almost 25% in moderate smokers and 65% in heavy smokers. Placenta previa occurs 25% more often in moderate smokers and 90% in heavy smokers. For further information on these problems, see Chapter 15.

In addition, cigarette smoking during pregnancy increases the risk of miscarriage, death of the fetus or death of a baby soon after birth. This risk is directly related to the number of cigarettes a woman smokes each day. It can increase as much as 35% for a woman who smokes more than a pack of cigarettes a day.

What can I do about it if I smoke?

The best way you can help yourself is to quit smoking completely before and during your pregnancy. If you can't do this—it's hard to quit cold turkey—reduce the number of cigarettes you smoke. It may help reduce your risks.

I want to quit smoking. Is it OK for me to use the Nicoderm® patch or Nicorette® gum while I'm pregnant?

Many studies have shown the harmful effects of cigarette smoking during pregnancy. The *specific* effects of Nicoderm and Nicorette on fetal development are unknown. However, if you are pregnant, researchers advise *avoiding* both of these "stop-smoking" systems.

I don't smoke, but my husband does. Will this hurt me or the baby?

Some research indicates a non-smoker and her unborn baby who are exposed to secondary smoke are exposed to carboxyhemoglobin and nicotine. These substances may harm you or your baby. It is a good idea to ask your husband to stop smoking while you are pregnant. You might suggest he quit smoking altogether.

Alcohol Use

Is it all right to drink alcohol while I'm pregnant?

Alcohol use by a pregnant woman carries considerable risk. Even moderate use of alcohol has been linked to an increase in the chance of miscarriage. Excessive alcohol consumption during pregnancy often results in abnormalities in the baby. Chronic use of alcohol during pregnancy can lead to *fetal alcohol syndrome (FAS)*, which is abnormal fetal development.

What is fetal alcohol syndrome?

Fetal alcohol syndrome (FAS) is a collection of problems that affect children born to alcoholic women. It is characterized by growth retardation before and after birth. Defects in the heart and limbs and unusual facial characteristics, such as a short, upturned nose, a flat upper jawbone and "different" eyes, have also been seen in FAS children. These children may also have behavioral problems, impaired speech and impaired use of joints and muscles.

How much alcohol is "too much"?

At this time, we believe *any* amount of alcohol is too much. Most studies indicate four to five drinks a day are required to cause FAS, but mild abnormalities have been associated with as little as two drinks a day (1 ounce of alcohol). It's best to avoid alcohol completely while you're pregnant.

I don't drink much. Can I drink socially while I'm pregnant?

There is a lot of disagreement about this because we do not know what is a "safe" level of alcohol consumption during pregnancy. I recommend not drinking any alcohol during pregnancy. Why take the risk of harming your baby?

Is this the reason alcoholic beverages carry warning labels?

Yes. The warning advises women to avoid alcohol during pregnancy because of the possibility of causing problems in the fetus, including FAS.

What about drinking before pregnancy, while I'm trying to get pregnant?

If you're trying to get pregnant, you probably won't know exactly when you do conceive. Why take chances? It's a good idea to stop drinking while you are trying to conceive—that way you'll avoid any problems.

I've heard taking drugs with alcohol can cause more problems. How is that?

If drugs are taken with alcohol, it increases the chance of damaging the fetus. Drugs that cause the greatest concern include analgesics, anti-depressants and anti-convulsants.

I read somewhere that my partner's use of alcohol before my pregnancy may affect the fetus. Is this true?

Some researchers believe heavy alcohol consumption by the baby's father may produce FAS in the baby. Alcohol intake by the father has also been linked to intrauterine-growth retardation.

Should I take any other precautions with regards to alcohol?

Be very careful about substances you use that may contain alcohol. Over-the-counter cough medicines and cold remedies often contain alcohol—as much as 25%!

Drug Use and Drug Abuse

I want to know more about drug use, drug abuse and pregnancy. First, how do you define "drug abuse"?

Drug abuse usually refers to drugs prohibited by law, but it can also include use of legal substances, such as alcohol, caffeine and tobacco. Legal medications, such as benzodiazepine or barbiturates, may also have harmful effects, whether they are used for legitimate or illegal reasons.

What is "physical dependence"?

Physical dependence implies the drug must be taken to avoid unpleasant withdrawal symptoms—it does not always mean addiction or drug abuse. For example, many caffeine users develop withdrawal symptoms if they stop drinking coffee, but they are not considered drug abusers or drug addicts.

What is "psychological dependence"?

Psychological dependence means the user has developed an emotional need for a drug or medication. This need may be more compelling than a physical need and can provide the stimulus for continued drug use.

Can the use of drugs impact on my pregnancy?

Yes! Certain drugs damage the developing fetus. In addition, a woman who abuses drugs often has more complications of pregnancy because of her lifestyle.

What kind of problems do you mean?

With use of certain substances, nutritional deficiencies are common. Anemia and fetal-growth retardation can also occur. A pregnant woman may have an increased chance of toxemia or pre-eclampsia.

What about marijuana use during pregnancy? Can it hurt the baby?

Marijuana contains tetrahydrocannabinol (THC). Research has shown that the use of marijuana by a mother-to-be can cause problems including attention deficits, memory problems and impaired decision making in children; these appear between the ages 3 and 12.

How do amphetamines affect the baby?

Researchers have shown that use of central-nervous-system stimulants, such as amphetamines, during pregnancy is associated with an increase in cardiovascular defects in babies.

Some women use barbiturates. Are these harmful during pregnancy?

Barbiturate use may be associated with birth defects, although this has not yet been proved definitely. However, we have seen withdrawal, poor feeding, seizures and other problems in babies born to mothers who abused barbiturates during pregnancy.

Can other tranquilizers affect a pregnant woman?

Tranquilizing agents include benzodiazepines (Valium® and Librium®) and other, newer agents. Several studies have related the use of these drugs to an increase in congenital malformations.

What are opioids?

Opioids are derived from opium and synthetic compounds with similar actions. They produce euphoria, drowsiness or sleepiness, and decreased sensitivity to pain. Habitual use can lead to physical dependence.

What common drugs are opioids?

Opioids include morphine, Demerol®, heroin and codeine.

What kind of problems can opioids cause?

These drugs are associated with a variety of congenital abnormalities and complications of pregnancy. Women who use opioids during pregnancy are often at high risk for premature labor, intrauterine-growth retardation and pre-eclampsia.

What can happen to a baby if the mother uses opioids?

A baby born to a mother who uses opioids may experience withdrawal symptoms after birth.

Are there any other problems associated with using opioids during pregnancy?

If the mother uses the drugs intravenously, other problems may occur, such as AIDS, hepatitis and endocarditis. Any of these is considered *very* serious during pregnancy.

Is the use of hallucinogens declining?

The use of some hallucinogens, such as LSD, mescaline and peyote, is not as common as it was several years ago. However, phencyclidine (PCP) is a powerful hallucinogen whose use is growing.

How does use of PCP affect a pregnancy?

PCP, also called *angel dust,* can cause severe mental illness and loss of contact with reality in the mother. Research has shown it causes abnormal development in some humans, so

we believe it can cause abnormal development in human babies, although it has not been definitely proved.

Can use of hashish hurt a growing baby?

Hashish contains tetrahydrocannabinol (THC). Because we do not have definite answers as to how THC affects a developing baby, it is best to avoid using it during pregnancy.

I know cocaine use is more common today. How does it affect a pregnancy?

Today, use of cocaine is a more-common complication of pregnancy. Often a user consumes the drug over a long period of time, such as several days. During this time, the user may eat or drink very little, which can have serious consequences for a developing fetus.

How does cocaine affect the mother-to-be?

Use of cocaine has been associated with convulsions, arrhythmias, hypertension and hyperthermia in a pregnant woman. Continual use of cocaine can affect maternal nutrition and temperature control, which can harm the fetus. Cocaine use has been linked with miscarriage, placental abruption and congenital defects.

I've heard that use of cocaine during early pregnancy can cause serious problems. Is this true?

If a woman uses cocaine during the first 12 weeks of pregnancy, there is an increased risk of miscarriage. Damage to the developing baby can occur as early as 3 *days* after conception!

How does cocaine use by the mother-to-be affect the baby?

Infants born to mothers who use cocaine during pregnancy often have lower IQs and long-term mental deficiencies. Sudden infant death syndrome (SIDS) is also more common in these babies. Many babies are stillborn.

What about crack use?

All that I have stated about cocaine use can be applied to the use of crack.

I know someone who used drugs a few times while she was pregnant. Her baby seems all right. Aren't you exaggerating the dangers?

No. Your friend was lucky. A fetus is totally dependent on the mother-to-be for all of its needs, so everything a mother-to-be does can affect her baby. What may seem like a small amount to a woman can have a major effect on the fetus whose organs are still being formed. It is up to you to do all you can to help your baby have the best possible start in life.

⋄ 14 ⋄

Special Concerns of the Single Mother-to-Be

I've included this chapter in the book because many women today are having their babies alone, either by choice or because the baby's father is unwilling or unable to be with them. Others will have the support of the father-to-be, but have decided not to get married. My goal in writing it is to give you a foundation for seeking information about your unique situation. I feel comfortable answering the first group of questions because I have been asked many of them before.

I have not answered the second group of questions because they concern legal matters that I am not qualified to answer. However, they are included because there are many legal ramifications to this decision. I hope you will use the questions to help formulate questions about your personal situation to ask your attorney, a patient advocate, a hospital social worker, your health-care provider or family members.

I'm a single woman who has chosen to have my baby alone. What should I tell people who ask me why I am doing this?

It doesn't matter what people ask you—really it's none of their business. What is important is how you feel about the pregnancy. It's up to you to decide what you want to tell people and how much of an explanation you want to provide.

Some people think I'm crazy to have a baby alone. What should I say to them?

Your friends won't treat you this way. Once they understand your situation, they will support you. If others give you a hard time, don't talk with them about your pregnancy or your reasons for having your baby alone.

I feel as if I have no one close to share my pregnancy problems and concerns with. What can I do?

Share your problems and concerns with your family and friends. Mothers of young children can identify with your experiences—they had the same or similar experiences recently. If you have friends or family members who have young children, talk with them. Even if you were married, you would probably share your concerns with all of these people. Try not to let your situation alter this.

My family is against my decision to have my baby alone. Is there anything I can do about this?

If this is a decision you are comfortable with, deal with their discomfort by asking them to talk about the reasons they are against your pregnancy. You will never change some people's minds, so you will have to learn to live with their disapproval or ignore it.

Some people seem very interested in my situation but hesitate to talk to me. Should I encourage them to ask questions?

Only if you are comfortable with their questions. Some people are genuinely concerned about you; others are just nosy. Before you answer, decide if the people are truly interested in you. Then share with them as much or as little as you are comfortable discussing.

I'm having a lot of trouble emotionally with this pregnancy. Who should I talk to about it?

Begin by talking with your health-care provider. Office personnel can direct you to a counselor or a support group, depending on what you need.

Your health-care provider is a good person to talk to about your pregnancy concerns. If she can't help you, she'll be able to direct you to someone who can.

Will I have to make special plans for when I go into labor? What should they cover?

Just as any pregnant woman does, you must decide who will be with you when you labor and deliver, and who will be there to help afterward. The only special plan I can think of is to decide how you will get to the hospital. One woman decided to have her friend drive her, but couldn't reach her in time. Her next option (all part of her plan) was to call a taxi, which got her to the hospital in plenty of time.

I don't have a particular person in mind to ask—what can I do about a labor coach?

Ask a good friend, a relative or someone else who is close to you. Not all women have their partner as their labor coach. I've found that often a woman who has already given birth using the same methods is an excellent labor coach. She will understand your discomfort and be able to identify with your experience.

If I am a single mother, will the nurses treat me differently?

In all my experiences in medical school, during my residency and in my practice, the nurses I have dealt with are professionals. Their job is to provide the best care they possibly can, and they pride themselves in taking care of their patients. I have never known any of them to treat anyone differently for any reason.

How will it be different for me when I take my baby home by myself?

A new baby is always an incredible challenge, in any situation. You will probably need more support from family and friends because you will not have anyone to share the responsibilities with at home. Don't hesitate to ask for their assistance. If you have no one you can ask to give of their time, you might consider hiring someone to stay with you at night for the first week or two, to allow you to get back on your feet.

Do you think people will treat me or my baby differently because I am a single mother?

Today, being a single mother isn't that unusual. Many women of all ages have made this decision. Some people may treat you differently; others won't care. Good friends and family members should draw closer to you.

Because I had donor insemination, my baby won't have another set of grandparents, aunts and uncles. Do you think this will be a problem?

Families today are different than they were in the past. Many children don't have a complete set of parents or grandparents, even in the closest family units. I've found in these situations that an older family friend can be just as loving and giving to a child as a grandparent. Encourage older friends to take an active part in your child's life.

Are there support groups for single parents?

Yes, there are. Ask your health-care provider for the names of groups in your area.

I'm scared that if I get sick, no one will be there to take care of my baby. How can I deal with this problem?

You need to plan ahead for this situation. Find a family member or close friend who can be called upon to help out in case this happens. Knowing you have provided for this event should give you peace of mind.

***People seem to assume my partner and I are married, but
we aren't. What should we do about this?***

If you are pregnant and you are together, most people will
assume you are married. First, decide if it's important to clear
up the misunderstanding. If it's a sales clerk or a waitress, then
it probably isn't important to clarify your situation. If it's your
doctor, you should let him or her know what is going on.

Other Questions

The following questions are included without answers
because they are legal questions that should be covered with
an attorney who specializes in family law. Use them as a
guide to developing the questions you need to ask about
your particular situation.

***A friend who's been through this told me I'd better consider
the legal ramifications of this situation. What was she
talking about?***

***I've heard that in some states, if I'm unmarried I have to get
a special birth certificate. Is that true?***

***I'm having my baby alone, and I'm concerned about who can
make medical decisions for me and my expected baby. Is
there anything I can do about this concern?***

***I'm not married, but I am deeply involved with my baby's
father. Can my partner make medical decisions for me
if I have problems during or after the birth?***

***If anything happens to me, can my partner make medical
decisions for our baby after it is born?***

What are the legal rights of my baby's father if we are not married?

Do my partner's parents also have legal rights in regard to my child (their grandchild)?

My baby's father and I went our separate ways before I knew I was pregnant. Do I have to tell him about the baby?

I chose to have donor (artificial) insemination. If anything happens to me during my labor and/or delivery, who can make medical decisions for me?

Who can make medical decisions for my baby?

I got pregnant by donor insemination. What do I put on the birth certificate under "father's name"?

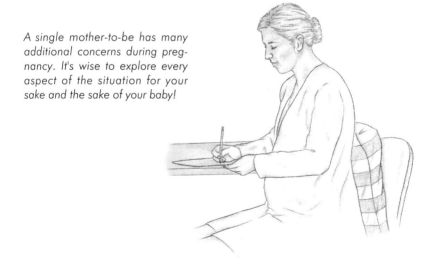

A single mother-to-be has many additional concerns during pregnancy. It's wise to explore every aspect of the situation for your sake and the sake of your baby!

Is there any way I can find out more about my sperm donor's family medical history?

Will the sperm bank send me updates if medical problems appear in my sperm donor's family?

I had donor insemination. Does the baby's father have any legal right to be part of my child's life in the future?

Someone was joking with me that my child could marry its sister or brother some day (because I had donor insemination) and wouldn't even know it. Is this possible?

As my child grows up, he or she may need some sort of medical help (like a donor kidney) from a sibling. Will the sperm bank give out this kind of information?

⋄ 15 ⋄
Problems &
Warning Signs

I'm worried that I won't know when to call my doctor if there are problems during my pregnancy. Are there warning signs I should know about?

If you think there is something to worry about, don't be afraid to ask for help. General warning signs include the following:

- ⋄ vaginal bleeding
- ⋄ painful urination
- ⋄ severe abdominal pain
- ⋄ loss of fluid from the vagina, usually a gushing of fluid, but sometimes a trickle or continual wetness
- ⋄ a big change in the movement of the baby or a lack of fetal movement
- ⋄ high fever (more than 101.6F; 38.7C)
- ⋄ chills
- ⋄ severe vomiting or inability to keep food or liquids down
- ⋄ blurring of vision

✧ severe swelling of the face or fingers

✧ a severe headache or a headache that won't go away

✧ an injury or accident serious enough to give you concern about the well-being of your pregnancy, such as a fall or an automobile accident

Bleeding During Pregnancy

I'm 7 weeks pregnant and started to bleed a little last night. It scares me. What should I do?

Tell your doctor about any bleeding; he or she may want you to have an ultrasound. This early in pregnancy you are probably worrying about having a miscarriage. Be assured that bleeding during pregnancy is not unusual and doesn't always mean a problem. About one woman in five bleeds sometime in early pregnancy.

What causes the bleeding?

Usually we cannot give a definite answer as to what causes it, but we do know that it is *not* usually a problem. If you experience any vaginal bleeding during pregnancy, call your doctor.

I called my doctor and told him I had some bleeding, and he told me to rest and not to have intercourse. Isn't there some medicine I can take or something I can do to stop the bleeding and make sure everything is going to be OK?

Your doctor gave you good advice—there isn't any surgery or medicine that will stop the bleeding. If your concern or your doctor's concern is high, he may schedule you for an ultrasound. An ultrasound won't stop anything from happening; it may give some reassurance, but you may still bleed. Decisions about a course of treatment or actions to take are very individual and must be discussed with your doctor, who knows your past history and individual situation.

If I go to bed with bleeding, will that help?

If you have any bleeding, contact your physician before you do anything. Follow his or her instructions. Going to bed and resting may help. Your health-care provider knows your medical and pregnancy history, so follow his or her advice.

Falling While You're Pregnant

I fell down today. How do I know that my baby wasn't hurt?

A fall is the most frequent cause of minor injury during pregnancy. Fortunately, a fall is usually without serious injury to the fetus or to the mother.

If you have any pregnancy symptoms that worry you, call your health-care provider and discuss it with him or her.

If I fall, are there problems or warning signs I should look for?

Some signs and symptoms to alert you to a possible problem include:

- ✧ bleeding
- ✧ a gush of fluid from the vagina, indicating rupture of membranes
- ✧ severe abdominal pain

Movement of the baby after a fall is reassuring.

What should I do if I fall?

If you fall, contact your doctor; you may require attention. If it's a bad fall, your doctor may advise monitoring the baby's heartbeat or having an ultrasound.

Miscarriages

This is my first pregnancy, and I'm very nervous about having a miscarriage. What exactly is a miscarriage?

A *miscarriage* is a loss of a pregnancy before 20 weeks of gestation. An embryo or a fetus is delivered before it can survive outside the womb. This may also be called a *spontaneous abortion*.

Why do miscarriages occur?

Most of the time we don't know—a miscarriage can happen for many different reasons. The most common finding in early miscarriages is an abnormality of the development of the early embryo. Research indicates that more than half of these miscarriages have chromosomal abnormalities. Outside factors, called *teratogens,* can also cause miscarriage. Maternal factors are also believed to be relevant in some miscarriages.

Do miscarriages occur very often?

Miscarriages occur in one out of every four pregnancies; about 25% of all pregnancies end with miscarriage.

What kind of "outside factors" can cause a miscarriage?

Research has shown that radiation and some chemicals (drugs or medications) may cause a miscarriage.

What "maternal factors" can cause a miscarriage?

There are many maternal factors that can result in a miscarriage.

* Research has shown that unusual infections in the mother-to-be, such as listeria, toxoplasmosis and syphilis, may cause miscarriage.
* A deficiency of progesterone is believed to be a cause of early miscarriage; if detected early enough, it can be treated.

❖ Genital infections have been shown to trigger miscarriage. When an infection is found, the woman and her partner are treated.

❖ Sometimes a woman's body makes antibodies that attack the fetus or disrupt the function of the placenta.

❖ Women who smoke have a higher rate of miscarriage.

❖ Alcohol also been blamed for an increased rate of miscarriage.

I've heard that sometimes a couple can cause a miscarriage. Can you explain this?

This does cause some confusion for many people, but it is fairly easy to understand. When their genes unite upon fertilization of the egg by the sperm, the union can produce genetic abnormalities that can cause a miscarriage. Genetic screening can reveal this, if this is the problem.

Can nutrient deficiency cause a miscarriage?

We have no concrete evidence that deficiency of any particular nutrient or even moderate deficiency of all nutrients can cause a miscarriage.

Can a woman cause a miscarriage to occur?

Not usually, so don't blame yourself if you have a miscarriage. It's a normal reaction to look for a reason for losing a pregnancy and to think you might have done something wrong. Many women try to blame stress, emotional upset or physical activity for causing a miscarriage. These things do not usually cause miscarriages.

I've heard that there are different types of miscarriage. What does this mean?

The medical descriptions for different types of miscarriage include:

- ✧ threatened miscarriage
- ✧ inevitable miscarriage
- ✧ incomplete miscarriage
- ✧ missed miscarriage
- ✧ habitual miscarriage

What is a "threatened miscarriage"?

A *threatened miscarriage* occurs when there is a bloody discharge from the vagina during the first half of pregnancy. Bleeding may last for days or weeks. There may or may not be cramping and pain—pain may feel like a menstrual cramp or mild backache. Bed rest is about all a woman can do to try to prevent the miscarriage from happening, although being active does not cause miscarriage.

What is an "inevitable miscarriage"?

An *inevitable miscarriage* occurs with the rupture of membranes, dilatation of the cervix and passage of blood clots and even tissue. Loss of the pregnancy is almost certain under these circumstances. Contraction of the uterus usually occurs, expelling the embryo or products of conception.

What is an "incomplete miscarriage"?

In an *incomplete miscarriage,* the entire pregnancy is not immediately expelled. Part of the pregnancy may be passed while the rest remains in the uterus. Bleeding may be heavy and continues until the uterus is empty.

What is a "missed miscarriage"?

A *missed miscarriage* can occur when an embryo that has died earlier is retained in the uterus. A woman may not bleed or have any other symptoms. The period between the failure of the pregnancy and the discovery of the miscarriage is usually weeks.

What is a "habitual miscarriage"?

A *habitual miscarriage* usually refers to three or more consecutive miscarriages.

What are the warning signs of a miscarriage?

The first warning sign is bleeding from the vagina, followed by cramping. Call your health-care provider if you experience these problems! The longer you bleed and cramp, the more likely you are to have a miscarriage.

What can I do if I think I'm having a miscarriage?

Talk to your doctor. In nearly all instances, there is nothing you can do to stop a miscarriage from happening. There is no surgery that can be done or medicine you can take to stop a miscarriage. Most physicians recommend bed rest and decreased activity. Some recommend use of a hormone called *progesterone,* but not all agree with its use. Ultrasound and blood tests may be used to assist your health-care provider in determining whether you are going to miscarry, but you may have to wait and see.

What will my doctor do if I am having a miscarriage?

If you expel all of the products of the pregnancy and bleeding stops and cramping goes away, you may be done with it. If everything is not expelled, it will be necessary to perform a D&C (dilatation and curettage), which is minor surgery to empty the uterus. It is preferable to do this surgery so you won't bleed for a long time, risking anemia and infection.

I've heard a woman needs to be concerned about Rh-sensitivity if she has a miscarriage. Is this true?

If you're Rh-negative and have a miscarriage, you will need to receive RhoGAM. This applies *only* if you are Rh-negative.

If I have a miscarriage, will there be an embryo or a fetus? What will it look like?

You usually won't see a fetus. What you pass looks like white, gray or red tissue and will look like a piece of placenta.

If I miscarry, will it possible to tell if it was a boy or girl?

No, this is not possible.

When my sister had a miscarriage, they told her to save the tissue, but she had already flushed it. Why did they want her to save it?

Some doctors want you to bring the tissue to the lab to verify it was really the pregnancy that was passed and not just a blood clot.

My friend had a miscarriage when she was 3 months pregnant, and she blames herself. Is this possible?

A woman shouldn't blame herself or her partner for a miscarriage. It is usually impossible to look back at everything a woman did, ate or was exposed to and find the cause of a miscarriage. Remember, usually no reason can be found for a miscarriage.

If I am having a miscarriage, will my pregnancy test be positive?

Yes. The hormones will make your pregnancy test positive.

A friend of mine had a stillbirth last year. What's the difference between a miscarriage and a stillbirth?

In medical terms, loss of the fetus before 20 weeks is a *miscarriage*. Loss of the fetus after 20 weeks is a *stillbirth*.

Ectopic Pregnancy

What is an ectopic pregnancy?

Ectopic pregnancy, sometimes called a *tubal pregnancy,* is not common. It occurs about once in every 100 pregnancies. An ectopic pregnancy happens when implantation occurs *outside* the uterine cavity, usually in the Fallopian tube.

I'm 8 weeks pregnant and have pain on my side where I think my ovary is. Could it be an ectopic pregnancy.

It isn't unusual to have mild pain early in pregnancy from a cyst on the ovary or stretching of the uterus or ligaments. It probably isn't an ectopic pregnancy, but if the pain is bad enough to cause you concern, call your doctor.

What are the factors that increase the risk of having an ectopic pregnancy?

There are quite a few factors that can increase your risk for an ectopic pregnancy, including:

- ❖ pelvic infections (PID or pelvic inflammatory disease)
- ❖ previous ruptured appendix
- ❖ previous ectopic pregnancy
- ❖ surgery on your Fallopian tubes (such as reversal of a tubal ligation)
- ❖ use of an IUD

How is an ectopic pregnancy diagnosed?

Diagnosis of an ectopic pregnancy can be difficult and may require a couple of tests and some waiting. Tests used include

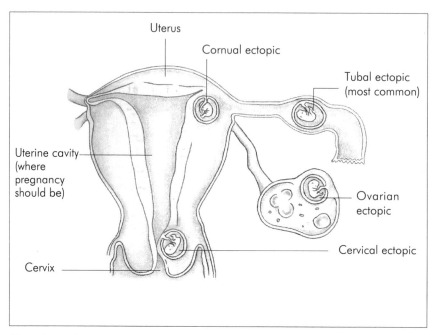

Sites of ectopic pregnancies.

ultrasound, quantitative HCGs and laparoscopy (a visual examination inside the abdomen). Even with these tests, it may be a few days or weeks before a definitive diagnosis can be made.

I've had some pain and bleeding, and my doctor is concerned about an ectopic pregnancy. Yesterday I had a quantitative HCG, and I'm supposed to have another one tomorrow. What is a quantitative HCG?

A *quantitative HCG (human chorionic gonadotropin)* is a special pregnancy test done on your blood. HCG is a hormone produced during pregnancy; it increases very rapidly early in pregnancy. A regular pregnancy test, using blood or urine, gives you a positive or negative ("yes" or "no") answer. A quantitative HCG assigns a number to tell how pregnant you are. The numbers aren't exact, but in a normal pregnancy they increase in a way that can help your doctor decide if it is a normal pregnancy. This test is not used in normal pregnancies but can be very helpful when you are concerned about a miscarriage or ectopic pregnancy.

If I have an ectopic pregnancy, will a pregnancy test be positive?

Yes. The hormones produced with an ectopic pregnancy still make your pregnancy test positive.

If I have an ectopic pregnancy, what can they do for me?

An ectopic pregnancy almost always requires surgery to correct the problem, which results in loss of the pregnancy.

Blood Clots During Pregnancy

My sister had thrombophlebitis during her pregnancy. Is that the same as a blood clot in the leg?

Yes, it is. The problem has several names, including *venous thrombosis, thromboembolic disease, thrombophlebitis* and *lower deep-vein thrombosis.*

Why do blood clots in the leg occur in pregnancy?

This condition is more likely to occur during pregnancy because of the changes in blood circulation. There is a slowing of blood flow in the legs because of pressure from the uterus on blood vessels and because of changes in the blood and its clotting mechanisms. Blood clots occur in less than 1% of all pregnancies.

What causes blood clots during pregnancy?

The most likely cause of a blood clot in the legs during pregnancy is decreased blood flow, called *stasis.*

I had a blood clot a few years ago. Is that relevant to my pregnancy?

Yes. Tell your doctor about it. This is important information!

I have a blood clot in my leg, but my doctor said it isn't serious because it's "superficial." What does that mean?

If a blood clot occurs in the veins near the surface of the leg, it is called *superficial* and is not serious. This type of thrombosis does not require hospitalization and is treated with mild pain relievers, elevation of the leg, heat and support of the leg with an Ace® bandage or support stockings.

I have a deep-vein thrombosis, and my doctor said it was a serious problem. Why?

This type of thrombosis is more serious because of the risk of the blood clot breaking loose and traveling to another part of the body, such as the lungs. This is called a *pulmonary embolus.*

What are the signs and symptoms of a deep-vein thrombosis?

Signs and symptoms of a deep-vein thrombosis can vary widely and include:

- ✦ paleness of the leg
- ✦ leg is cool to the touch
- ✦ a portion of the leg may be tender, hot and swollen
- ✦ skin of the leg may have red streaks over the veins
- ✦ squeezing the calf or walking may be very painful
- ✦ rapid, abrupt onset of the above symptoms

How is a deep-vein thrombosis diagnosed?

In a pregnant woman, an ultrasound of the legs is the only test that is done. In a non-pregnant person, either X-ray or ultrasound is used.

How is deep-vein thrombosis treated during pregnancy?

Treatment usually consists of hospitalization and the administering of heparin to thin the blood and allow the clot to be dissolved. While heparin is being given, the woman is required to stay in bed with heat applied to her elevated leg.

I had a blood clot with my last pregnancy and just found out I'm pregnant. What should I do?

Call your doctor. If you have had a blood clot with a previous pregnancy, you will probably need heparin during this pregnancy. It should be started right away.

If heparin is to be given to prevent another blood clot, how is it given?

This is done either by injections that you give yourself 2 or 3 times a day, by a long-dwelling I.V. or by a heparin pump.

Isn't there a blood thinner that can be taken as a pill?

Yes, it is called *warfarin* (Coumadin®), but it cannot be given during pregnancy because it is not safe for the baby. Heparin is safe for use during pregnancy. After you deliver, you may have to take warfarin for a few weeks, depending on the severity of the blood clot.

How common is a pulmonary embolism in pregnancy?

It is an uncommon problem in pregnancy and occurs only once in every 3,000 to 7,000 deliveries.

Breast Lumps in Pregnancy

I'm pregnant and just found a lump in my breast. What should I do?

Tell your doctor immediately! It's normal for your breasts to change and get larger during pregnancy, but lumps need to be checked out.

Are there any tests that can be done if I am pregnant and have a breast lump?

The first test is to examine yourself, then have your doctor check you if you find a lump. After examination by your doctor, either a mammogram or an ultrasound may be done. If a mammogram is done, be sure to tell them you are pregnant. They will cover your abdomen with a lead shield.

What can be done for a breast lump during pregnancy?

Often a lump in the breast can be drained or aspirated. If it cannot be drained, biopsy or removal of the lump may be necessary. Depending on how serious it is, surgery or other treatment may be needed.

Does a breast lump always mean cancer?

No, it doesn't, but it is very important to get breast lumps checked.

Does pregnancy make a breast cancer grow faster?

Not everyone agrees on the answer to this question. Most medical experts don't believe pregnancy accelerates the course or growth of a breast cancer.

Toxemia of Pregnancy

I've heard about toxemia of pregnancy. What is it?

Toxemia of pregnancy, also called *pre-eclampsia,* is development of the following symptoms:

- ❖ hypertension
- ❖ protein in the urine
- ❖ swelling, usually in the legs, or elsewhere in the body
- ❖ changes in muscle reflexes

Toxemia develops in about 5% of pregnancies, usually in a woman's first pregnancy.

Why is toxemia serious during pregnancy?

Toxemia occurs only during pregnancy. It is serious because it can lead to eclampsia.

What is eclampsia?

Eclampsia refers to seizures or convulsions in a woman with toxemia (pre-eclampsia).

What is a seizure?

A *seizure* is a loss of body control, such as passing out. Seizures often include twitching, shaking or convulsions of the body. If you think you've had a seizure, contact your doctor immediately!

How can I know if my toxemia is getting worse and I am beginning to develop eclampsia?

Warning signs that toxemia is getting worse include:
- pain under the ribs on the right side
- headache
- seeing spots or other changes in your vision

If my legs are swollen, does it mean I have toxemia?

No, it does not. Most pregnant women experience some swelling in various parts of the body. Development of toxemia includes evidence of the other symptoms in addition to swelling.

Does an elevation in my blood pressure mean I am getting toxemia?

Again, you may experience some of the symptoms without having toxemia.

What causes toxemia?

Researchers have not been able to isolate a definite cause for toxemia, but it occurs most often during a woman's first pregnancy.

How is toxemia treated?

The goal in treating toxemia is to avoid seizures, which occur if the woman develops eclampsia. To treat toxemia, the first step is bed rest. The woman is also advised to drink lots of water, and avoid salt and foods containing large amounts of sodium.

If toxemia doesn't get better with bed rest, drinking fluids and avoiding salt and sodium, then what?

In some cases, medication is prescribed to prevent seizures. These medications include magnesium sulfate or anti-seizure medicines, such as phenobarbital.

When Your Water Breaks

I've heard about my "water breaking." What does this mean?

When your water breaks, the amniotic sac, which surrounds the baby and placenta, actually ruptures. The amniotic fluid that is inside the sac may gush out, then leak out more slowly. This occurrence often signals the beginning of labor.

What is the "bag of waters"?

This is another name for the amniotic sac.

Every once in a while I feel a little wetness—as though I'm losing urine. Why does this happen?

As your pregnancy grows, your uterus grows larger and gets heavier. The uterus sits on top of the bladder—as it increases in size, it can put a great deal of pressure on your bladder and prevent your bladder from holding as much. Leakages can occur, especially when you lift something or bounce up and down. You may notice that your underwear or clothing is damp.

How do I know my water isn't broken when I find my clothing wet?

It may be very difficult to tell the difference between losing a little urine and your water breaking. However, when your membranes rupture, you usually experience a gush of fluid or a continual leaking from inside the vagina. If you think your water has broken, call your doctor.

What does amniotic fluid look like?

It is usually clear, but it may have a bloody appearance or it may be yellow or green.

What should I do when my water breaks?

If you think your water has broken, call your health-care provider. Don't have sexual intercourse if you think your water has broken; it can increase the possibility of an infection inside your uterus.

Are there any tests that can be done to determine if my water has broken?

Yes, there are. One is a *nitrazine test.* Fluid is placed on a piece of nitrazine paper; if membranes have ruptured, the paper changes color. Another test is a *ferning test.* When viewed under a microscope, dried amniotic fluid looks like a fern or the branches of a pine tree.

Problems with the Placenta

I've heard of a woman having problems with the placenta. What is the placenta?

The placenta is a flat, spongy structure that grows inside the mother's uterus. It is attached to the fetus by the umbilical cord and carries nourishment and oxygen from the mother to the baby. It also carries waste products from the baby to the mother for excretion.

I have a friend who had placenta previa. What is it?

With *placenta previa,* the placenta covers part or all of the cervix.

Why is this a problem?

It's a problem because when the cervix begins to dilate (open) the placenta is pulled away from the uterus, causing heavy bleeding. This can be dangerous for the mother-to-be and the baby.

What are the signs and symptoms of placenta previa?

The most characteristic symptom in placenta previa is painless bleeding.

If I experience this painless bleeding, what will my doctor do?

If your doctor is concerned about placenta previa, he or she will order an ultrasound exam to determine the location of the placenta. Your physician will *not* do a pelvic exam if he or she is concerned about placenta previa because a pelvic exam may cause heavier bleeding. If you see another doctor or when you go to the hospital, tell whoever examines you that you have placenta previa and should not have a pelvic exam.

Are there things I shouldn't do if I know I have placenta previa?

Most physicians recommend avoiding intercourse, not traveling and not having a pelvic exam.

If I have placenta previa, will I have to have a Cesarean section?

With placenta previa, the baby is more likely to be in a breech position. For this reason, and also to avoid bleeding, a C-section is almost always performed.

How common is placenta previa?

It occurs in about 1 birth in 200.

In an article about pregnancy problems, I read about placental abruption being very serious. Can you explain what it is?

Placental abruption is separation of the placenta from the wall of the uterus during pregnancy. Normally the placenta does not separate until after delivery of the baby.

Is placental abruption dangerous?

When the placenta separates before birth, it can be very serious for the baby, and even cause fetal death.

How often does it occur?

The frequency of placental abruption is estimated to be about 1 in every 80 deliveries.

What causes placental abruption?

The cause of placental abruption is unknown, however certain conditions may make it more likely to occur. These include:

- trauma to the mother, such as from a fall or a car accident
- an umbilical cord that is too short
- very sudden change in the size of the uterus, such as with the rupture of membranes
- hypertension
- dietary deficiency
- an abnormality of the uterus, such as a band of tissue in the uterus called a *uterine septum*

How will I know if I have placental abruption?

The signs and symptoms of placental abruption include:

- heavy bleeding from the vagina
- uterine tenderness
- uterine contractions
- premature labor
- lower-back pain

Placental abruption may occur without the presence of any or all these symptoms.

Are there any tests available to help diagnose placental abruption?

Ultrasound may be helpful, but it does not always provide an exact diagnosis.

What are the risks to the mother-to-be with placental abruption?

Risks to the mother-to-be include shock, severe blood loss and the inability of the blood to clot.

How is it treated?

The most common treatment of placental abruption is delivery of the baby. However, the decision of when to deliver the baby varies, depending on the severity of the problem.

If I have placental abruption, does it mean I have to have a C-section?

In some situations, if the baby needs to be delivered rapidly, you will need a Cesarean section. But each case *must* be handled on an individual basis.

Can a woman do anything to prevent placental abruption?

We now believe deficiency of folic acid may play a role in causing placental abruption. Extra folic acid may be prescribed during pregnancy. Maternal smoking and alcohol use may make it more likely for a woman to have placental abruption. If you smoke or drink alcohol, you may be advised to stop both activities.

I've heard about something called a "retained placenta." What is this?

One complication following the birth of a baby is an abnormally adherent placenta, which means a placenta that does not deliver following the birth of the baby. This is called a *retained placenta*. Usually the placenta separates on its own from the implantation site on the uterus a few minutes after delivery. In some cases, it doesn't separate because it is attached to the wall of the uterus. This can be very serious and can cause extreme blood loss.

What causes a retained placenta?

Some reasons for a retained placenta include a placenta attaching:

* ✧ over a previous C-section scar or other incision scar on the uterus
* ✧ in a place that has been curetted (scraped), such as with a D&C
* ✧ over an area of the uterus that was infected

What kind of problems does a retained placenta cause?

The most significant problem is heavy bleeding after delivery. If the placenta is not delivered, it must be removed some other way. One solution is to perform a D&C. However, if the placenta has grown into the wall of the uterus, it may be necessary to remove the uterus by performing a hysterectomy.

Is a retained placenta common?

No. It occurs in about 1% of all deliveries.

✧ 16 ✧

You Should Also Know

How does the doctor determine my due date?

Your due date is set as 38 weeks after the date the baby was conceived. If you don't know the exact date of conception, it is estimated to be near the middle of your menstrual cycle, or two weeks after the beginning of your last period. Once your doctor knows the date of conception, he counts 38 weeks from that date to determine your due date.

Another way to estimate the date of delivery is to take the date of the beginning of your last period, add 7 days and go back 3 months. Both methods give the same result.

I get confused by the terms "gestational age" and "fertilization age." Why are two ages used?

Gestational age is the length of time since the beginning of your last period. If your doctor says you are 15 weeks pregnant, she's referring to your gestational age. *Fertilization age* is the actual age of the fetus, which would be 13 weeks in this case.

What about "trimesters"? My sister told me there are three trimesters during pregnancy.

That's correct. *Trimesters* divide pregnancy into three stages, each about 13 weeks long. It helps group together times of development.

I'm 13 weeks pregnant, but I don't show yet and don't feel very pregnant. How do I know everything is OK?

At this point, you have ended the *embryonic* period and begun the *fetal* period. A lot has happened with the development of your baby. There a few outward signs that can help reassure you. If you have seen your doctor in the last couple of weeks, you have probably heard the baby's heartbeat. In the middle of your abdomen just above your pubic bone you may feel your uterus, which will feel like the top of a smooth ball, about the size of a large grapefruit.

Some Common Physical Concerns

My feet are huge—I can't wear any of my shoes. What can I do about it?

Some swelling in your feet is normal during pregnancy. Wear sneakers, flats or shoes with low heels (no higher than 2 inches). If swelling becomes extreme, especially during the last trimester, consult your physician; it could be a sign of problems. Rest lying down on your side as frequently as possible. You may need to buy larger shoes toward the end of your pregnancy.

What is sciatic-nerve pain?

Sciatic-nerve pain is an occasional excruciating pain in your buttocks and down the back or the side of your leg. You may experience it as your pregnancy progresses. The sciatic nerve runs behind the uterus in the pelvis to your legs. Pain is believed to be caused by pressure on the nerve from the growing uterus.

What can I do about sciatic-nerve pain?

The best way to treat the pain is to lie on your opposite side. It helps relieve pressure on the nerve.

I've heard that backaches are a normal part of pregnancy. What causes them?

Nearly every woman experiences backache at some time during her pregnancy. It usually occurs as you get bigger. You may also experience backache after walking, bending, lifting, standing or excessive exercise. Be careful about lifting and bending—do it correctly.

How do I take care of problems with my back?

You can treat backache with heat, rest and analgesics, such as acetaminophen (Tylenol). Special maternity girdles can provide some support. Keep your weight under control, and participate in mild exercise, such as swimming, walking and stationary-bike riding. Try to lie on your side when resting or sleeping.

Should I be concerned about lower-back pain?

Lower-back pain is common during pregnancy. However it may be an indication of a more-serious problem, such as pyelonephritis or a kidney stone. If pain becomes constant or more severe, it's important to discuss it with your health-care provider.

I've heard that lying on my side in the third trimester will help with any swelling I have. Is this true?

Yes, it is. By the third trimester, your uterus is quite large and puts a lot of pressure on your blood vessels, which blocks their flow. Lying or sleeping or your side during the third trimester will help relieve this.

The Emotions of Pregnancy

Now that I know I'm pregnant, I'm not as excited as I thought I'd be. Is this normal?

If you aren't immediately thrilled about pregnancy, don't feel alone. A very common feeling and response to pregnancy is to question your condition. Some of this may be because you're not sure of what lies ahead.

When will I begin to think of the fetus as my "baby"?

This is different for everyone. Some women begin to feel this way as soon as they know they are pregnant. For others, it occurs when they hear their baby's heartbeat, around 12 or 13 weeks, or when they first feel their baby move, between 16 and 20 weeks.

I'm not very far along in my pregnancy, but I seem to be very emotional about everything. Is this normal?

Yes, it's perfectly normal to get very emotional about many things. You may feel moody, cry at the slightest thing or find yourself daydreaming. Emotional swings are very normal during pregnancy.

Will these emotional swings continue during my pregnancy?

They continue to some degree throughout pregnancy. These swings are caused by the changing hormones in your body. Explain to your partner and other family members that you may experience these swings.

Your Maternity Wardrobe

Now that I know I'm pregnant, I'm excited about wearing maternity clothes. When will I need them?

It's very hard to predict exactly when you'll need to start wearing maternity clothes. You may have some clothes that are loose enough to wear for a while. You might be able to wear some of your partner's shirts. A rule of thumb to follow is when you become uncomfortable wearing your regular clothes, it's time to start wearing maternity clothes.

Are there any points I should keep in mind when selecting maternity clothes?

Choose natural fabrics when possible—avoid synthetic fabrics. During pregnancy, your metabolic rate increases, and you may feel warmer than usual. You'll want to wear fabrics that "breathe." Wear cotton in the summer, and layer your clothing in winter.

There are so many different styles of clothing for a pregnant woman. Are any styles better than others?

It depends on your preference, but I'll share with you some of the tips my patients have given me. They have found the following styles added to their comfort:

- ✧ wide, elastic bands or panels that fit under your abdomen to provide support
- ✧ wrap-around openings that tie and are easy to adjust
- ✧ elastic waists that expand
- ✧ button or pleated waistbands that are adjustable
- ✧ waistbands that have sliders to adjust fit

My friend told me that I should wear special maternity underwear while I'm pregnant. What did she mean?

Undergarments that add support to your abdomen, breasts or legs may make you feel more comfortable during pregnancy. These undergarments include maternity bras, nursing bras, maternity panties and maternity support hose. Be sure to choose panties and support hose with a cotton crotch.

What are maternity bras?

Maternity bras are designed to provide your enlarging breasts the extra support they need during pregnancy. They have wider sides and stretchier backs than your regular bras. They usually have four sets of hooks on the back, instead of two or three, providing more room for you to grow.

Can't I just wear my normal bra in a larger size?

It's probably better to buy a maternity bra. They can help combat the stretch marks and sagging of your breasts, which are associated with pregnancy.

What is a nursing bra?

A nursing bra is worn for breastfeeding; it has cups that open so you can breastfeed without having to get undressed. Buy a nursing bra *only* if you plan to breastfeed your baby. You won't need one if you bottlefeed.

When should I buy a nursing bra?

Wait until the final weeks of your pregnancy; don't buy one before the 36th week of pregnancy. Your breasts won't be large enough to get a correct fit before then.

How will I know a nursing bra will fit correctly?

Choose a nursing bra with about a finger's width of space between any part of the cup and your breast. This allows for the enlargement of your breasts when your milk comes in. Take nursing pads with you when shopping for a nursing bra for a better fit. Choose a bra that is comfortable when fastened on the loosest row of hooks to allow for shrinkage in your ribcage after pregnancy.

What are maternity panties?

These panties provide support for your enlarging abdomen. Some have panels for your abdomen; others have a wide elastic band that fits under your abdomen to provide support. These panties may be most comfortable in the last trimester of pregnancy.

Will I have to wear maternity support stockings?

Many women do *not* have to wear support hose during pregnancy. However, if you have a family history of varicose veins or if you develop them during pregnancy, you may need to wear them. Don't depend on over-the-counter support hose. You'll need to visit a vein specialist to have maternity support stockings personally fitted. See Chapter 9 for additional information on varicose veins and support stockings.

Can I wear regular pantyhose?

If you don't have any problems with varicose veins, regular pantyhose are OK. Choose hose with a stretchy, wide, nonbinding waistband, and wear them over or under your abdomen, whichever is more comfortable. You might also be able to buy maternity pantyhose.

Choosing Your Baby's Pediatrician

My friend told me that I should pick my baby's pediatrician before the baby is born. Is this true?

Yes. It's best to choose and visit a pediatrician *before* your baby is born. An interview will help you build a partnership for your child's health and well-being with this physician. You can talk with the pediatrician about the care of your baby, ask questions about feeding and receive some guidelines about dealing with a new baby.

How do I find a pediatrician?

Ask your health-care provider, friends, co-workers and family members for references to pediatricians they know and trust. If you cannot find one that way, contact your local medical society and ask for a reference.

When should this visit be arranged?

It's usually most beneficial to visit the pediatrician 3 or 4 weeks before your due date. In that way, if the baby comes early, you will have already made these arrangements.

Should I take the baby's father with me to this visit?

I think it's a very good idea for both of you to visit the pediatrician. I'm sure your partner has some questions he would like answered, and this is the perfect time for the two of you to sit down and discuss them with your baby's doctor.

Why is it important to have a pediatrician before the birth?

It's important to meet this person under *calm* circumstances, to discuss the doctor's philosophy, to learn his or her schedule and to clarify what you can expect of this physician. When your baby is born, the pediatrician will be notified so he or she can come in to the hospital and check the baby. If you select a pediatrician before the birth, your baby will see the same doctor for follow-up visits at the hospital and at the doctor's office.

I'm sure there are certain questions we should bring up at this interview. What are some of them?

There are many things you will want to cover in this initial interview. Below is a list of questions that I believe will help you create a dialogue with this important health-care provider for your child.

- ✧ What are your qualifications and training?
- ✧ What is your availability?
- ✧ Are your office hours compatible with our work schedules?
- ✧ Can an acutely ill child be seen the same day?
- ✧ How can we reach you in case of an emergency or after office hours?
- ✧ Who responds if you are not available?
- ✧ Is the office staff cordial, open and easy to talk to?
- ✧ Do you return phone calls the same day?
- ✧ Are you interested in preventive, developmental and behavioral issues?
- ✧ How does your practice operate?
- ✧ Does it comply with our insurance?
- ✧ What is the nearest (to our home) emergency room or urgent-care center you would send us to?

What other things should we consider when selecting the pediatrician?

There are some issues that can be resolved only by analyzing your feelings after your visit—examining your "gut reactions" to certain issues. Below is a list of questions you and your partner might want to discuss after your visit.

❖ Are the doctor's philosophies and attitudes acceptable to us, such as use of antibiotics and other medications, child-rearing practices or medical-related religious beliefs?

❖ Did the doctor listen to us?

❖ Was he or she genuinely interested in our concerns?

❖ Did the physician appear interested in developing a rapport with our expected child?

❖ Is this a person I feel comfortable with and with whom our child will be comfortable?

What if we belong to an HMO and I cannot choose a particular physician?

It's still a good idea to meet this person *before* the birth of your baby. If you have a conflict or don't see eye to eye on important matters, you may be able to choose another pediatrician within the practice. Ask your patient advocate for information and advice.

Traveling During Pregnancy

I've got to make a business trip soon, and I'm pregnant. Can I go?

Travel during pregnancy can be fatiguing and frustrating, but if your pregnancy is normal, you should be able to travel during the first and second trimesters without too much trouble. Consult your physician if you're considering traveling during your third trimester.

What should I keep in mind about traveling while I'm pregnant?

Take frequent breaks to stretch your legs during trips. Don't overdo it—rest when possible. You might want to avoid places where good medical care is not available or where changes in climate, food or altitude could cause you problems.

Is it all right to fly?

Flying in itself should not cause you any problems. Try to get an aisle seat, so you can stretch your legs and get up to walk more easily. Drink plenty of fluids, such as water and juice, because recirculated air in an airplane is extremely dry. Discuss any plans you have for flying with your physician. I've heard of some airlines refusing to carry a pregnant passenger without written consent of her physician.

I'm just finishing my first trimester, and we are planning a trip. Is it OK?

Ask your doctor. Most will tell you it's OK to travel during pregnancy, but each situation is different. Some general considerations about traveling during pregnancy include the following.

  ❖ Don't plan a trip during your last month of pregnancy.
  ❖ If you're having any problems, such as bleeding or cramping, don't travel.
  ❖ If you are uncomfortable or have problems with swelling, traveling, sitting in a car or doing a lot of walking may make things worse (and it probably won't be much fun either).
  ❖ If your pregnancy is considered high risk, a trip during pregnancy is not a good idea.

Remember you are pregnant when you plan a trip. Be sensible in your planning—don't overdo it—and take it easy!

What are the greatest risks for me if I decide to travel during my pregnancy?

The biggest risk of traveling during pregnancy is the development of a complication while you are away from home and away from those who have been involved in your pregnancy and know your history. Other concerns include your discomfort or trouble sleeping, especially if you are cooped up in a car for hours or are trying to sleep in a strange bed. Consider these things and discuss them with your doctor before making plans, buying tickets or making reservations.

I've heard I shouldn't travel during the last month of my pregnancy. Why?

At this point, labor could begin at any time, your water could break or other problems could occur. Your doctor knows what has happened during your pregnancy and has a record of tests done—these things are important. If you check into a hospital in a strange place, they don't know you and you don't know them. Some doctors won't accept you as a patient in this situation, and it can be awkward. It doesn't make sense to take this kind of a chance.

Can't my doctor check me and tell if I will be in labor soon so I'll know if I can go on a trip?

First of all, *no one* can predict when your labor will begin. No one can guarantee you can go on a trip and not go into labor or have other problems. You can't guarantee it—even if you're at home! Plan ahead, and discuss it with your doctor *before* you make plans or buy airplane tickets.

My husband has to go out of town for a business trip, and I'm due in 3 weeks. Can't my doctor check me and tell if I will go into labor while he's gone?

If your husband goes on his trip, he may miss the delivery. Your doctor can check you, but this really only tells you where you are at *that* point in time. Nothing will *guarantee* your husband won't miss the delivery. The last month of pregnancy isn't a good time for either one of you to be traveling.

Driving and Seat-Belt Use in Pregnancy

Is it safe for me to drive during pregnancy?

Yes, it's safe to drive throughout your pregnancy. It may become uncomfortable for you to get in and out of the car as pregnancy progresses, but being pregnant should not interfere with your ability to drive.

I always wear a seat belt when I drive, but I'm wondering if a seat belt could cause me problems now that I'm pregnant. Should I wear one?

Yes! Many women are confused about wearing seat belts or shoulder harnesses during pregnancy, but don't be misled. These safety restraints are necessary during pregnancy, just as they are necessary when you're not pregnant. Seat-belt use is so important that the National Highway Safety Administration

Seat-belt use is extremely important during pregnancy. Always buckle up!

has recently designed a "pregnant dummy" to use in simulated accidents to record how an accident could affect a pregnant woman (and her unborn baby).

Will wearing a safety belt hurt my baby?

There is no evidence use of safety restraints increases the chance of fetal or uterine injury. You have a better chance of survival in an accident wearing a seat belt than not wearing one.

Is there a proper way for me to wear a seat belt while I'm pregnant?

Yes. Place the lap-belt part of the restraint *under* your abdomen and *across* your upper thighs so it's snug and comfortable. Adjust your sitting position so the belt crosses your shoulder without cutting into your neck. Position the shoulder harness between your breasts; don't slip this belt off your shoulder.

The Costs of Having a Baby

What does it cost to have a baby?

It costs a lot to have a baby! Costs vary from one part of the country to another, depend on how long you stay in the hospital and whether you or your baby have complications. Prices in 1995 range from $4,000 to $12,000 for a delivery. Total cost depends on how long you and your baby are in the hospital, if you have an epidural and if you deliver vaginally or by Cesarean section.

How can I find out more about exactly what it will cost?

You may need to check with the hospital and your insurance company, if you have insurance. Someone in your doctor's office can usually help you with this. Don't be embarrassed or afraid to ask about it. Most offices have a person who works with insurance companies all the time and knows about things you haven't thought about.

What things does insurance cover?

There is no simple answer to this question—it can vary quite a bit. You can find out by asking your insurance company the following questions:

- ❖ Are there maternity benefits?
- ❖ Does insurance coverage pay for some things and not for others, such as ultrasound?
- ❖ Will it pay for complications?
- ❖ Does it specify which doctor or hospital I must use?
- ❖ How long will my insurance allow me to stay in the hospital?
- ❖ Will it cover a specialist if I need one?
- ❖ How is the baby covered?
- ❖ Does it pay for an epidural anesthesia?

Often the personnel in your doctor's office know the answers to these questions or can help you get answers.

Is it really OK to ask my doctor's office questions about insurance? I don't want to bother them.

Yes, it's OK, so don't be afraid to ask. Most offices have at least one person who spends all of his or her time working with insurance companies. They realize how important this is.

I live in Canada. Is insurance for a baby different here?

Yes, the Canadian health-care system is very different from the health-care system in the United States. Canadians pay a health-care premium on a monthly basis, and cost varies depending on the province you live in. The doctor who delivers your baby is paid by the government.

Prenatal Classes

When should I register for prenatal classes?

Plan ahead. When you are around 20 weeks pregnant, begin looking into classes that are offered in your area. You should be signed up or just beginning classes by the beginning of the third trimester or about 27 weeks. It's a good idea to plan to finish the classes at least a few weeks before you are due.

Why should I take prenatal classes?

Classes are a good way to prepare for a very important and exciting time of your life! You will find that other people have the same concerns you have.

Where are prenatal classes held?

Childbirth classes are offered in various settings. Most hospitals that deliver babies offer prenatal classes at the hospital. They are often taught by labor-and-delivery nurses or by a midwife. Ask your health-care provider about which classes would be best for you.

Are prenatal classes only for first-time moms?

No. Classes are recommended for first-time pregnant women, women with a new partner, if it has been a few years since you've had a baby, if you have questions or if you would like a review of labor and delivery.

I want to take some childbirth-education classes to prepare me for my baby's birth. How do I find them?

First, ask your health-care provider to recommend classes in your area. He or she is familiar with what is being offered. Check local hospitals; many offer these classes. Friends can also be good sources. You might also look in your yellow pages under "Childbirth Education."

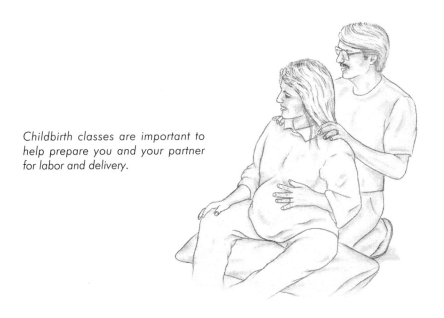

Childbirth classes are important to help prepare you and your partner for labor and delivery.

Do many couples take childbirth-education classes?

Yes. Nearly 90% of all first-time expectant parents take some type of childbirth-education class.

Do these classes really help?

They seem to. Studies have shown that women who have taken classes need less medication, have fewer forceps deliveries and feel more positive about the birth than women who do not take classes.

What kind of things will we learn about in childbirth classes?

Classes cover many aspects of labor and delivery, including breathing techniques, vaginal birth, Cesarean delivery, hospital procedures, ways to deal with the discomfort and pain of labor and delivery, various pain-relief methods and the postpartum or recovery period.

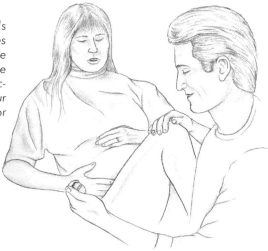

Some childbirth methods teach breathing techniques to help you deal with the pain of labor. If you choose one of these methods, practice your breathing with your partner to prepare you for labor and delivery.

Does insurance cover childbirth-education classes?

Some insurance companies and a few HMOs offer at least partial reimbursement for class fees.

What are Lamaze classes?

Lamaze is the oldest technique of childbirth preparation. It emphasizes relaxation and breathing as ways to relax during labor and delivery.

What are Bradley classes?

These classes teach the Bradley method of relaxation and inward focus, using many types of relaxation. Bradley class members are typically people who have decided they do not want to use any type of medication for labor-pain relief.

How will I know a class is right for me?

There are quite a few things you can do.

- ✧ Find out what is available in your area.
- ✧ Talk to friends and relatives who have taken various classes.

❖ Decide whether you want a drug-free birth or whether you are willing to consider pain relief if it is necessary.

❖ Learn about the qualifications of the instructors in various programs.

❖ Visit some classes in your area to choose the best one for you.

Other Pregnancy Questions

I have a couple of friends who got pregnant at about the same time I did, but we all look as if we're at different stages of pregnancy. Is there anything wrong?

No, not usually. Everyone's pregnancy is different, and every woman reacts to pregnancy differently. A lot of what you look like depends on your size (how tall you are, your weight) and the size of your growing baby. Don't expect to look the same as other women or to have the same experiences as your friends.

Is it OK to have sexual relations while I am pregnant? My partner and I don't want to do anything that would be dangerous to our baby.

In most situations and in most cases, it's OK to have sexual relations during pregnancy. If you're having any problems with bleeding, cramping or later in your pregnancy you think your water has broken, then it's best not to have relations. For more information on this subject, see Chapter 10.

I don't usually use sunscreen, but a friend suggested it's important during pregnancy. Why?

The use of sunscreen on your face is very important during pregnancy. It lessens the likelihood of getting the "mask of pregnancy," which is a darkening of skin pigment on cheeks, forehead and chin. Use products with an SPF of 15 or higher.

If you are prone to acne breakouts, use a water-based or oil-free product.

How safe is it for me to take a bath during pregnancy?

Most health-care providers believe it is safe to bathe during pregnancy. The only precaution is to avoid slipping and falling as you get in or out of the tub.

Someone said I shouldn't bathe during pregnancy, that it's better to shower. Is this true?

There is no medical reason to choose showering over bathing during pregnancy. In the last few weeks of pregnancy, as you get bigger, you must be careful about slipping and falling in the shower or the tub. If you think your water has broken (ruptured membranes), your doctor may recommend that you don't bathe.

I've always heard that a pregnant woman shouldn't have her hair colored or get a permanent. Is there any real reason to avoid these?

I don't think these should be problems for you. However, it's probably a good idea to avoid these activities during the first trimester, especially if you have morning sickness. The fumes from the hair dye or the permanent solution could make you feel ill.

I love to have a massage because it relaxes me so much. Can I continue to have massages while I'm pregnant?

It's probably OK to have a massage during pregnancy. You may find it more difficult as your pregnancy progresses and you get bigger. If you want to have a massage when you are further along in your pregnancy, lie on your side instead of on your stomach. Always be careful not to get overheated in any activity.

My breasts are really sore. Is this normal?

Changes in your breasts can begin early in your pregnancy; it isn't unusual for them to tingle or be sore. You may also notice your breasts getting larger, or see a darkening areola or an elevation of the glands around the nipple.

It seems like I am always in the bathroom urinating since I found out I'm pregnant. Is this normal?

More-frequent urination is common in pregnancy. Watch for signs of a urinary-tract infection, such as blood in your urine, a fever or burning or pain when you urinate.

We have a dog that has been our "baby" for 6 years. Now we are expecting a real baby. Will we have problems with our pet?

When a baby is born to a couple with a dog that has been the center of attention for a long while, problems may arise.

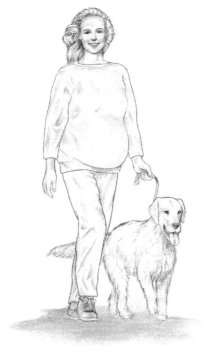

You may discover your animals have a difficult time being replaced by the new baby. There are techniques you can use to help your animal accept the baby when you bring it home.

Sometimes the dog resents the attention the baby gets and growls at the infant, barks or demands attention. The animal may even revert to unacceptable behavior, such as wetting or tearing things up.

What can we do to help our pet accept the new baby?

If your dog has never been around children, begin introducing her to the sights, sounds and smells of a new baby before your baby is born. When you bring the baby home, give your dog positive attention while introducing her to the new baby. Be firm when your dog misbehaves—don't let her get away with bad behavior. Be sure your dog is neutered; unneutered dogs are more apt to growl, snap and bite. Don't isolate your dog when you bring the baby home. Make her a part of the interactions with the baby. Don't leave the dog alone with the baby. Use common sense, and take things slowly.

We have a cat. Should we expect problems with him when we bring the baby home?

Cats are affected in many of the same ways as dogs, and much of the advice on dogs applies to cats. Expect a cat to take longer to adjust to a new baby than a dog does. You will have to train your cat to stay out of the baby's crib.

We've been considering names for our baby; some of them are unusual. Should we discuss our choices with others?

I have one patient who told me she and her husband decide on a name together, but don't tell anyone else until after the baby is born. She said it's very easy for people to criticize a name when you're thinking about it, but few people will tell you they don't like a name when you've already named your baby!

Is it OK to use the microwave during my pregnancy?

We don't know for sure if there is danger to your pregnancy from being around a microwave oven, so follow the directions provided with your microwave oven. It's a good idea not to stand next to or directly in front of it while it's in use.

Would it be all right to take my partner to my appointments with me?

It's a great idea! It will help him realize what is happening to you and to feel a part of your pregnancy. And it's nice for your partner and your health-care provider to meet before labor begins.

Can I take anyone else with me to my appointments?

It's all right to take your mother or mother-in-law to an appointment with you to hear the baby's heartbeat. Things have really changed since your mother carried you; she might enjoy this type of visit. If you want to bring anyone else, discuss it with your health-care provider first.

My kids are curious and ask a lot of questions about my pregnancy. Is it OK to take them with me to my prenatal appointments?

Many offices don't mind if you bring your children with you; other offices ask that you not bring children along. Ask about the office policy. If you're having problems and need to talk with your doctor, it can be very difficult to talk if you're also trying to take care of a young child.

Do you have any suggestions for me if I do bring my children with me?

Some suggestions for bringing children include the following.
- ✧ Ask about office policy ahead of time.
- ✧ Don't bring them on your first visit when you will probably be having a pelvic exam.

✧ If you're bringing your children to hear the heartbeat, don't bring them the first time your doctor tries to hear it; wait until after you have heard it first.

✧ Bring one or two children at a time rather than a large group.

✧ Bring something to "entertain" your child in case you have to wait—not all offices have toys or books for kids.

✧ Be considerate of other patients; don't bring a child who has a cold or is sick. I've had patients bring their children with them then tell me the child had chicken pox or strep throat! This could be very serious for other pregnant women sitting in the waiting room.

I've been hearing about how important the placenta is during pregnancy. Can you tell me more about it?

The placenta, which attaches to the umbilical cord of the baby, transports oxygen to the baby and carries away carbon dioxide. It is involved in the baby's nutrition and the baby's excretion of waste products. It also plays a very important role in hormone production during pregnancy.

Does the placenta protect my baby?

The placenta acts as a filter for many substances passing from you to your baby, including certain medications and infections that can't pass through the placenta to the baby.

I'm confused about the placenta and the birth of my baby. Is the placenta delivered separately?

Yes. Stage 3 of labor involves the delivery of the placenta. After the birth of your baby, the uterus contracts and expels the placenta. Once the placenta has been delivered, the birthing process is complete. For further information, see Chapter 17.

Some Pregnancy Warnings

I like to sit in a hot tub after I exercise, but I read I shouldn't while I'm pregnant. Why?

Your baby relies on you to maintain the correct body temperature. Research has shown that an elevated temperature for several minutes may harm a developing fetus, so for this reason, it's best to avoid hot tubs, saunas, steamrooms and spas during pregnancy.

I like to look tan all year long, so I use a tanning booth. This won't harm my baby, will it?

Researchers have not studied the effects on a growing fetus when a pregnant woman lies in a tanning booth. Until we know that there is no reason for concern, don't do this while you're pregnant.

Is it all right to douche during pregnancy?

No. Most doctors agree douching can be dangerous during pregnancy.

What's the problem with douching during pregnancy?

Using a douche may cause an infection or bleeding or even break your bag of waters (rupture your membranes). It can cause more serious problems, such as an *air embolus*. An air embolus results when air gets into your circulation from the pressure of the douche. It is rare but can be a serious problem.

I usually have electrolysis for some facial hair I have. Can I have this done during pregnancy?

No one knows for sure whether this procedure is safe or not. Because there is no information available, I would suggest you wait until after your baby is born to have your facial hair removed.

To take care of leg hair, I have my legs waxed. Is this permissible while I'm pregnant?

I don't believe there is any risk to you with this procedure. Just be sure you don't get overheated while having this done. You shouldn't raise your body temperature above 102F (39C) for more than 15 minutes.

When I was 15, I got a tattoo on my shoulder, but I want to have it removed now. My dermatologist told me to wait till after the baby is born. Why?

Many tattoos are removed using lasers, and we are unsure how safe it might be for you to have this done during pregnancy. I agree with your dermatologist—wait until after your baby is born to have it removed.

I just got a gift certificate for an herbal wrap, and I'm 14 weeks pregnant. Should I wait to have it until after my baby is born?

Definitely wait until after your baby is born to have an herbal wrap. Being wrapped in hot towels will cause your body to become very heated, which is not advisable during pregnancy.

Can I continue to use my electric blanket now that I'm pregnant?

There has been controversy about using electric blankets during pregnancy. At this time, no one knows the answer to this question. Until we know more, the safest thing to do is not to use an electric blanket but to find other ways to stay warm, such as with down comforters or extra blankets.

Everybody at work seems to have advice for me. How do I handle this?

Unwelcome advice, unwarranted questions, even physical contact, are common during pregnancy. Use humor to deflect some of the questions. You can listen to unasked-for advice, nod wisely and say "thanks," without making any commitment. Try not to let this attention annoy you.

I find it annoying when people (even total strangers) pat my pregnant abdomen. How can I stop them or keep them from doing this?

You can ask people to look and not touch! When someone reaches out to touch your abdomen, tell them you are uncomfortable with that.

Down's Syndrome

What is Down's syndrome?

Down's syndrome is a condition in which a baby is born mentally retarded and often physically deformed. His or her appearance may include a sloping forehead, short, broad hands, a flat nose and low-set ears. There may also be heart problems, gastrointestinal defects or leukemia. Down's syndrome is caused by a defective chromosome.

Can Down's syndrome be diagnosed before the baby is born?

Yes. Traditionally amniocentesis has been used to diagnose Down's syndrome. Other tests that may prove useful include alphafetoprotein, chorionic villus sampling and, in some cases, ultrasound.

What are the chances of my baby developing Down's syndrome?

The risk of delivering a baby with Down's syndrome increases with the age of the mother, as shown in the following statistics:

- ❖ at age 25 the risk is 1 in 1,300 births
- ❖ at 30 it is 1 in 965 births
- ❖ at 35 it is 1 in 365 births
- ❖ at 40 it is 1 in 109 births
- ❖ at 45 it is 1 in 32 births
- ❖ at 49 it is 1 in 12 births

In a more-positive light, even at age 49, you have a 92% chance of delivering a child *without* Down's syndrome.

·17·
Labor
& Delivery

I've already felt some contractions, and I'm only 6 months pregnant. Am I going into labor?

Probably not. You are probably experiencing Braxton-Hicks contractions, which are painless, non-rhythmical contractions. They can begin early in pregnancy and continue off and on until your baby is born. They are felt at irregular intervals and may increase in number and strength when your uterus is massaged.

I heard a woman describe her baby as "dropping." Does this mean the baby was falling out?

No, it doesn't. The feeling of having your baby drop, also called *lightening*, means the baby's head has moved down deep into your pelvis. It is a natural part of the birthing process and can happen a few weeks to a few hours before labor begins.

Will I feel better when my baby drops?

You may feel that you have more room to breathe when the baby descends into your pelvis, but there may also be more pelvic pressure or discomfort.

I've heard horror stories about a woman's water breaking when she is out in public. Does this happen often?

Many mothers-to-be worry about the embarrassment of having their bag of waters break when they are in a public place. Although it doesn't happen very often, it is possible. Don't waste energy worrying about it. If it should happen to you, people would be very understanding and helpful. At that stage of your pregnancy, your condition would be very obvious to them!

Does the water usually break before a woman goes into labor?

Many times the water will break shortly before labor begins. However, in most cases the physician must rupture the membranes after the woman goes to the hospital.

How will I know when my water breaks?

Your baby is surrounded by *amniotic fluid* in the uterus. Often, as labor begins, the membranes that surround the baby break and fluid leaks from your vagina. You may feel a gush of fluid, followed by slow leaking, or you may just feel a slow leaking, without the gush of fluid. A sanitary pad will help absorb the slow leaking so you are not embarrassed by it.

What should I do when my water breaks?

Contact your health-care provider immediately; some precautions must be taken. If labor and delivery are imminent, you may be advised to go to the hospital. If you are not near term, your doctor may ask you to come to his office, where you will be examined. You may not be ready to deliver your baby yet, and your doctor wants to prevent you getting an infection. The risk of infection increases when your water breaks.

My doctor said she might have to induce me. How is this done?

If labor is induced, your bag of waters will be broken or you will receive oxytocin (Pitocin®) intravenously. The medication is given in gradually increasing doses until contractions begin.

Why is labor induced?

Your doctor may decide to induce labor if you or your baby are at risk, such as if you are overdue. If the cervix is dilated and contractions have not begun or are not strong enough, your labor may be induced.

Is there any way for my doctor to know when I will go into labor?

No one knows when labor will begin.

How long does labor last?

The length of your labor is extremely individual. It varies from pregnancy to pregnancy and depends on how many pregnancies you have already had.

How long can I expect to be in labor with a first baby?

With a first pregnancy, the first and second stages of labor can last 14 to 15 hours, or more. A woman who has already had one or two children will probably have a shorter labor, but that's not always the case.

Premature Labor

What is "preterm birth"?

Preterm birth refers to a baby born more than 4 weeks early. It is also called *premature birth*.

How common is preterm birth?

About 10% of all babies are born more than 4 weeks early.

I've heard preterm birth can be dangerous for the baby. Why?

Preterm delivery of a baby can be dangerous because the baby's lungs and other organ systems may not be ready to function on their own.

What causes premature labor?

In most cases, the cause of premature labor is unknown. Causes we do understand include:

- a uterus with an abnormal shape
- a large uterus
- hydramnios
- an abnormal placenta
- premature rupture of the membranes
- incompetent cervix
- abnormalities of the fetus
- fetal death
- retained IUD
- maternal illness, such as high blood pressure, or some maternal infections
- incorrect estimate of gestational age, which means the baby is really *not* premature

What will my doctor tell me to do if I go into labor too early?

It is important to try to halt the contractions if you go into labor too early. Most doctors start by recommending bed rest and increased fluids to stop labor. Bed rest means lying in bed on your side. Either side is OK, but the left side is best.

Why do I have to lie in bed?

It works. It may mean you have to modify or to stop your activities, but we have found that bed rest helps end premature labor. Before we had medications, bed rest was the only treatment for premature labor. It is still often successful in halting premature labor.

I've heard there are medications to stop premature labor. Can't I take one of those medications instead of going to bed?

Even if you take medication, you will probably be advised to rest in bed. Bed rest is an essential part of the treatment plan for premature labor.

What kind of medications are used to treat premature labor?

Medications that relax the uterus and decrease contractions include three types:

- ❖ magnesium sulfate, which is usually given through an I.V.; sometimes it is given orally.
- ❖ beta-adrenergics, including ritodrine and terbutaline, which are given orally, through an I.V. or by injection.
- ❖ sedatives or narcotics, which may be used in early attempts to stop premature labor.

What are the benefits of stopping premature labor?

It is better for both mother and baby if premature labor is stopped. Premature delivery increases the risks of fetal problems and maternal problems, such as an increased risk of C-section.

Going to the Hospital

I'm nervous about preparing to go to the hospital. What should I be concerned about?

Going to the hospital to have a baby can cause anyone a little nervousness, even an experienced mom. If you make some plans before you have to go, you'll have less to worry about.

- ❖ Tour the labor and delivery area of your hospital.
- ❖ Ask about preregistering at the hospital.
- ❖ Plan the trip; know who will take you, and have a backup person available
- ❖ Make a personal plan.
- ❖ Pack your bag.

I've never had a baby before. What do I need to take with me to the hospital?

There are a lot of things to consider, but the list below should cover most of what you might need.

- ❖ 1 cotton nightgown or T-shirt for labor
- ❖ extra pillows to use during labor
- ❖ lip balm, lollipops or fruit drops to use during labor
- ❖ light diversion, such as books or magazines, to use during labor
- ❖ 1 nightgown for after labor (bring a nursing gown if you are going to breastfeed)
- ❖ slippers with rubber soles
- ❖ 1 long robe for walking in the halls
- ❖ 2 bras (nursing bras and pads if you breastfeed)
- ❖ toiletries you use, including brush, comb, toothbrush, toothpaste, soap, shampoo, conditioner
- ❖ hairband or ponytail holder, if you have long hair
- ❖ eyeglasses (you can't wear contact lenses)
- ❖ underwear and loose-fitting clothes for going home
- ❖ sanitary pads, if the hospital doesn't supply them

Should I bring anything to the hospital for my partner?

It's a good idea to include some things in your hospital kit for your partner to help him get through the experience. You might consider the following items:

- ✧ completed insurance or preregistration information
- ✧ talc or cornstarch for massaging you during labor
- ✧ a paint roller or tennis ball for giving you a low-back massage during labor
- ✧ tapes or CDs and a player, or a radio to play during labor
- ✧ labor handbook
- ✧ camera and film
- ✧ list of telephone numbers and a long-distance calling card
- ✧ change for telephones and vending machines

What should I bring for my new baby?

The hospital will probably supply most of what you will need for your baby, however there are a few things you should have ready:

- ✧ clothes for the trip home, including an undershirt, sleeper, outer clothes (a hat if it's cold)
- ✧ a couple of blankets
- ✧ diapers, if your hospital doesn't supply them

Be sure you have an approved infant car seat to take your baby home. It's important to start your baby in a car seat the very first time he or she rides in a car!

Do I need to preregister at the hospital?

It will save you time if you register at the hospital a few weeks before your due date. It is wise to do this before you go to the hospital in labor because you may be in a hurry or concerned with other things.

How do I preregister at the hospital?

You will be able to preregister with forms that you receive from your doctor's office or from the hospital.

When I preregister, what do I need to know?

Take your insurance card or insurance information with you. It is important to know your doctor's name, your pediatrician's name and your due date. It is also helpful to know your blood type and Rh-factor.

If I am in labor, what can I expect once I get to the hospital?

After you are admitted, you will probably be settled into a labor room, and you will be checked to see how much you have dilated. A brief history of your pregnancy will be taken. Vital signs, including blood pressure, pulse and temperature, are noted. You may receive an enema, or an I.V. may be started. Blood will probably be drawn. You may have an epidural put in place, if you have requested it.

When I get to the hospital, can they tell if my membranes have ruptured?

There are several ways to confirm if your membranes have ruptured.

  - ❖ By your description of what happened, such as a large gush of fluid from your vagina.
  - ❖ With *nitrazine* paper. Fluid is placed on the paper; if membranes have ruptured, the paper changes color.
  - ❖ With a *ferning test*. Fluid is placed on a glass slide, allowed to dry and examined under a microscope. If it has a "fern" appearance, it is amniotic fluid.

Does a woman always need to have her pubic hair shaved before the birth of her baby?

No. Most are not shaved these days. However, some patients who chose *not* to have their pubic hair shaved later told me they experienced discomfort when their pubic hair became entangled in their underwear due to the normal vaginal discharge after the birth of their baby.

Is an I.V. always necessary?

An I.V. is necessary with an epidural. However if you have chosen not to have an epidural, it is not always required. Most physicians agree an I.V. is helpful if the woman needs medications or fluids during labor.

Can I refuse to have an I.V.?

Discuss this with your health-care provider before the birth of your baby. In some situations, an I.V. can save your life.

A friend told me that when she got to the hospital, she found out her doctor was on vacation and someone she didn't know was going to deliver her baby. Is there anything I can do to prevent this from happening to me?

Talk to your doctor about this possibility. If your doctor believes he or she might be out of town when your baby is born, ask to meet doctors that "cover" when your doctor is unavailable. Although your physician would like to be there for the birth of your baby, sometimes it is not possible.

Labor

What does labor feel like?

Your entire abdomen (the uterus) contracts (tightens) like a hard muscle then relaxes. The tightening of the uterus can cause pain.

I've heard friends describe labor differently. One said her back hurt, another said it felt like the pain she had with diarrhea. Are these different types of labor?

No, these are not different types of labor. Labor is different for every woman; that's the reason we can't predict what your labor will be like before it begins. You may also find you labor differently from one pregnancy to the next.

I've heard all sorts of stories about labor, but I don't really know what it is. Can you explain it for me?

Labor is defined as the *dilatation* (stretching and expanding) of your cervix. This occurs when your uterus, which is a muscle, tightens (contracts) to squeeze out its contents (your baby).

True Labor or False Labor?

Considerations	True Labor	False Labor
Contractions	Regular	Irregular
Time between contractions	Come closer together	Do not get closer together
Contraction intensity	Increases	Doesn't change
Location of contractions	Entire abdomen or back	Various locations
Effect of anesthetic or pain relievers	Will not stop labor	Sedation may alter frequency or stop contractions
Cervical change	Progressive cervical change (effacement and dilatation)	No cervical change

How will I know the difference between true labor and false labor?

There *are* differences between the two. Look at the chart on the opposite page so you'll be better able to distinguish the difference.

I've heard about different stages of labor. What are they?

Labor is divided into three stages—each stage is distinctly different and has a specific purpose. Review the chart on pages 314 to 315 to see what you might expect during the various stages of labor and delivery.

What is the first stage of labor?

Stage 1 of labor is the longest and consists of three phases—early, active and transition. This first stage of labor usually lasts 6 to 8 hours but can be longer for a first birth.

In the early phase, labor is just getting started and dilatation of the cervix has just begun. In the active phase, the cervix dilates at a fairly constant rate; transition includes complete dilatation. Contractions help the cervix dilate and thin out. They also help move the baby down the birth canal for delivery.

At the transition phase, the pace and intensity of labor increases, signaling that labor is moving into the second stage.

What is the second stage of labor?

In *stage 2 of labor,* you are fully dilated and begin to push. Contractions change and become much harder, longer and more frequent. Along with your pushing, these contractions help deliver the baby. This stage can take 2 hours or longer. Anesthesia at this point, especially an epidural block, may prolong this stage of labor because your urge to push is decreased. At the end of the second stage, your baby is born.

The Three Stages of Labor

Stage	What's Happening	Your Experience	What You Can Do
Stage 1 Early phase	•Uterine contractions cause cervix to dilate (open) and efface (thin out) •Cervix dilates to 4 to 5cm	•Pinkish discharge ("show" or "bloody" show") •Membranes may rupture, causing a gush or trickle of amniotic fluid from your vagina •Mild contractions occur at 15- to 20-minute intervals in the beginning and last about 1 minute. Gradually they become more regular and closer together	•To prevent vomiting, don't eat or drink anything once labor begins. •You may be able to stay at home for a while if you are at term. Ask your doctor when you should go to the hospital. If it is preterm labor, if you have intense, constant pain or if you have bright red bleeding, call your doctor immediately. •Use relaxation and breathing techniques learned in childbirth class
Active phase	•Cervix dilates from 4 to 8cm and continues to thin out	•Contractions are more intense and frequent •Contractions will be about 3 minutes apart and last about 45 seconds	•Continue using relaxation and breathing techniques •If labor is very painful, you may ask for an epidural after the cervix dilates to 4 to 5cm
Transition phase	•Stage 1 is changing to Stage 2 •Cervix dilates from 8 to 10cm and continues to thin out	•Contractions are 2 to 3 minutes apart and last about 1 minute •You may feel very uncomfortable •You may feel strong pressure, causing the urge to push; don't push until your health-care provider says your cervix is completely dilated •You may be moved to delivery room	•Continue relaxation and breathing techniques to counteract urge to push

Stage	What's Happening	Your Experience	What You Can Do
Stage 2	•Cervix is completely dilated •Baby continues to descend •As you push, your baby is born; doctor will suction baby's nose and mouth, and clamp its umbilical cord	•Contractions occur at 2- to 5-minute intervals and last 60 to 90 seconds •If you received an epidural, you may find it hard to push • You may receive an episiotomy to prevent tearing of vaginal tissues as the baby is born	•After cervix is completely dilated, you will begin to push with each contraction •You may be able to get an injection of analgesic or a tranquilizer, or you may get a low spinal block if you didn't have a regional anesthetic
Stage 3	•After the baby is born, the placenta separates from the wall of the uterus and is expelled •Doctor will examine placenta to ensure it is intact and all of it has been delivered	•Contractions may be closer together and less painful •Doctor will repair your episiotomy	•When baby is being delivered, listen to your doctor, who will tell you when and when not to push to prevent baby from being born too quickly •As you push, you may be able to watch your baby born if an overhead mirror is available •You'll meet and hold your baby •You may need to push to expel the placenta •You may be able to hold your baby while the doctor repairs your episiotomy

What is the third stage of labor?

Stage 3 of labor usually takes only a few minutes. During stage 3, the uterus contracts and expels the placenta (afterbirth).

Somewhere I read there's a fourth stage of labor. Is this true?

Some doctors describe a fourth stage of labor, referring to the time period after delivery of the placenta, while the uterus continues to contract. Uterine contraction is important in controlling bleeding after the birth of your baby.

My sister-in-law said it's important for me to know how to contact my doctor when I go into labor. Why?

It's a good idea to ask your health-care provider certain questions about preparing to go to the hospital. She may have specific instructions for you. You might want to ask your health-care provider the following questions.

- ✧ When should I go to the hospital once I am in labor?
- ✧ Should I call you before I leave for the hospital?
- ✧ How can I reach you after regular office hours?
- ✧ Are there any particular instructions to follow during early labor?

My best friend told me she had a "bloody show" just before she went into labor. What is it?

You may bleed a *small* amount of blood following a vaginal exam or at the beginning of labor. This bloody show occurs as the cervix stretches and dilates. If it causes you concern or appears to be a large amount of blood, contact your health-care provider immediately.

Timing contractions provides your health-care provider with information so he or she can decide whether you should go to the hospital.

I read that I may pass a "mucus plug" at the beginning of labor. Is this dangerous?

Along with a bloody show, you may pass some mucus, sometimes called a *mucus plug*. Passing this mucus doesn't always mean you'll have your baby soon or that you are beginning labor.

I've heard how important it is to time contractions once labor begins. Why?

There are two reasons for timing contractions:

❖ to find out *how long* a contraction lasts
❖ to find out *how often* contractions occur

It's important for your doctor to have this information so he or she can decide if it's time for you to go to the hospital.

How do we time a contraction for how long it lasts?

Begin timing when the contraction *starts,* and end timing when the contraction *lets up and goes away.*

How do we time a contraction for how often it occurs?

Be sure to ask your doctor which method he or she prefers because there are two ways to time contractions.

♦ Start timing when the contraction *starts* and time it until the next contraction *starts*. This is the most-common method.

♦ Start timing when the contraction *ends* and note how long it is until the next contraction *starts*.

What if I go into labor and my partner isn't with me?

Well before your delivery date, sit down and talk with your partner about how you will stay in touch as your due date approaches. Some of my patients rent personal pagers for the last few weeks for the partner to carry. (Some hospitals or HMOs supply pagers for expectant couples the last few weeks.) Line up a backup support person, in case your partner cannot be with you or if you need someone to take you to the hospital.

I understand my partner can be very important during labor and delivery. How?

Your partner can help in many ways. He can help prepare you for labor and delivery and can support you as you labor. He can share in the joy of the delivery of your baby. He can support you emotionally throughout the entire birthing process, which can be very important to you both.

What does a labor coach do during labor and delivery?

A labor coach can do a lot to help you through labor. He or she can:

♦ time your contractions so you are aware of the progress of your labor

♦ encourage and reassure you during labor

♦ help you deal with your physical discomfort

✧ help create a mood in the labor room
✧ report symptoms or pain to the nurse and/or doctor
✧ keep a watch on the door, and protect your privacy
✧ control traffic into your room

I've heard I can't drink anything during labor. Why?

Women often get nauseated, which may cause vomiting. It is for your safety that you are not allowed to eat or to drink anything during labor to keep your stomach empty.

If my labor is a long one, can I have anything to drink?

No, just sips of water or ice chips to suck on. If labor is long, you may be given fluids through an I.V.

What about food—if my labor is extremely long, can I eat anything?

No, you can't. As I have explained, it's for your safety that you will not be allowed anything to eat.

I'm nervous about whether my baby is too big for me to deliver. Can my doctor tell if I'll have problems before labor begins?

Even with an estimation of how much your baby weighs, your doctor cannot really know if the baby is too big for you until after labor begins. Usually labor must begin so your doctor can see how the baby fits into your pelvis and if there is enough room for the baby to pass through the birth canal.

I've heard many different stories from friends, but I need an answer. Will I have to have an enema when I go to the hospital to have my baby?

You may not be required to have an enema—it is usually a choice. You need to discuss this with your health-care provider at one of your prenatal appointments. There *are* benefits to having an enema early in labor. It decreases the amount of contamination by bowel movement or feces during labor and at the time of delivery. It may also help you after delivery if you have an episiotomy because having a bowel movement very soon after delivery can be painful.

What can I expect when I have my first bowel movement after delivery?

Your first bowel movement usually occurs a day or two after delivery. If you had an enema, it could take a few days longer. It could be painful, especially if you have an episiotomy.

A friend said her doctor prescribed stool softeners for her, and they helped. Is this common?

Yes. Most doctors prescribe stool softeners after delivery to help with your bowel movements. They are safe to take, even if you are nursing.

What is back labor?

Back labor occurs when the baby comes out through the birth canal looking straight up. This type of presentation often causes lower-back pain.

If my baby is looking up, will that make my labor longer?

This type of labor may take longer for delivery. It may require rotation of the baby's head so it comes out looking down at the ground rather than looking up at the sky.

My sister-in-law had all sorts of friends present during her labor and when she gave birth last year. I don't want anyone but my husband with me. Is this unusual?

Whatever you want should be OK with your husband or partner. As I've said before, the birth experience can be stressful for you. As long as it's acceptable to your doctor, you should be allowed to make a lot of the decisions about the birth experience.

Tests During Labor

My health-care provider was mentioning fetal monitoring during labor and delivery. What is this?

In many hospitals, a baby's heartbeat is monitored throughout labor, making it possible to detect any problems early so they can be resolved.

What kind of monitoring do they do?

There are two types of fetal monitoring during labor—*external fetal monitoring* and *internal fetal monitoring*.

What is external fetal monitoring?

This type of monitoring can be done before your membranes rupture. A belt with a receiver is strapped to your abdomen, and it records the baby's heartbeat. See the illustration below and the one on page 83.

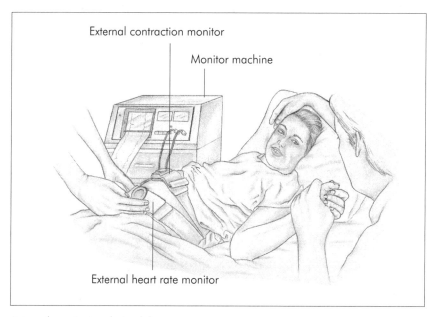

External monitoring during labor.

What is internal fetal monitoring?

Internal fetal monitoring is a more-precise method of monitoring the baby. An electrode is placed on the fetal scalp to record the fetal heart rate; it gives a more-exact reading. See the illustration on page 84.

I recently read about fetal blood sampling during labor. What is this test?

It is another way of evaluating how well a baby is tolerating the stress of labor.

How is fetal blood sampling done during labor?

Membranes must be ruptured, and the cervix must be dilated at least 2cm. An instrument is applied to the scalp of the baby to make a small nick in the skin. The baby's blood is collected in a small tube, and its pH (acidity) is checked.

What can the doctor learn from fetal blood sampling?

The pH level can help determine whether the baby is having trouble during labor. Results help the physician decide whether labor can continue or if a Cesarean section needs to be done.

Dealing with the Pain of Childbirth

I've never had a baby before, and I'm terrified of the pain of childbirth. Is it really awful?

Childbirth *is* accompanied by pain; expectation of this pain can evoke fear and anxiety in you. This is normal. If you're concerned about pain and how you'll handle it, the best way to deal with it is to become informed about it.

My friend told me I wouldn't feel like a "real woman" unless I have my baby without any pain relief. Is this true?

Many women believe they'll feel guilty after their baby is born if they ask for pain relief during labor. Sometimes they believe the baby will be harmed by the medication. Some believe they'll deprive themselves of the complete birth experience. I tell my patients that the main goal of any labor and delivery is a *healthy baby*. If a woman needs pain relief to help her, it doesn't mean she's failed in any way!

How can I find out more about the different pain-relief methods available during labor and delivery?

Discuss it with your health-care provider. Your childbirth preparation class is also a good place to ask about these medications.

I've heard about "analgesia" and "anesthesia" for pain relief. What's the difference?

Analgesia is pain relief without total loss of sensation. *Anesthesia* is pain relief with total loss of sensation.

How does analgesia work?

An analgesic is injected into a muscle or vein to decrease the pain of labor, but it allows you to remain conscious. It provides pain relief but can make you drowsy, restless and nauseous. You may experience difficulty concentrating. It may slow the baby's reflexes and breathing, so it is usually given during the early and middle parts of labor.

How does anesthesia work?

There are two types of anesthesia—*general anesthesia* and *local anesthesia,* sometimes called *regional anesthesia.* With general anesthesia, you are completely unconscious, so it is used only for some Cesarean deliveries and emergency vaginal deliveries. Local anesthesia affects a small area and is very useful for an episiotomy repair.

Is general anesthesia dangerous?

There are some disadvantages to using a general anesthesia—it is not used as much today as it was in the past. The advantage of general anesthesia is that it can be administered very quickly in an emergency. Disadvantages include causing the mother to vomit or to aspirate vomited food or stomach acid into her lungs.

Does local anesthesia affect the baby?

Local anesthesia rarely affects the baby and usually has few lingering effects.

I've heard there are several types of local anesthesia. What are they?

The three most common types of local anesthesia are pudendal block, spinal block and epidural block.

What is a pudendal block?

A *pudendal block* is medication injected into the vaginal area to relieve pain in the vagina, the perineum and the rectum. It allows the mother to remain conscious during its use. Side effects are rare. It is considered one of the safest forms of pain relief, however it does not relieve uterine pain.

What is a spinal block?

With a *spinal block,* medication is injected into spinal fluid in the lower back, which numbs the lower part of the body. The mother remains conscious during delivery with a spinal block. This type of block is administered only once during labor, so it is often used just before delivery. It works quickly and is an effective pain inhibitor.

What is an epidural block?

In an *epidural block,* a tube is inserted into a space outside the mother's spinal column in the lower back. Medication is administered through the tube for pain relief, and the mother remains conscious during delivery. The tube remains in place until after delivery so additional medication can be administered when necessary.

An epidural causes some loss of sensation in the lower part of the body. It helps relieve painful uterine contractions, pain in the vagina and rectum as the baby passes through the birth canal and the pain of an episiotomy. A woman can still feel pressure, so she can push adequately during vaginal delivery.

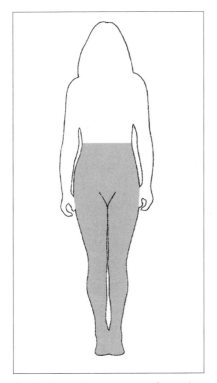

Regional anesthesia—area of anesthesia with spinal or epidural.

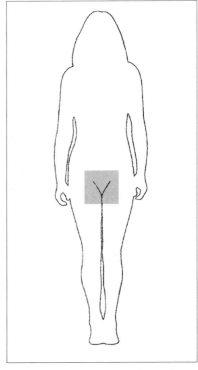

Local anesthesia—area of anesthesia with local anesthetic.

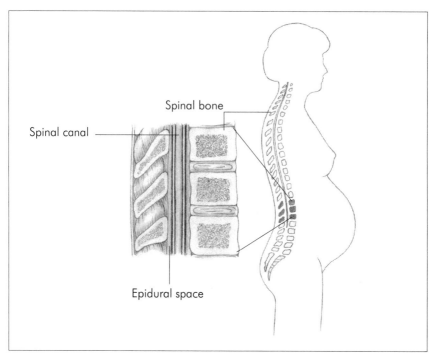

Epidural anesthesia.

An epidural block is not effective in some women. Because an epidural may make it harder to push, vacuum extraction or forceps may be necessary during delivery.

What are the side effects of a spinal block or an epidural block?

Both a spinal block and an epidural block can cause a woman's blood pressure to drop suddenly, which in turn can cause a decrease in the baby's heart rate. These blocks are not used if the woman is bleeding heavily or if the baby has an abnormal heartbeat. A woman may experience a severe headache if the covering of the spinal cord is punctured during needle insertion with either type of anesthesia.

I recently read about an anesthesia called a "walking spinal." What is it?

A *walking spinal,* also called *intrathecal anesthesia,* can be given to women who suffer extreme pain in the early stages of labor (less than 5cm dilated). A small amount of narcotic, such as Demerol, is injected through a thin needle into the spinal fluid, which eases the pain and causes few side effects.

Because the dose is small, neither the mother nor baby becomes overly drowsy. Sensory and motor functions remain intact, allowing the mother to walk around with help or sit in a chair.

Is a walking spinal available everywhere?

Unfortunately, its use at this time is very limited. By the beginning of 1995, only 12 teaching hospitals in the United States were using it. However, the number of places planning to use this type of anesthesia is growing. Further testing is necessary before the procedure becomes routine and widely available.

Cesarean Delivery

My doctor just told me I may need to have a Cesarean delivery, and I'm scared. What is it exactly?

When a woman has a *Cesarean delivery* (also called a *C-section*), her baby is delivered through an incision made in the mother's abdominal wall and uterus.

Why is a Cesarean operation performed?

There are many reasons for doing a C-section, but the main goal of doing one is to deliver a healthy baby. Specific reasons include:

      ✧ a previous Cesarean delivery

❖ to avoid rupture of the uterus
❖ the baby is too big to fit through the birth canal
❖ fetal distress
❖ compression of the umbilical cord
❖ baby is in the breech position
❖ placental abruption
❖ placenta previa
❖ multiple fetuses—twins, triplets or more

I've read that more Cesareans are being done today. Is this true?

Yes. There has been an increase in the rate of C-sections. In 1965, only 4% of all deliveries were Cesarean. Today in the United States, nearly 25% of all deliveries are Cesarean deliveries.

Why are there more Cesarean deliveries today?

We believe the increase is related to better monitoring during labor and safer procedures for C-sections. Women are also having bigger babies. A third factor in this increase may be rising malpractice rates and the fear of litigation. However, the goal is the same—a doctor wants to deliver the baby safely.

How is a C-section done?

An incision is made through the skin of the abdominal wall down to the uterus, and the wall of the uterus is cut. Then the amniotic sac containing the baby and placenta is cut, and the baby is removed through the incisions. After the baby is delivered, the placenta is removed. The uterus is closed in layers with sutures that are absorbed (they don't have to be removed). The abdomen is then sewn together.

If I have to have a Cesarean, can I be awake?

With many C-sections, the anesthesiologist will give you an epidural or a spinal anesthetic. You are awake with these.

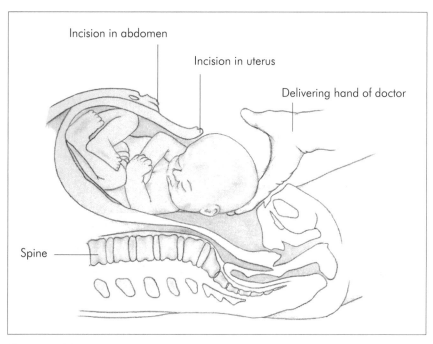

Cesarean delivery.

Can't my doctor tell if I'll need a C-section before I go into labor?

It would be nice to know this so you wouldn't have to go through labor, but it isn't that easy. We usually have to wait for labor contractions to see if your baby is stressed by them. And we have to wait to see if the baby fits through the birth canal.

Are there any advantages to having a Cesarean delivery?

The most important advantage is delivery of a healthy baby.

I'm sure there are disadvantages to having a C-section. What are they?

This is major surgery and carries with it certain risks, including infection, bleeding, shock through blood loss, the possibility of blood clots and injury to other organs, such as the bladder or rectum. You will probably have to stay in the hospital a couple of extra days.

How long does it take to recover from a Cesarean?

Recovery at home takes longer with a Cesarean than it does with a vaginal delivery. The normal time for full recovery is 4 to 6 weeks.

How many Cesarean deliveries can a woman have?

There is no exact number. Many doctors recommend no more than two or three, but this is evaluated at the time of each delivery. I have one patient on whom I recently performed her *eighth* C-section. This is unusual however.

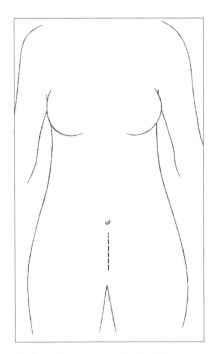

Midline Cesarean-section incision.

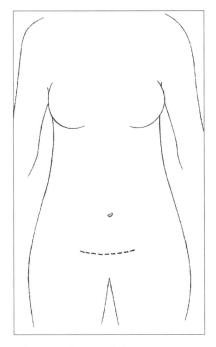

Bikini or pfanensteil Cesarean-section incision.

Some women at my childbirth preparation class said if you have a Cesarean, you've failed as a woman. Is this true?

No! If you have a Cesarean, you have *not* failed in any way! The goal in pregnancy, labor and delivery is a healthy baby and a healthy mother. In many situations, the *only* way to achieve that is with a Cesarean delivery.

If a woman has repeat Cesarean sections, how does the doctor perform the surgery? Does he or she make a new, different incision for every birth?

Usually the same incision site will be used. If you have a large scar, your doctor may cut out the old scar.

My sister has systemic lupus erythematosus and had to have two Cesarean deliveries. She said it was because the prednisone she has to take kept her from actively going into labor. Is this true?

Yes. Prednisone may prevent labor in some women, and so a Cesarean delivery could be required.

I've heard that once you have a Cesarean, you must always have one. But don't some women deliver vaginally after having a Cesarean?

In the past it was felt that once a woman had a C-section, any later deliveries would have to be Cesarean also. Today it is becoming quite common for women who have had a C-section to deliver vaginally with later pregnancies. This is called *vaginal birth after Cesarean (VBAC)*.

How does a woman know whether she can have a VBAC?

There are various factors that must be considered in making this decision. The type of incision done with the Cesarean delivery is important. With a classical incision, which goes high up on the uterus, labor is *not* permitted in subsequent pregnancies. If the woman is small and the baby is large, it may cause problems. Multiple fetuses and medical complications, such as diabetes or high blood pressure, may require a repeat C-section.

How many C-sections can I have and still be a candidate for VBAC?

The American College of Obstetricians and Gynecologists states two Cesarean deliveries are all right, other factors permitting.

What factors determine whether I can have a vaginal birth after having had a C-section?

Women who have the best chance of having a successful vaginal delivery after a C-section include women:

   ❖ whose original cause for a Cesarean delivery is not repeated with this pregnancy
   ❖ who have no major medical problems
   ❖ who had a low-transverse incision (incision on the uterus) with their previous C-section
   ❖ who have a normal-size baby
   ❖ whose babies are in the normal head-down position

If I want to try a vaginal delivery after a C-section, what can I do?

The most important thing to do is to discuss it with your doctor well in advance of labor so plans can be made. It may be helpful to get the records from your other delivery. Discuss the benefits and risks, and ask your doctor for his or her opinion as to your chances of a successful vaginal delivery. He or she knows your health and pregnancy history. Include your partner in this decision-making process.

Will I Need an Episiotomy?

What is an episiotomy?

An *episiotomy* is a surgical incision in the area behind the vagina, above the rectum; it is made during delivery to avoid tearing the vaginal opening and/or rectum.

Will my physician require me to have an episiotomy?

This is something you need to discuss with your physician at your prenatal visits. There are some situations that do not require an episiotomy, such as a small baby or a premature baby. Often this decision cannot be made until the time of delivery.

Does every woman have to have an episiotomy?

No, it is not necessary for everyone. Most women having their first or second baby will have an episiotomy. The more children a woman has had, the less likely it will be for her to need an episiotomy. It depends on the size of the baby.

My friend said she didn't need an episiotomy. Why does a woman have an episiotomy?

An episiotomy is done to allow room for the baby to fit through the birth canal and to avoid tearing into other organs in the mother. Again, if a woman has had a few pregnancies and deliveries, she may not need an episiotomy with her later children.

What factors determine whether I have to have one?

Some factors leading to an episiotomy include:
- the size of the mother's vaginal opening
- the size of the baby's head and shoulders
- the number of babies previously delivered
- a forceps or vacuum delivery

I've heard some episiotomies are bigger than others. What does this mean?

Description of an episiotomy includes a description of the depth of the incision. There are four degrees that describe incision depth:

 ✧ *1st degree*—cuts only the skin
 ✧ *2nd degree*—cuts the skin and underlying tissue, called *fascia*
 ✧ *3rd degree*—cuts the skin, underlying tissue and rectal sphincter, which is the muscle that goes around the anus
 ✧ *4th degree*—goes through the three layers described above and the rectal mucosa, which is the lining of the rectum

How painful is an episiotomy?

After delivery of your baby, the most painful part of the entire birth process might be your episiotomy. Don't be afraid to ask for help with this pain. Many things can be done to help relieve the pain, including pain medication, ice, Sitz baths and laxatives.

The Baby's Birth Position

I heard a woman at the doctor's office say her baby was in a "breech position." What did she mean?

A *breech position* means the baby is not in a head-down position, and the legs or buttocks come into the birth canal first.

If my baby is in a breech position, is that bad?

Early in pregnancy, breech is common. By the last 4 to 6 weeks, your baby should be in a head-down position. If your baby is breech when it is time to deliver, your doctor may try to turn the baby or you may need a Cesarean delivery.

What causes a baby to be in a breech position?

One of the main causes is prematurity of the baby. Near the end of the second trimester, it's more common for the baby to be in a breech position. As you progress through the third trimester, the baby usually turns into the head-down position for birth.

Are there different kinds of breech positions and other abnormal positions?

Yes. There are three different breech presentations and two other abnormal positions:

- ✧ Frank breech—lower legs are flexed at the hips and extended at the knees. Feet are up by the face or head.
- ✧ Complete breech—one or both knees are flexed, not extended.
- ✧ Incomplete breech—a foot or knee enters the birth canal ahead of the rest of the baby.
- ✧ Face presentation—the baby's head is hyperextended so the face enters the birth canal first.
- ✧ Shoulder presentation—the baby is lying almost as if in a cradle in the pelvis. The head is on one side of the mother's abdomen, and the bottom is on the other side.

How is a baby in the breech position delivered?

There is some controversy about this. For a long time, breech deliveries were performed vaginally, then it was believed the safest method was by C-section. Many doctors still believe a Cesarean delivery is the safest way to deliver a baby in the breech position. However, some doctors believe a woman can deliver a breech baby without difficulty if the situation is right.

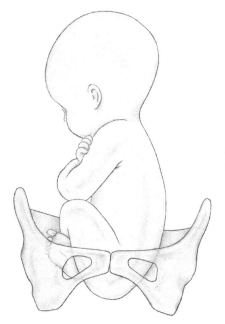

Complete-breech presentation of baby.

I've heard that sometimes the doctor will try to turn a baby in the breech position. Is that true?

Yes. If your baby is in a breech position, your physician may attempt to change its position by using *external cephalic version (ECV)*.

How is the baby turned?

The doctor places his or her hands on your abdomen. Using gentle movements, he or she manually shifts the baby into the head-down position. An ultrasound is usually done first so the doctor can see the position of the baby. Ultrasound is used during the procedure to guide the doctor in changing the baby's position.

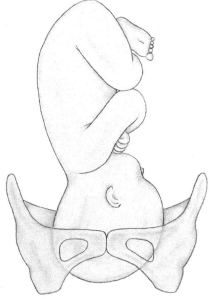

Preferable alignment for birth.

When is external cephalic version usually done?

Most physicians who use this method do so before labor begins or in the early stages of labor.

How successful is ECV?

It is successful in about 50% of the cases in which it is used.

Can every doctor do ECV?

Not every doctor is trained in the procedure. If your physician suggests it, find out if he or she has been trained to do it.

Delivery of Your Baby

How long does a vaginal delivery take?

The actual delivery of the baby and placenta (not including the laboring process) takes anywhere from a few minutes to an hour.

How long does a Cesarean delivery take?

It usually takes from 30 to 60 minutes. However the part that takes the longest is not the birth of the baby—that is performed rather quickly. Stitching closed the various skin and muscle layers after the baby is born takes the greatest amount of time.

Will I deliver in the same room I labor in?

This is the setup in some hospitals and is called *LDRP,* which means *labor, delivery, recovery and postpartum.* With LDRP, you labor and deliver in the same room, then remain there during recovery and your stay at the hospital. Not all hospitals or birthing centers are equipped this way. In many places you will labor in a labor room and move to a delivery room to deliver. Then you will recover in a wardlike setting before being moved to your room, where you will remain until you go home.

I've read that there are other birth positions that are acceptable besides lying on my back with my feet in stirrups. Is that true?

Yes there are. You may not have to use stirrups, or you may deliver lying on your side.

Will my doctor have to use forceps during the delivery?

It depends on the situation at the time of delivery. The factors involved include the size of the baby, the size of your pelvis, how well you are able to push and whether your baby needs to be delivered immediately.

Exactly what are forceps?

Forceps look like two metal hands and are used to help deliver the baby. However, they are not used as much today as the were in the past. Instead, physicians more often use a vacuum extractor or perform a Cesarean section.

What is a vacuum extractor?

A *vacuum extractor* is a plastic cup that fits on the baby's head by suction. When you push during labor, your doctor is able to pull and help to deliver the baby more easily.

What is the Lamaze method of childbirth?

The *Lamaze method* is a very popular, widely available method of childbirth. It provides education and practice for

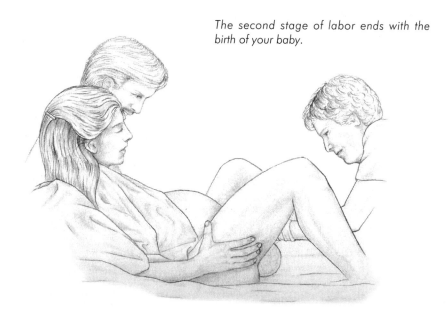

The second stage of labor ends with the birth of your baby.

the mother and labor coach in the weeks before birth. The woman learns breathing exercises to help her through her labor and learns ways to concentrate on objects to block out pain or to help reduce pain.

Can every woman use the Lamaze method?

The Lamaze method works very well for many women in labor. However, this approach requires a very serious commitment from the woman and her labor coach. It takes a great deal of practice and a lot of hard work during labor, but it can be very rewarding.

My partner wants to take a video of the birth, but I don't want him to. Am I being unreasonable?

No, you're not. The birth process is very private for many women, and they don't want to be videotaped, photographed or forced to share it with others. If this is your wish, explain it to your partner. He should respect your wishes. If he won't listen, discuss the problem with your health-care provider. Ask him or her to explain your objections to your partner.

After Your Baby Is Born

What happens to my baby after it is born?

First, the baby's mouth and throat are suctioned to clear out any secretions. Then the doctor clamps and cuts the umbilical cord. The baby is wrapped in clean blankets and may be placed on your abdomen. At 1 minute and 5 minutes after birth Apgar scores are recorded to show the baby's response to birth and to life on its own. An ID band is placed on the baby's wrist. Usually a brief physical or an assessment is done right after delivery. The baby receives drops in its eyes to prevent infection and is given a vitamin-K shot to prevent bleeding.

You will be asked if you want your baby to receive the hepatitis vaccine. You will probably have discussed this with your doctor. The vaccine is given to protect the baby against hepatitis in the future. However, you might decide not to have it given.

Once the initial evaluation is complete, the baby is returned to you. Later, the baby is placed in a heated bassinet for a period of time. See the chart on page 343 for a description of tests commonly performed on newborns.

My husband wants to cut the umbilical cord after the baby is delivered. Can he do this?

Talk to your doctor about your husband's participation in the delivery. What he is allowed to do varies from place to place.

I've heard my uterus will contract after my baby is born. How much will it shrink?

After you deliver your baby, the uterus shrinks from the size of a watermelon to the size of a volleyball. The uterus contracts and becomes smaller so it won't bleed.

How serious is bleeding after the birth of the baby?

You can expect to bleed after you deliver, but heavy bleeding is not very common. Bleeding is controlled by massaging the uterus (called *Credé*) and medications; it lessens gradually over time then stops.

Is it normal to bleed heavily after my baby is born?

It's not unusual to lose blood during labor and delivery. However, heavy bleeding after the baby is born can be serious. A loss of more than 17 ounces (500ml) in the first 24 hours after your baby's birth, called *postpartum hemorrhage,* is cause for concern.

What causes heavy bleeding?

The most common causes of heavy bleeding include the following:

- ✧ a uterus that won't contract
- ✧ tearing of the vagina or cervix during birth
- ✧ a large or bleeding episiotomy
- ✧ a tear, rupture or hole in the uterus
- ✧ failure of blood vessels inside the uterus to compress
- ✧ retained placental tissue
- ✧ clotting or coagulation problems

What if bleeding becomes heavy after a few days or weeks?

Contact your doctor. Sometimes the bleeding is normal, but it is best to talk to your health-care provider about it. He or she may want to see you to determine if the amount of bleeding is normal and, if necessary, to prescribe medication.

I've heard that we can have our baby's umbilical-cord blood saved and frozen for later use, if it is needed. Why would we want to do this?

Cord blood — blood saved from the umbilical cord — may be "banked" and saved for future use. Umbilical-cord blood can be used to treat cancer and genetic diseases that are now treated by bone-marrow transplants. Cord blood has been used successfully to treat childhood leukemia, some immune diseases and other blood diseases.

Blood is collected directly from the umbilical cord immediately after delivery. It is then transported to a bank facility where it is frozen and stored. There is no risk to the mother or baby.

It is expensive and it may not be for everyone. If you are interested, your doctor can tell you more.

If Your Baby Is Late

What is a "postdate birth"?

Babies born 2 weeks or more past their due date are called *postdate* or *post-term births.*

How common is postdate birth?

About 10% of all babies are born more than 2 weeks past their due date.

Is a postdate birth dangerous for my baby?

The majority of babies born more than 2 weeks late are delivered safely. However, carrying a baby longer than 42 weeks can cause some problems for the fetus and the mother, so health-care providers conduct tests on these babies and induce labor, if necessary.

Why do they test a postdate baby?

A health-care provider can determine if a baby is moving around in the womb and if the amount of amniotic fluid is healthy and normal. If it is determined the baby is healthy and active, the mother-to-be is usually monitored until labor begins on its own. Tests are usually done as reassurance that an overdue baby is OK and can remain in the womb. These tests include a non-stress test, a contraction stress test and a biophysical profile. If signs of fetal stress are found, labor is often induced.

Emergency Childbirth

What should I do if I go into labor and can't make it to the hospital?

Emergency childbirth can happen to anyone, so the best thing to do is to be prepared. Read and study the information in the following boxes. Be sure you have the names and telephone numbers of your doctor or health-care provider and those of friends or family written down and near the phone. And if it happens to you, try to relax and follow the instructions provided.

	Emergency Delivery if You Are Alone
1	Call 911 for help.
2	Call a neighbor, close member or friend (have phone numbers available).
3	Try not to push or bear down.
4	Find a comfortable place, and spread out towels or blankets.
5	If the baby comes before help arrives, try to use your hands to ease the baby out while you gently push.
6	Wrap the baby in a clean blanket or clean towels; hold it close to your body to keep it warm.
7	Use a clean cloth or tissue to remove mucus from the baby's mouth.
8	Do not pull on the umbilical cord to deliver the placenta—it is not necessary.
9	If the placenta delivers on its own, save it.
10	You don't need to cut the cord.
11	Try to keep yourself and your baby warm until medical help arrives.

Emergency Delivery at Home

1   Call 911 for help.

2   Call a neighbor, family member or friend (have phone numbers available).

3   Encourage the woman *not* to push or to bear down.

4   Use blankets and towels to make the woman as comfortable as possible.

5   If there is time, wash the woman's vaginal and rectal areas with soap and water.

6   When the baby's head delivers, encourage the woman to pant or blow, and to concentrate on *not* pushing.

7   Try to ease the baby's head out with gentle pressure. Do not pull on the head.

8   After the head is delivered, gently push down on the head and push a little to deliver the shoulders.

9   As one shoulder delivers, lift the head up, delivering the other shoulder. The rest of the baby will quickly follow.

10   Wrap the baby in a clean blanket or towel.

11   Use a clean cloth or tissue to remove mucus from the baby's mouth.

12   Do not pull on the umbilical cord to deliver the placenta—it is not necessary.

13   If the placenta delivers on its own, wrap it in a towel or clean newspapers, and save it.

14   You don't need to cut the cord.

15   Keep the placenta at the level of the baby or above the baby.

16   Keep both mother and baby warm with towels or blankets until medical help arrives.

Emergency Delivery on the Way to the Hospital

1   Stop the car.

2   Try to get help, if you have a cellular phone or a CB radio.

3   Put on your flashing warning lights.

4   Place the woman in the back seat, with a towel or blanket under her.

5   Encourage the woman not to push or bear down.

6   When the baby's head delivers, encourage the woman to pant or blow, and to concentrate on *not* pushing.

7   Try to ease the baby's head out with gentle pressure. Do not pull on the head.

8   After the head is delivered, gently push down on the head and push a little to deliver the shoulders.

9   As one shoulder delivers, lift the head up, delivering the other shoulder. The rest of the baby will quickly follow.

10   Wrap the baby in a clean blanket or clean towels. Clean newspapers can be used if nothing else is available.

11   Use a clean cloth or tissue to remove mucus from the baby's mouth.

12   Do not pull on the umbilical cord to deliver the placenta—it is not necessary.

13   If the placenta delivers on its own, wrap it in a towel or clean newspapers and save it.

14   You don't need to cut the cord.

15   Keep the placenta at the level of the baby or above the baby

16   Keep both mother and baby warm until you can get them to the hospital or medical help arrives.

·*18*·

After Your Baby's Birth

How long will I have to stay in the hospital?

Most women are discharged within a day or two, if labor and delivery are normal and the baby is doing well. If you have a Cesarean delivery, you need to stay a few days longer.

What can I expect during my recovery from a vaginal delivery?

Your blood pressure and bleeding will be checked closely for the first hours after the birth. You will be offered medication for pain relief, and you will be encouraged to nurse your baby.

What can I expect during recovery if I have a Cesarean delivery?

You will be in a recovery area where you will be monitored by a nurse. You will be offered pain medication. After about an hour, you will be moved to your room.

I've heard the nurse will measure my urine output after delivery. Why?

This is checked to make sure your kidneys and bladder are working.

What is the pain after childbirth like? What can I expect?

There are two main areas of pain—your abdomen and your episiotomy (if you have one). You can ask for pain medication for both.

How can I tell if my episiotomy is OK?

It will be hard for you to tell. The nurses will check it for you.

What should I do if I get an infection in the episiotomy incision?

This type of infection is unusual and doesn't usually show up for a few days. It requires antibiotics to treat it.

If I don't want any more children, is it a good idea to have my tubes tied after I deliver my baby?

Some women choose to have a tubal ligation done while they are in the hospital after the birth of their baby. However this is not the time to make a decision about a tubal ligation if you haven't thought seriously about it before.

Are there advantages to having a tubal ligation after delivery?

Yes, there are. You are already in the hospital; if you have an epidural, you already have the anesthesia necessary for a tubal ligation.

What are the disadvantages to having a tubal ligation after delivering my baby?

Consider tubal ligation permanent and irreversible. If you have your tubes tied within a few hours or a day after having your baby, then change your mind, you will regret it.

If I didn't have an epidural, what kind of anesthesia is used for a tubal ligation?

In most cases, it requires general anesthesia.

Are there any activities I should avoid after my baby is born?

Avoid lifting any objects heavier than the baby the first few weeks. If possible, avoid climbing stairs whenever you can.

I've decided not to breastfeed. Will my doctor give me pills or a shot to dry up my milk?

You may be given pills to stop your milk from coming in, although it is not done as often now as was in the past. It is more common now to bind or wrap the breasts to stop the milk flow.

When you hold your baby, be sure to support his or her head with your hand.

What if I decide I want to breastfeed later. Can I?

No. If you stop your milk from coming in by taking medicine or not breastfeeding, you won't be able to start it later.

My friend said she was really tired after her baby was born. Is this normal?

Many women are surprised by how tired they are emotionally and physically the first few months after the birth of the baby. Be sure to take time for yourself—you'll have a period of adjustment.

I've heard I should get lots of sleep after the baby is born. Why?

Sleep and rest *are* essential after the baby is born to help you get back in shape. To get the rest you need, go to bed early when possible. Try taking a nap or resting when the baby naps.

I feel exhausted having to deal with my baby. How can I get my husband to help me?

Parenthood is easier and more enjoyable when both partners share the responsibilities and chores. Couples should form an equal parenthood partnership. It will take a cooperative effort from both of you, but it can be done.

How do we form this partnership?

Try to sit down together *before* the baby is born and discuss what changes you are going to be facing. You may be able to avoid problems before they occur. Sharing tasks, such as bathing and diaper changing, seems to work out the best.

My mother told me that there are some warning signs of problems I may experience after birth. What are they?

You should not feel ill after birth. Call your doctor immediately if you have any of the following problems:

♦ unusually heavy or sudden increase in vaginal bleeding (more than your normal menstrual flow or soaking more than two sanitary pads in 30 minutes)
♦ vaginal discharge with strong, unpleasant odor
♦ a temperature of 101F (38.3C) or more, except for the first 24 hours after birth
♦ breasts that are painful or red
♦ loss of appetite for an extended period of time
♦ pain, tenderness, redness and/or swelling in your legs
♦ pain in the lower abdomen or in the back

What are "after-baby blues"?

The term *after-baby blues* refers to a feeling of depression a woman may experience after her baby is born. It is also called *postpartum depression*. The condition is marked by anxiety, crying, depression, irritability and restlessness. It usually lasts only a week or two and is caused by the change in hormone levels in a woman's body after her baby is born.

What can I do about after-baby blues?

If you don't feel better in a few days, call your health-care provider. Discuss your concerns with him or her; you'll be advised what to do. You may be referred to outside help, if it is needed. If you don't take care of yourself, your depression can worsen and can affect your physical health as well as your relationships with your baby and your partner.

Will I ever regain the tightness of my abdominal skin now that my baby is here?

For some women, skin returns to normal naturally. For others, it never returns to its prepregnancy state. Abdominal skin is not like muscle, so it can't be strengthened by exercise. One of the main factors that affects your skin's ability to return to its prepregnancy tightness is connective tissue, which provides suppleness and elasticity. As you get older, your skin loses connective tissue and elasticity. Other factors include your state of fitness before pregnancy, heredity and how greatly your skin was stretched during pregnancy.

My breasts grew quite a bit during pregnancy. Will they return to their normal size?

Most women find their breasts return to their prepregnancy size or decrease a little in size. This is a result of the change in the connective tissue that forms the support system in a woman's breasts. Exercise will not make breasts firmer, but it can improve the chest area so breasts have better support.

I thought I'd feel thinner now that I'm no longer pregnant, but I still feel fat. What can I do about my weight?

It's normal to lose 10 to 15 pounds (4.5 to 6.75kg) immediately after your baby is born. Extra weight may be harder to lose. Your body stored about 7 to 10 pounds (3.15 to 4.5kg) of fat to provide energy for the first few months after birth. If you eat properly and get enough exercise, these pounds will slowly come off.

Shouldn't I go on a strict diet to lose the weight?

No! Don't go on a strict diet right away—wait until later. Even if you don't breastfeed your baby, your body requires a well-balanced, nutritious diet for you to stay healthy and keep your energy levels up.

I've heard I shouldn't diet if I'm breastfeeding. Why?

All the nutrients your baby receives while breastfeeding depend on the quality of the food you eat. Breastfeeding places more demands on your body than pregnancy. Your body burns up to 1,000 calories a day just to produce milk. When breastfeeding, you need to eat an extra 500 calories a day. Be sure to keep fluid levels up.

I really want to get back to exercising now that my baby is here. How should I approach exercising?

Exercise is important to your total feeling of well-being. Do something you enjoy, and do it on a regular basis. Walking and swimming are excellent exercises to help you get back in shape. However, before you start any postpartum exercise program, be sure to check with your doctor. He or she may have some particular advice for you.

I want to get in shape as soon as possible, now that my baby's here. What can I do?

Be careful about beginning an exercise program too soon. Discuss it with your health-care provider first. Be sure you don't overtire yourself. Get adequate rest.

What kind of activities can I start with?

Walking is a good exercise, but take it slowly. Ask your doctor when and how you can increase your exercise program.

Your Postpartum Checkup

I'm scheduled for a postpartum checkup in 6 weeks. Do I really need to go?

Yes. Your postpartum checkup is the last part of a complete prenatal-care program. It is just as important as seeing your health-care provider during pregnancy. A postpartum checkup is scheduled between 2 and 6 weeks after delivery, depending on the circumstances of the birth.

What will my postpartum checkup cover?

You will have a physical exam, similar to the one at your first prenatal exam. Your health-care provider will also do an internal exam. If you had any birth tears or incisions, your health-care provider will examine them to see how they are healing. This is a good time to discuss birth control, if you haven't already made plans.

Why do I have to have a pelvic exam now that my baby is born?

Your health-care provider does an internal exam to determine if your uterus is returning to its prepregnant size and position. This normally takes about 6 weeks. If there are any problems, they can be taken care of at this time.

Birth Control After Pregnancy

When can I resume sexual relations with my partner?
Six weeks after delivery, if your recovery is normal.

I've heard that breastfeeding is a good way to keep from getting pregnant. Is this true?
Breastfeeding decreases your chances of getting pregnant, but you *cannot* rely on breastfeeding or the lack of menstruation to protect you against getting pregnant again. You need to use some type of protection when you resume intercourse.

What type of birth control can I use while breastfeeding?
There are many types of contraception you can use—condoms, birth-control foam or jelly, diaphragms, IUDs, Norplant. Talk about your options with your health-care provider.

Should I talk to my doctor about contraception at my postpartum checkup?
This is the perfect time to discuss it. If you are not planning another pregnancy immediately, you need to discuss this with your doctor. You can ask about contraceptive methods. You may decide on oral contraceptives, Norplant or an IUD. You will need a prescription for an oral contraceptive. If you decide on Norplant or an IUD, you will have to make arrangements for the procedure.

I've heard I can't use birth-control pills while I'm breastfeeding. Why?
Do not use oral contraceptives if you are breastfeeding. The hormones in oral contraceptives can get into your milk and be passed along to your baby. Choose some other form of birth control until you are finished breastfeeding.

Making Your Home Safe for Baby

I recently heard on TV that baby-proofing a house is important, even when the baby is very young. What did they mean?

First, you cannot baby-proof a house. All you can do is make it baby-safe. Accidents can and do happen, so it's best to try to safeguard your baby's environment. Keep in mind the following.

⋄ Crib slats should be no farther apart than 2-3/8 inches (6cm).

⋄ Be sure the mattress fits securely.

⋄ Keep the crib away from windows, wall decorations, heating units, climbable furniture, blind and drapery cords, and other possible dangers.

⋄ Never use a pillow in the crib.

⋄ Keep the dropside up and locked when baby is in the crib.

⋄ Keep mobiles and other crib toys out of baby's reach. You may have to remove them as baby grows older.

⋄ Never hang a pacifier or anything else around your baby's neck.

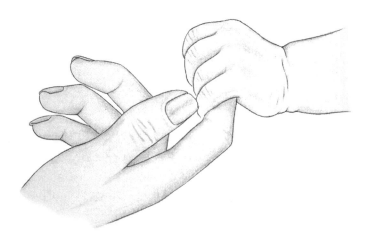

- ✧ Never leave baby unattended on a sofa, chair, changing table or any other surface above the floor.
- ✧ Never put an infant seat on the counter or a table.
- ✧ Use safety straps with all baby equipment.
- ✧ Never leave a baby unattended in *any* water. A baby can drown in 1 inch of water.
- ✧ Never hold your baby while you're cooking or drinking any hot beverage.
- ✧ If you warm formula or baby food in the microwave, it can heat unevenly, causing hot spots. Be sure to shake the bottle or stir the food well before serving.
- ✧ Don't hang anything on stroller handles, such as a purse or bag. The extra weight could cause the stroller to tip over.
- ✧ Always put your baby in a car seat, even for a 2-block ride. Be sure the car seat is safety approved and installed correctly.

◈ 19 ◈

Your
New Baby

**I've heard that my baby will have to have a lot of tests after
it's born. What are they?**

After delivery, the hospital staff conducts a variety of tests to
evaluate your baby. The tests that are performed depend on
your medical history, findings obtained during examination of
the newborn and other factors. Tests performed on the baby
include:

- ◈ Apgar test
- ◈ screening for hyperphenylketonuria, anemia and hypothyroidism
- ◈ Coombs test
- ◈ reflex assessment
- ◈ assessment of neonatal maturity
- ◈ Brazelton neonatal behavioral assessment scale
- ◈ additional blood tests

See the following chart for an explanation of these tests.

Tests on the Newborn

Test	How Test Is Performed	What Test Indicates
Apgar test	At 1 and 5 minutes after birth, baby is assessed for color, heart rate, muscle tone, reflex response, breathing. Each category receives a score from 0 to 2 points, for a maximum of 10 points.	Gives an indication of baby's general condition at birth. Helps hospital staff decide if newborn needs extra care. Does not indicate what future may hold.
Blood screen	Blood is taken from baby's heel.	Detects phenylketonuria, anemia and hypothyroidism.
Coombs test	Blood is taken from umbilical cord if mother's blood is Rh-negative, type O or has not been tested for antibodies.	Detects whether Rh-antibodies have been formed.
Reflex assessment	Tests several specific reflexes, including the rooting and grasp reflexes.	If a particular reflex is not present, further evaluation is necessary.
Assessment of neonatal maturity	Many characteristics of baby are assessed to evaluate neuromuscular and physical maturity.	Each characteristic is assigned a score; sum indicates infant's maturity.
Brazelton neonatal behavioral assessment scale	Tests broad range of behaviors in babies where a problem is suspected. Some hospitals test all babies.	Provides information to doctors and parents about how a newborn responds to the environment.
Other blood tests	Blood is taken from heel to test for sickle-cell anemia, blood-glucose levels or other problems.	Results indicate whether baby needs further evaluation.

Someone said there are differences in the birth weight of babies. Can you tell me more about it?

Yes, we've found three distinct differences in the birth weight of babies. However, these are general statements and do not apply in all cases.

- ❖ Boys weigh more than girls.
- ❖ Birth weight of an infant increases with the increasing number of pregnancies or babies you deliver.
- ❖ White babies at term weigh more than black babies at term.

Your Newborn's Appearance

What does the baby look like at birth?

The baby is wet and usually has some blood on it. *Vernix,* a white or yellow waxy substance, may cover part or much of its body.

I always thought all newborns were beautiful, but my new baby isn't very pretty. Her head looks too big. What's wrong with her?

A baby's head is large in proportion to the rest of her body. At birth, it measures one-quarter of her entire length. As she grows, this will change until her head is one-eight of her adult height.

My little girl looks like she's been in a fight—her nose is flat and lumpy. Will she need plastic surgery?

The shape of your little girl's nose at birth has little to do with what it will look like when she's an adult. A newborn's nose may look too flat to breathe through, but babies manage to breathe through them.

My little boy's head is misshapen. Will it always be like this?

If your baby made his appearance into this world through the birth canal, he may have an elongated head. The shape is only temporary and will become more "normal" in the next few days.

My husband and I each have lots of hair, but our son is completely bald. Our daughter had lots of hair when she was born. Why the difference?

Your baby may be born with lots of hair or none at all. Don't worry about it. If he has lots of hair, this first hair will fall out during the first 6 months and will be replaced by hair that may be entirely different in color and texture. If he doesn't have any hair, it's not a permanent condition either. He will eventually grow hair.

Your newborn's head may appear misshapen, but it will become more "normal" looking as time passes.

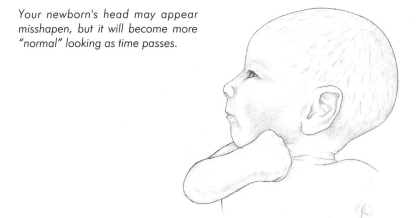

My baby's eyes seem to be swollen. What causes this?

A newborn's eyes are often swollen or puffy immediately after birth. This is caused by the pressure in the birth canal and subsides in a few days.

When they brought my baby to me in my room, his eyes looked greasy and were kind of red. What did they do to him?

Your baby's eyes were probably slightly irritated and reddened by the drops or ointment applied to his eyes shortly after birth. This is used to prevent eye infections. Redness usually disappears within 48 hours after birth.

My little girl has one eye that seems to wander when she looks at me. Is this an indication of some major problem?

One of your baby's eyes may wander when she looks at you, or she may look cross-eyed. Don't worry. Her eye muscles aren't strong enough yet to control her eye movements. A wandering eye usually corrects itself by the time the baby is 6 months old. If she still has a problem after that, discuss it with your health-care provider.

My little boy looks as if he's squinting at me. Are his eyes all right?

The skin folds at the inner corners of his eyes make it look as if he's squinting. As time passes, these folds become less prominent, and he won't look as if he's squinting any more.

My baby's skin seems dry and flaky. I always heard a baby's skin is soft and beautiful. Should I be concerned?

Within hours after birth, a baby's skin begins to dry out and may become flaky and scaly. This can last for a few weeks after birth. You really don't need to treat it, but you may want to rub a little lotion on your baby's delicate skin.

A friend told me my baby will probably get a lot of different rashes. Is this normal?

It is normal for babies to get various types of rashes in the first few months after birth. Don't be too alarmed about them. Contact your health-care provider if any rash lasts longer than a few days or if your baby seems to be extremely uncomfortable.

What kinds of rashes can I expect my baby to get?

  ❖ The most-common rash is *diaper rash*. Keep the area dry and clean, and apply a protective ointment that contains zinc oxide.
  ❖ A red, blistery rash may be *prickly heat*. Apply cornstarch to the affected area, and don't overdress the baby.
  ❖ Tiny yellow bumps on the face, called *milia*, affect about half of all newborns.
  ❖ Large yellow pimples on splotchy skin is called *newborn rash*. This affects about 70% of all newborns.
  ❖ Swollen pink pimples are called *newborn acne*.

Treatment for milia, newborn rash and newborn acne is time—you don't need to do anything. They will disappear on their own in a short time.

I know a baby's skin is sensitive. Is it OK to take my baby out in the sun?

It's best to avoid exposing your baby to sunlight. A newborn's skin has little or no ability to protect itself from damage by the sun. Sunscreens are not recommended for babies under 6 months, so keep your little one in the shade for the best protection. Put a hat and protective clothing on the baby for even a brief outing in the sun, especially in very hot, sunny areas like the Southwest.

Your Baby's Health

I've never had a baby before. I'm concerned that I won't know when he's ill or when I should call the doctor. Do you have any recommendations?

If your baby exhibits any of the following symptoms, call your health-care provider:

✧ fever higher than 101F (38.3C)

✧ inconsolable crying for long periods of time

✧ problems with urination

✧ projectile vomiting, in which stomach contents come out with great force

✧ baby appears lethargic or floppy when held

✧ severe diarrhea

✧ unusual behavior

✧ poor appetite

Any of these could be an indication your baby is ill.

My brother's baby suffers from ear infections. I'm uncertain I'll be able to tell if my baby has an ear infection. What should I look for?

It may be difficult for you to determine that your baby has an ear infection. Symptoms that may indicate an ear infection in babies under 6 months of age include:

✧ irritability that lasts all day

✧ sleeplessness

✧ lethargy

✧ feeding difficulties

These symptoms may be hard to discern and may not be accompanied by fever. For babies between 6 and 12 months of age, symptoms are similar, except that fever is more common. The onset of ear pain may be sudden, acute and more noticeable.

I understand that dehydration is extremely dangerous in a baby. How will I know if my baby is dehydrated?

Dehydration in an infant can be *very* serious. If it occurs, call your health-care provider immediately. There are some warning signs to watch for.

- ✧ Baby wets fewer than six cloth or five disposable diapers a day.
- ✧ Baby's urine is dark yellow or orange. It should be pale yellow.
- ✧ Baby has fewer than two loose stools a day.
- ✧ Baby seems to be having trouble sucking.
- ✧ The soft spot on baby's head is sunken in.
- ✧ Baby is listless or otherwise unhealthy.

I've heard it's dangerous for a baby to have diarrhea. How will I know if my baby has diarrhea?

If you are concerned, call your health-care provider. A change in the number of diapers used or the consistency of the bowel movement is the first clue.

What should I do if my baby has diarrhea?

The first thing to do is call your health-care provider. If your baby has diarrhea, he or she will need extra water and minerals to prevent dehydration. Your health-care provider may recommend an oral electrolyte solution to help replenish your baby's lost fluids and minerals.

Jaundice

I've heard about newborns with jaundice. What is jaundice?

Jaundice is the yellow staining of the skin, sclera (eyes) and deeper tissues of the body. It is caused by the newborn's inability to handle *bilirubin,* a chemical produced in the liver.

Is jaundice dangerous for a newborn?

Yes. Jaundice is caused by too much bilirubin in the baby's blood, a condition called *hyperbilirubinemia.* It can be dangerous for the baby if it is left untreated. Problems for the baby may include central-nervous-system damage (brain damage) or kernicterus (very high hyperbilirubinemia). Kernicterus can result in spasticity, lack of coordination in muscles, mental retardation and even death.

How is jaundice diagnosed?

The baby's color is observed by the pediatrician and the nurses in the baby nursery. The baby looks yellow because of the excess amounts of bilirubin in the blood.

How is it treated?

Phototherapy is the treatment of choice for jaundice. The baby is placed under special lights; the light penetrates the baby's skin and destroys the bilirubin. In some parts of the country, such as the Southwest, special lights may not be necessary. The baby is merely placed in the sunshine for short periods of time, and the sunlight destroys the excess bilirubin. In more severe cases, blood-exchange transfusions may be necessary.

Colic

Both of my sister's babies had colic. What is it exactly?

Colic is a condition marked by episodes of loud, sudden crying and fussiness, which can often last for hours, in a baby that is otherwise healthy. About 20% of all babies experience the pain and crying caused by colic. In full-blown colic, the abdomen becomes distended and the infant passes gas often.

What should I do if I think my baby may have colic?

The only way to know if your baby has colic is to see your pediatrician or family physician. He or she can determine if it is colic or if your baby is having some other problem.

When does colic appear?

It usually appears gradually in the infant about 2 weeks after birth. As days pass, the condition worsens, then often disappears around the age of 3 months but occasionally lasts until 4 months. Colic attacks usually occur at night beginning in the late afternoon and early evening and last 3 to 4 hours. The attacks cease as quickly as they begin.

What causes colic?

Researchers have been studying colic and its causes for a long time, but we still have little proof why it occurs. Theories about its causes include:

- ❖ immaturity of the digestive system
- ❖ intolerance to cow's-milk protein in formula or breast milk
- ❖ fatigue in the infant

If our baby suffers from colic, what can we do?

At this time, we cannot offer a definitive answer on ways to stop the colic. Most doctors recommend using a variety of methods to try to ease the baby's discomfort.

- ✧ Offer the baby the breast or a bottle of formula.
- ✧ Try non-cow's milk formula, if you bottlefeed.
- ✧ Carry your baby in a sling during an attack. Motion and closeness often help somewhat.
- ✧ Try a pacifier to soothe the baby.
- ✧ Put the baby on its stomach across your knees and rub its back.
- ✧ Wrap the baby snugly in a blanket.
- ✧ Massage or stroke the baby's tummy.

Your Baby's Sleeping Habits

I've heard stories about how difficult it is to get a baby to go to sleep at night. What can I do about this?

The wisest thing is to establish a routine to help your baby develop healthy sleeping habits.

- ✧ Wait until your baby is tired to put him to bed.
- ✧ Develop a regular, predictable routine for bed.
- ✧ Develop good sleep associations, such as a favorite blanket or toy, or a pacifier. Don't put your baby to bed with a bottle!
- ✧ Never leave your baby alone on a water bed.

My brother's new baby wants to sleep all day and stay up all night. Is there any way to get a baby to sleep at night and be up during the day?

There are some things a parent can do to try to change the day/night situation with the baby.

- ✧ Limit daytime naps to a few hours each.

♦ Don't overstimulate the baby when you get up for nighttime feedings.

♦ By day, let baby nap in a light area, with some noise. At night, put baby in a very quiet, dark room to sleep.

♦ Keep baby up during the day by talking and singing or providing other stimulation.

I heard that it's better to put a baby down to sleep on its side or back, rather than on its stomach. Is this true?

Research has proved that it *is* better to place a baby on its side or back when putting it down to sleep. We have discovered this position greatly reduces the incidence of SIDS (sudden infant death syndrome).

Someone told me that there's a difference in the sleep habits between bottlefed and breastfed babies. Is this true?

Yes, it is. Sleep patterns develop differently for bottlefed and breastfed babies. Bottlefed babies sleep longer at night as they mature. Breastfed infants don't shift to longer sleep patterns until around the time they are weaned. See the chart below for a comparison of bottlefed and breastfed babies' sleep patterns.

Taking Care of Baby

I'm nervous about dealing with the baby's umbilical cord. What should I do?

It isn't that difficult to deal with the stump of the umbilical cord. It will fall off 7 to 10 days after birth. Until it does, clean your baby with sponge baths instead of tub baths.

My baby's eyes are all gooey. How can I safely clean them?

To remove sleepers from your baby's eyes, use a moistened cotton ball. Place the cotton ball at the inner corner of the eye, and wipe vertically down the nose.

Length of Nighttime Sleep Patterns

	Bottlefed Babies	*Breastfed Babies*
Newborn	5 hours	4 to 7 hours
4 months	8 to 10 hours	4 to 7 hours
6 months	9 to 10 hours	4 to 7 hours
Total Sleep in 24 hours	13 to 15 hours	11 to 14 hours

How can I clean my baby's nose?

Never put anything inside your baby's nose. If you need to remove dried nasal secretions, gently wipe around the nose. Dried nasal secretions are usually sneezed out.

Is there an easy way to clean my baby's ears?

Never probe in your baby's ears with any object! Ear wax is there for a purpose. It's OK to clean around the outside of the ears with a soft washcloth, but don't put anything inside your baby's ears.

I've been trying to decide between cloth and paper diapers for my new baby. Is one better than the other?

This is a tough question to answer because you must take into consideration your lifestyle, budget and baby. *Disposable diapers* are very convenient. You don't need pins or plastic pants, and you never have to wash them. *Cloth diapers* can be used many times. Some styles don't need pins or plastic pants. You will need adequate washing and drying facilities, or you may choose a diaper service. Many of my patients use a combination of disposable and cloth diapers.

My little girl was pretty big when she was born, and I don't want her to be fat. Should I be concerned about how fat she is now?

No, that's not really a concern at this early age. You should focus on whether your baby is growing and developing appropriately, not how fat she is. Do *not* put your baby on a diet to keep her slim!

Will my doctor tell me if my baby is too fat?

Your doctor will be more concerned about where your child fits on the growth charts in relation to other children. Usually a child's weight (and height) are given using a percentile. For example, if you are told your daughter is in the 80th percentile, it means 80 out of 100 children weigh less than she does and 20 children weigh more.

Is there any way I can keep my baby from being obese?

There are some tips to help you give your baby the best nutritional start possible.

- ✧ Breastfeed your baby.
- ✧ Do not introduce solid foods until the age of 4 to 6 months.
- ✧ Feed your baby in response to hunger, not to meet other needs or just because it's "time to eat."
- ✧ Encourage physical activity and sound eating habits for everyone in your family.

Car Restraints—For the Safety of Your Baby

Does my baby need to ride in a car safety-restraint seat all the time?

Every time your baby rides in the car, he or she should be in an approved safety-restraint seat. In an accident, an unrestrained child becomes a missilelike object in a car. The force of a crash can literally pull a child out of an adult's arms!

What about short trips, like going home from the hospital— what can happen to my baby?

It's incredible, but one study showed more than 30 deaths a year occur to unrestrained infants *going home from the hospital after birth!* In nearly all these cases, if the baby had been in an approved infant-restraint system, he or she would have survived the accident. Don't take chances—keep your baby safely restrained.

*Buckling up your baby in an approved
car safety-restraint system is essential for
every trip you make!*

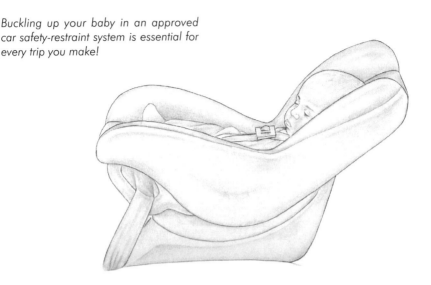

**My mother said that it's against the law to let babies ride in
a car without a safety-restraint system. Is this true?**

Many states now have laws that govern safety-restraint systems. Call your local hospital or police department, and ask
for information. Some hospitals won't let you take the baby
home if he or she is *not* going to ride in an approved safety-restraint seat. Many hospitals have loaners you can borrow
until you get your own.

Where is the safest spot in the car to put the baby's car seat?

The safest spot is in the middle of the back seat. In this
position, it is more protected in the event of a side collision.
Manufacturers recommend *not* putting the car seat in the
front seat if you have a passenger-side air bag. If the bag
inflates, it can knock the car seat around or even injure the
baby.

✧ 20 ✧

Feeding Your Baby

How will I know when my baby is hungry?

A baby exhibits definite signs of hunger, including:

- ✧ fussing
- ✧ putting his hands in his mouth
- ✧ turning his head and opening his mouth when his cheek is touched

How often does a baby need to feed?

Early in life, most babies eat every 3 to 4 hours, although some babies feed as often as every 2 hours. It may help your baby get on a schedule if you feed at regular intervals. Or you can let your baby set your schedule—some babies need to nurse more often than others. Sometimes your baby will need to feed more often than she usually does. See how often your baby wants to feed and whether she is growing properly. These are the best guides to feeding your baby. Usually as the baby grows older, she waits longer between feedings and feeds longer at each feeding.

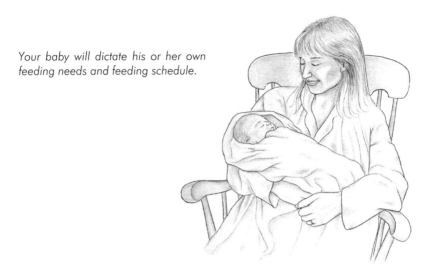

Your baby will dictate his or her own feeding needs and feeding schedule.

How much should I feed my baby at each feeding?

A baby is usually the best judge of how much he or she should take at each feeding. Usually a baby will turn away from the nipple (mother or bottle) when it is full.

I've heard that babies don't need to be fed breast milk or formula every time they're thirsty, that water is OK sometimes. How do I know when I should give water?

Discuss this with your health-care provider. Much depends on your baby's weight, how well he is doing and whether he is hungry or thirsty. Your health-care provider will give you answers.

Do all babies need to be burped?

It's a good idea to burp your baby after each feeding. Some babies need to be burped during a feeding as well. Hold your baby over your shoulder or sit your baby in your lap, and gently rub or pat the back. You will probably want to place a towel over your shoulder or at least have one handy in case he or she spits up. If your baby doesn't burp, don't force it.

Is spitting up common in babies?

It is common during the early months of life because the muscle at the top of the stomach is not yet fully developed. When a baby spits up enough to propel the stomach contents several inches, it is called *vomiting*. If your baby vomits after a feeding, do not feed him or her again immediately—the stomach may be upset. It may be wise to wait until the next feeding.

Is it true breastfeeding is the best choice for my baby?

If you can breastfeed, we have found it is best for the baby. Breast milk contains all the nutrients a baby needs, and it's easy to digest. Breastfed babies have lower rates of infections because of the immunological content of breast milk. And breastfeeding provides the baby a sense of security and the mother a sense of self-esteem. However, if there are reasons you cannot or choose not to breastfeed, be assured that your baby will do well on formula.

My sister had problems and couldn't breastfeed. What if something like that happens to me and I can't breastfeed—will it harm my baby?

No, it will not harm your baby if you cannot or choose not to breastfeed. I don't want any mother to feel guilty because she doesn't breastfeed her baby. Sometimes you cannot breastfeed because of some physical condition or other problem. Sometimes you choose not to breastfeed because of other demands on your time, such as a job or other children to care for. Your baby can still get all the love and attention *and* nutrition it needs if breastfeeding is not possible for you.

Bottlefeeding as One Option

I may be in the minority, but I want to bottlefeed, not breast-feed. Will I be a terrible mother because I feel this way?

No, you will not be a terrible mother because you choose not to breastfeed. In fact, statistics show that more women choose to bottlefeed than breastfeed their babies. We know that through the use of iron-fortified formula, your baby can receive good nutrition if you bottlefeed. So don't berate your-self or feel guilty if you bottlefeed—it's a personal decision that *you* must make.

I've heard all the great things about breastfeeding. Aren't there any good things to be said about bottlefeeding?

There *are* advantages to bottlefeeding that are often over-looked. Some women enjoy the freedom bottlefeeding pro-vides. Someone else can help care for the baby. Fathers can be more involved in the care of the baby. Bottlefed babies are often able to last longer between feedings because formula is usually digested more slowly than breast milk. And you can determine exactly how much formula your baby is taking in at each feeding.

I've definitely decided I want to bottlefeed. Is there any special way to bottlefeed a baby?
  - ✧ Snuggle your baby close to you during feeding.
  - ✧ Heat the formula to body temperature by running under warm water.
  - ✧ Place the bottle's nipple right side up, ready to feed.
  - ✧ Don't touch the tip of the nipple.
  - ✧ Brush the nipple lightly over the baby's lips, and guide it into the baby's mouth. Don't force it.
  - ✧ Tilt the bottle so the neck is always filled, keeping the baby from sucking in too much air.

Bottlefeeding is a choice for many women. It allows them more freedom and the opportunity for other members of the family to participate in feeding the baby.

♦ Remove the bottle during feeding to let the baby rest. It usually takes 10 to 15 minutes to finish feeding.

♦ Don't leave the baby alone with the bottle. *Never* prop up a bottle and leave the baby alone to suck on it.

♦ *Never* put a baby down to bed with a bottle.

Do I have to warm up the formula before I feed it to my baby?

There's no evidence that feeding refrigerated formula without warming it will harm your baby. If you usually warm it, your baby will probably prefer it that way. If your baby is usually breastfed, he or she will probably prefer a warmed bottle. Be careful formula is not *too hot*.

I'm concerned about the formula to use. Are there different types?

Yes, there are. Most babies do very well on milk-based formula, but some babies need specialized formulas.

What types of formulas are there besides regular milk-based formula?

Several types are available on the market today, including:

   ❖ *milk-based, lactose-free formula*—fed to babies with feeding problems caused by lactose intolerance, such as fussiness, gas and diarrhea

   ❖ *soy-based formula*—milk-free and lactose-free for babies with milk allergies or sensitivity

   ❖ *hypoallergenic protein formula*—easier to digest and lactose-free for babies with colic or other symptoms of milk-protein allergy

I recently read that bottlefeeding with a bottle that is slanted is better for the baby. Why?

Research has shown that feeding a baby with a bottle that is slanted is better. This design keeps the nipple full of milk, which means baby takes in less air. A slanted bottle also helps ensure baby is sitting up to drink. When a baby drinks lying down, milk can pool in the eustachian tube, where it can cause ear infections.

How long should a baby receive formula?

The American Academy of Pediatrics recommends that a baby be fed iron-fortified formula for the first year of life. Feeding for this length of time helps maintain adequate iron intake.

Breastfeeding as Your Other Option

When can I begin breastfeeding?

You can usually begin breastfeeding your baby within an hour after birth. This provides your baby with *colostrum*, the first milk your breasts produce. Colostrum contains important factors that help boost the baby's immune system. Breastfeeding also causes your pituitary gland to release oxytocin, a hormone that causes the uterus to begin contracting and to stop bleeding.

I'm nervous about breastfeeding. How do I start?

Don't be discouraged if you don't feel natural at first. It takes some time to find out what will work best for you and your baby. Hold your baby so she can reach the breast easily while nursing. Hold the baby across your chest, or lie in bed. Your baby should take your nipple into her mouth fully, so her gums cover the areola. She can't suck effectively if your nipple is only slightly drawn into her mouth.

Breastfeeding is best for baby and provides him or her the best start in life.

I've heard that breastfeeding is the best way to bond with my baby. Is this true?

Breastfeeding is an excellent way to bond with your baby because of the closeness between mother and child established during the feeding process. However, there are also other ways you can bond with your baby. Studies have shown that carrying your baby close to your body in a slinglike carrier helps the bonding process. It's great because dads can bond this way with baby, too.

I read that breastfeeding can prevent milk allergies. How?

It's nearly impossible for a baby to become allergic to its mother's breast milk. This is important if there is a history of allergies in your family or your partner's family. The longer a baby breastfeeds, the less likely he or she is to be exposed to substances that could cause allergic problems.

Everyone always mentions the good things about breastfeeding. What are some of the disadvantages?

The greatest disadvantage for many mothers is the fact they are tied down to the baby so completely. They must be available when their baby is hungry. Breastfeeding can also make other family members feel left out. Mothers who breastfeed must pay careful attention to their diet, both for the nourishment they take in and the avoidance of foods that pass into their breast milk and cause problems for the baby. Also, caffeine, alcohol and some medications can pass into breast milk.

I've heard stories about friends having to be up half the night to breastfeed. How long does it usually take for a baby to nurse?

Usually most babies will breastfeed every 2 to 3 hours for 5 to 15 minutes per breast.

How Breastfeeding Affects You

Someone told me I had to drink lots of fluids (water mostly) while I'm breastfeeding. Is this true?

It's a good idea to keep your fluid intake up if you breast-feed.

Can I diet if I'm breastfeeding?

No, it's best not to diet while breastfeeding. All the nutrients your baby receives from breastfeeding depend on the quality of the food *you* eat. Breastfeeding places more demands on your body than pregnancy. Your body burns up to 1,000 calories a day just to produce milk. When breastfeeding, you need to eat an extra 500 calories a day, and be sure to keep fluid levels up.

I've heard that breastfeeding is a good way to keep from getting pregnant. Is this true?

No. Do *not* rely on breastfeeding to protect you against getting pregnant again. You need to use some type of protection when you resume intercourse.

My doctor said I shouldn't use birth-control pills while I'm breastfeeding. Why?

Do not use oral contraceptives if you are breastfeeding. The hormones in oral contraceptives can get into your milk and be passed along to your baby, possibly causing problems with the baby's development. Choose some other form of birth control until you are finished breastfeeding.

My sister told me not to eat spicy food while I'm breastfeeding. Does this cause some problem?

Most substances you eat or drink (or take orally, as medication) can pass to your baby in your breast milk. Spicy foods, chocolate and caffeine are just a few things your baby can react to when you ingest them. Be careful about what you eat and drink during breastfeeding.

How is caffeine a problem during breastfeeding?

Caffeine in breast milk can cause irritability and sleeplessness in a breastfed baby.

I read an article the other day about a condition called "insufficient milk syndrome." What is it?

Insufficient milk syndrome is rare, but it does occur. The baby becomes dehydrated because of breastfeeding problems, such as the mother's low milk supply or the baby's failure to drink enough milk.

What kind of problems can insufficient milk syndrome cause?

If it is not detected in the baby and treated, it can cause stroke, blood clot, brain damage and even death of the infant.

How does this syndrome occur?

It can happen when a mother has the idea that breastfeeding is the only "right" method of feeding and takes it to extremes. This woman views using a bottle, even when breastfeeding complications occur, as personal failure. It can also happen when a mother is unable to produce enough breast milk, due to genetic defect, injury or breast surgery. However, this problem is very rare.

Your Milk Production

My mother said she couldn't nurse me because she didn't have enough milk. Is this a common problem?

This is *not* a common problem. With some practice and lots of patience, nearly all women can breastfeed their babies.

I have a cousin whose breast milk never came in after her triplets were born. Is this common with multiple births?

No, it isn't.

I recently read that I can express my breast milk so my baby can drink it when I'm away from home. How do I do that?

By using a breast pump that is hand, battery or electrically operated. Expressed milk can be frozen and saved.

How long does it take to express my breast milk?

You'll need 10 to 30 minutes to do this, depending on the type of pump you have, and you'll need to do it one to four times a day (around the time you would normally nurse). You also need a refrigerated place to store the milk and a comfortable, private place where you can relax enough for milk letdown to occur.

How can I store breast milk after it is pumped?

There are several steps you must take to store breast milk safely.

- ✧ Pump or express milk into a clean container.
- ✧ Label the container with the date and amount of milk collected.
- ✧ Freshly pumped breast milk can be kept at room temperature for up to 2 hours, but it's best to refrigerate milk as soon as possible.
- ✧ You may store breast milk safely in the refrigerator for up to 72 hours.

I've heard I can freeze breast milk. How do I do that?

For longer storage, you can freeze your breast milk. You can keep it in a refrigerator freezer for 6 months or in a deep freezer (-20F; -29C) for up to 12 months. Fill container only

3/4 full to allow for expansion during freezing. Freeze milk in small portions, such as 2 to 4 ounces (56 to 112g), because these amounts thaw more quickly.

Is it possible to combine fresh breast milk with frozen breast milk?

Yes, this is possible. First, cool breast milk before combining it with previously frozen milk. The amount of thawed breast milk must be more than the amount of fresh breast milk. Never refreeze breast milk!

What's the best way to thaw frozen breast milk?

- ✧ Put the container of frozen milk in a bowl of warm water for 30 minutes, or hold container under warm running water.
- ✧ *Never* microwave breast milk; it can alter the composition of the milk.
- ✧ Swirl the container to blend any fat that might have separated during thawing.
- ✧ Feed thawed milk immediately, or store in the refrigerator for up to 24 hours.

The lady at La Leche League told me that if I bottlefeed part of the time, my milk supply will be reduced. Is this true?

Yes, it is. Your milk supply is driven by the baby's demand. If you bottlefeed part of the time, your baby will not be demanding the breast milk from you, and your body will slow down its production.

Some Common Problems During Breastfeeding

Will it be painful when my milk comes in?

Breast milk becomes more plentiful between 2 and 6 days after birth, when it changes from colostrum to more-nourishing mature milk. Your breasts may become engorged and cause you some pain for 24 to 36 hours. Continue breastfeeding during this time. Wear a supportive bra, and apply cold compresses to your breasts for short periods. Take acetaminophen (Tylenol) if pain is severe, but don't take anything stronger.

My friend says she feels a tingling in her breasts when her baby nurses. What causes this?

Soon after a baby begins to nurse, the mother experiences tingling or cramping in her breasts called *milk letdown*, which means milk is flowing into the breast ducts. It occurs several times during feeding. Occasionally a baby will choke a bit when the rush of milk comes too quickly.

I've read that many new mothers have problems with sore nipples. Why?

If your baby doesn't take your nipple into his or her mouth fully during breastfeeding, the jaws can compress the nipple and make it sore. But take heart—sore nipples rarely last longer than a couple of days. Continue breastfeeding while your breasts are sore.

Is there any other way to prevent sore nipples?

Nipple shields, worn inside your bra between the nipple and fabric, provide some relief. (It keeps tender skin from rubbing on the bra fabric.) A mild cream can also be applied to sore nipples to provide some soothing relief. Ask your pharmacist or health-care provider for the names of some products that are OK to use during nursing.

My best friend had a very bad breast infection with her last baby. How will I know if I have one?

Large red streaks that extend up the breast toward the armpit usually indicate a breast infection. If you experience this, call your health-care provider immediately. An infection can cause a fever to develop within 4 to 8 hours after the appearance of the red streaks. Antibiotic treatment needs to be started immediately because antibiotics work well only in the first 12 to 16 hours of infection. Treatment can clear up the infection within 24 hours.

How is a breast infection treated?

If you have a plugged duct, apply a warm compress to the affected area or soak the breast in warm water. Then express milk or breastfeed while massaging the tender area. If you develop flulike symptoms with a sore breast, call your health-care provider immediately. Antibiotic treatment will be started. You'll also need to rest in bed, and empty the infected breast by pumping or breastfeeding every hour or two.

What happens if a breast infection isn't treated?

It can turn into an abscess. This is very painful and may need to be opened and drained.

Is there any way to prevent breast infections?

Yes, there are several things you can do to help prevent an infection.

> ✧ Eat right, and get enough rest. Doing these two things helps reduce stress and keeps your immune system in top fighting form.

✦ Don't wear tight-fitting bras—especially underwire-bras—because they block milk flow. This can cause an infection.

✦ Be sure you empty your breasts on a regular schedule. This avoids engorgement.

✦ After each feeding or pumping, let nipples air-dry for a few minutes.

Should I stop nursing if I get a breast infection?

No, don't stop nursing. It's important to continue breast-feeding. If you stop, the infection may get worse.

I recently read that ducts in the breast can get plugged up. What does this mean?

A plugged milk duct in the breast prevents milk from flow-ing freely. It results in tender or firm areas of the breast that become more painful after breastfeeding. A plugged duct is not red, and you will not have a fever.

How is a plugged duct treated?

It usually takes care of itself if you continue to nurse fre-quently. Apply warm compresses to the sore area to help with the pain and to open the duct. Acetaminophen may also be taken.

If I'm sick, can I still breastfeed?

If you have a cold or other virus, it is all right to breastfeed. It's OK to breastfeed if you're taking an antibiotic, as long as you know the drug is not incompatible with nursing. Ask your health-care provider or pharmacist if any medication prescribed for you should not be taken while breastfeeding. Be sure to ask *before* you begin taking it.

You Should Also Know

My breasts are very small. How do I know I'll have enough breast milk?

The size of your breasts doesn't influence the amount of milk you have, so this usually isn't a problem.

I'm embarrassed when I think about breastfeeding my baby in public. Is it really acceptable?

In many countries, breastfeeding is a natural part of life. In North America, people are more accepting of breastfeeding than in the past. My best advice is to gauge each situation separately. If you are comfortable nursing at a friend's house, go ahead. If you feel uncomfortable nursing in a public place, go into the ladies' room or a lounge, and feed there. Look at each instance by itself—you'll soon learn how comfortable you feel feeding your baby away from home.

My sister-in-law said she didn't keep breastfeeding her son because he wouldn't settle into a pattern. Is this common?

You may be unprepared for how often your baby will want (and need) to nurse in the first week after birth. You may wonder if it's worth it to continue. Relax and be patient. It will take time for your baby to establish his or her nursing pattern. By the end of the second week, a pattern will probably be established, and your baby will sleep longer between feedings.

Is it OK to substitute bottles for some breastfeeding sessions?

It's best to avoid bottles, if possible, for the first month of breastfeeding. This is for two reasons—your baby may come to prefer feeding from a bottle (it's not as hard to suck) and your breasts will not produce enough milk.

I don't know how long I'll be able to breastfeed my baby because I have to go back to work. Is there a time that is the most important for me to nurse my baby?

Nursing the first 4 weeks of your baby's life provides the most protection for your baby and the most beneficial hormone release for you to help you recover after the birth. Nursing for the first 6 months is very beneficial for your baby—it provides excellent nutrition and protection for illness. After 6 months, the nutrition and protection aspects are not as critical for your baby. So if you can nurse only a short period of time, try to stick with it for the first 6 months or at least for the first 4 weeks.

I want to continue breastfeeding my baby after I go back to work. Is this possible?

It is possible to continue breastfeeding your baby after you return to work. If you breastfeed exclusively, you will have to pump your breasts or arrange to see your baby during the day. Or you can nurse your baby at home and provide formula for when you're away.

A friend told me that support at work for her breastfeeding seemed to disappear after 4 or 5 months. What can I do about this?

You may have to talk to your employer and co-workers about the situation and attempt to work out a solution that is equitable for everyone.

If I have to be out of town on business for a few days, will my breast milk dry up?

You probably will need to pump your breast milk while you are gone. You may be very uncomfortable if you don't because your milk will continue to come in. Take a breast pump with you and discard the breast milk after it is pumped.

I've heard there are special bras to wear while breastfeeding. What are they?

Nursing bras are worn for breastfeeding. They have cups that open so you can breastfeed without having to get undressed.

How soon can I buy a nursing bra?

Wait until at least the 36th week of your pregnancy. If you buy it sooner, it will be very difficult to buy one that fits.

How can I be sure a nursing bra will fit correctly?

Your breasts will become larger when your milk comes in, so buy a bra with at least a finger's width of space between any part of the cup and your breast. Be sure to make allowances for the room taken up by the nursing pads. When trying on the bra, fasten the hooks at their loosest setting. That will make it possible for you to tighten it as your ribcage shrinks after your baby is born.

Are there any other special clothes I should consider for breastfeeding?

Yes. Nighties, shift dresses and full-cut blouses have been designed with discreet breast openings so you don't have to get undressed to breastfeed. You can reach up inside your outer clothing, unhook your nursing bra and place your baby at your breast without anyone noticing. Draping a light towel or blanket over your shoulder, over the baby's head, adds further coverage.

A few years ago, I had my very small breasts enlarged. Can I breastfeed my baby after it is born?

Yes. Many women who have had breast-enlargement surgery are able to breastfeed successfully.

Because of back problems caused by extremely large breasts, I had the size of my breasts reduced. Will this affect my ability to breastfeed?

You should still be able to breastfeed. The surgery may result in a decreased production of milk, but usually there is enough.

Someone told me that if I breastfeed, my nipples will drip milk when my baby cries. This isn't true, is it?

It is true. This will occur when your baby, or any other baby you are around, cries. This reflex is called the *milk letdown response* and is normal. To protect your clothing, be sure you wear breast shields.

I'm sure my partner will feel left out if he can't feed the baby. Is there any way he can participate in feeding?

Your partner can help out by getting up at night and bringing the baby to you or by changing the baby. Your partner can also feed your baby expressed breast milk or water.

I know my stepdaughter will want to help me feed the baby, but I'll be nursing. How can I include her?

You can include your stepdaughter by letting her hold or burp the baby after it is fed. If you express your milk, she could feed the baby a bottle of it at some feeding.

Should I switch breasts during breastfeeding?

Yes, but wait until your baby finishes with one breast before switching to the other one. The consistency of breast milk changes from thinner to richer as the baby nurses. At the next feeding, start your baby on the breast you nursed last. This will help you keep both breasts stimulated. If your baby only wants to nurse from one breast each feeding, simply switch to the other breast the next feeding.

If I have any problems breastfeeding, what can I do?

Many hospitals have breastfeeding specialists you can call for help. Try the office of your health-care provider—they may be able to refer you to someone knowledgeable. You can also look in the telephone book for the *La Leche League*, which is an organization that promotes breastfeeding. Someone from the local group can give you advice and encouragement.

How do I discontinue nursing when my baby is old enough to stop?

You can either taper off gradually or stop cold turkey. Each way has its advantages. If you want to taper off gradually, start offering a bottle every other feeding or offer bottles during the day and nurse at night. If you stop "cold turkey," you may have some sleepless nights with a screaming baby, and you may be quite uncomfortable physically with engorged breasts. However, this method takes less time.

At what age (of the baby) do most women stop breastfeeding?

That varies from woman to woman. Some women like to nurse until they return to work. Others nurse through the first year. It depends on your situation and your desire.

Glossary

A

Abortion—Termination of pregnancy before 20 weeks of gestation.

Abruptio placenta—See *Placental abruption.*

Acquired-Immune-Deficiency Syndrome (AIDS)—Debilitating, usually fatal, illness that affects the body's ability to respond to infection. Caused by the human immune deficiency virus (HIV).

Aerobic exercise—Exercise that increases your heart rate and causes you to consume oxygen.

Afterbirth—See *Placenta.*

Albuminuria—See *Proteinuria.*

Alphafetoprotein (AFP)—Substance produced by the unborn baby as it grows inside the uterus. Large amounts of AFP are found in amniotic fluid. Larger-than-normal amounts are found in the maternal bloodstream if neural-tube defects are present in the fetus.

Alveoli—Ends of the ducts of the lung.

Amino acids—Substances that act as building blocks in the developing embryo and fetus.

Amniocentesis—Removal of amniotic fluid from the amniotic sac. Fluid is tested for some genetic defects.

Amnion—Membrane around the fetus. It surrounds the amniotic cavity.

Amniotic fluid—Liquid surrounding the baby inside the amniotic sac.

Amniotic sac—Sac that surrounds baby inside the uterus. It contains the baby, the placenta and the amniotic fluid.

Ampulla—Dilated opening of a tube or duct.

Anemia—Any condition in which the number of red blood cells is less than normal. Term usually applies to the concentration of the oxygen-transporting material in the blood, which are the red blood cells.

Anencephaly—Defective development of the brain combined with the absence of the bones normally surrounding the brain.

Angioma—Tumor, usually benign, or swelling composed of lymph and blood vessels.

Anti-inflammatory medications—Drugs to relieve pain and/or inflammation.

Apgar score—Measurement of a baby's response to birth and life on its own. Taken 1 minute and 5 minutes after birth.

Areola—Pigmented or colored ring surrounding the nipple of the breast.

Arrhythmia—Irregular or missed heartbeat.

Aspiration—Swallowing or sucking a foreign body or fluid, such as vomit, into an airway.

Asthma—Disease marked by recurrent attacks of shortness of breath and difficulty breathing. Often caused by an allergic reaction.

Atonic—Flaccid; relaxed; lacking tone. As in *atonic uterus*.

Autoantibodies—Antibodies that attack parts of your body or your own tissues.

B

Back labor—Pain of labor felt in lower back.

Beta-adrenergics—Substances that interfere with transmission of stimuli. They affect the autonomic nervous system. During pregnancy, they are used to stop labor.

Bilirubin—Breakdown product of pigment formed in the liver from hemoglobin during the destruction of red blood cells.

Biophysical profile—Method of evaluating a fetus before birth.

Biopsy—Removal of a small piece of tissue for microscopic study.

Birthing center—Facility in which a woman labors, delivers and recovers in the same room. It may be part of a hospital, or it may be a freestanding unit.

Bloody show—Small amount of vaginal bleeding late in pregnancy; often precedes labor.

Board certification—Doctor has had additional training and testing in a particular specialty. In the area of obstetrics, the American College of Obstetricians and Gynecologists offers this training. Certification requires expertise in care of a pregnant woman.

Braxton-Hicks contractions—Irregular, painless tightening of uterus during pregnancy.

Breech presentation—Abnormal position of the fetus. Buttocks or legs come into the birth canal ahead of the head.

C

Carcinogen—Any cancer-producing substance.

Cataract, congenital—Cloudiness of the eye lens present at birth.

Cesarean section (delivery)—Delivery of a baby through an abdominal incision rather than through the vagina.

Chadwick's sign—Dark-blue or purple discoloration of the mucosa of the vagina and cervix during pregnancy.

Chemotherapy—Treatment of disease by chemical substances or drugs.

Chlamydia—Sexually transmitted venereal infection.

Chloasma—Extensive brown patches of irregular shape and size on the face or other parts of the body.

Chorionic villus sampling (CVS)—Diagnostic test done early in pregnancy. A biopsy of tissue is taken from inside the uterus through the abdomen or the cervical opening to determine abnormalities of pregnancy.

Colostrum—Thin, yellow fluid that is the first milk to come from the breast. Most often seen toward the end of pregnancy. It is different in content from milk produced later during nursing.

Condyloma acuminatum—Skin tags or warts that are sexually transmitted. Also called *venereal warts*.

Congenital problem—Problem present at birth.

Conjoined twins—Twins connected at the body; they may share vital organs. Also called *Siamese twins*.

Constipation—Bowel movements are infrequent or incomplete.

Contraction stress test (CST)—Response of fetus to uterine contractions to evaluate fetal well-being.

Crown-to-rump length—Measurement from the top of the baby's head (crown) to the buttocks of the baby (rump).

Cystitis—Inflammation of the bladder.

Cytomegalovirus (CMV) infection—Infection caused by any of a group of viruses from the herpes virus family.

D

D&C (dilatation and curettage)—Surgical procedure in which the cervix is dilated and the lining of the uterus is scraped.

Developmental delay—Condition in which the development of the baby or child is slower than normal.

Diabetes, pregnancy-induced—See *Gestational diabetes*.

Diastasis recti—Separation of abdominal muscles.

Dilatation—Expansion of an organ or vessel.

Dizygotic twins—Twins derived from two different eggs. Often called *fraternal twins*.

Down's syndrome—Condition in which baby is born mentally retarded and with a generally dwarfed appearance, including a sloping forehead, short, broad hands, a flat nose and low-set ears.

Dysplasia—Abnormal, precancerous changes in the cells of the cervix.

Dysuria—Difficulty or pain urinating.

E

EDC (estimated date of confinement)—Anticipated due date for delivery of the baby. Calculated as 280 days after the first day of the last menstrual period.

Eclampsia—Convulsions and coma in a woman with *pre-eclampsia*. Not related to epilepsy.

Ectopic pregnancy—Pregnancy that occurs outside the uterine cavity.

Edema—Swelling of the feet or legs due to water retention.

Effacement—Thinning of cervix.

Electronic fetal monitoring—Use of electronic instruments to record the fetal heartbeat and the mother's contractions.

Embryo—Organism in the early stages of development.

Embryonic period—First 10 weeks of gestation (8 weeks of fetal development).

Endometrium—Mucous membrane that lines the inside of the uterine wall.

Enema—Fluid injected into the rectum for the purpose of clearing out the bowel.

Engorgement—Congested; filled with fluid.

Epidural block—Type of anesthesia. Medication is injected around the spinal cord during labor or some types of surgery.

Episiotomy—Surgical incision of the vulva (area behind the vagina, above the rectum). Used during delivery to avoid tearing or laceration of the vaginal opening and rectum.

Estimated date of confinement—See *EDC*.

External cephalic version (ECV)—Procedure done late in pregnancy in which doctor manually attempts to move a baby from the breech position into the normal head-down position.

F

Face presentation—Situation in which baby comes into the birth canal face-first.

Fallopian tube—Tube that leads from the cavity of the uterus to the area of the ovary. Also called *uterine tube*.

False labor—Tightening of uterus without dilatation or thinning of the cervix.

Fasting blood sugar—Blood test to evaluate the amount of sugar in the blood following a period of fasting.

Ferrous gluconate—Iron supplement.

Ferrous sulfate—Iron supplement.

Fertilization—Joining of the sperm and egg.

Fertilization age—Dating a pregnancy from the time of fertilization; 2 weeks earlier than the gestational age.

Fetal alcohol syndrome (FAS)—Birth defects in an infant born to mother whose alcoholic intake persisted during pregnancy. Infant will have physical abnormalities and/or mental deficiencies.

Fetal anomaly—Fetal malformation or abnormal development.

Fetal arrhythmia—See *Arrhythmia*.

Fetal distress—Problems with the baby that occur before birth and/or during labor. These endanger the baby and require immediate delivery.

Fetal monitor—Device used before or during labor to listen to and record the fetal heartbeat. Can be external monitoring (through maternal abdomen) or internal monitoring (through maternal vagina) of the baby inside the uterus.

Fetal period—Time period following the embryonic period (first 10 weeks of gestation) until birth.

Fetal-growth retardation—See *Intrauterine-growth retardation*.

Fetus—Refers to the unborn baby from 10 weeks of gestation until birth.

Forceps—Special instrument placed around the baby's head, inside the birth canal, to help guide the baby out of the birth canal during delivery.

Frank breech—Baby presenting buttocks first. Legs are flexed and knees extended.

Fraternal twins—See *Dizygotic twins*.

Full-term infant—Baby born between 38 and 42 weeks of pregnancy.

G

Genetic counseling—Consultation between a couple and a specialist about genetic defects and the possibility of presence or recurrence of genetic problems in a pregnancy.

Genital herpes simplex—Herpes simplex infection involving the genital area. It can be significant during pregnancy because of the danger to a newborn fetus infected with herpes simplex.

Gestational age—Dating a pregnancy from the first day of the last menstrual period; 2 weeks longer than fertilization age. See *Fertilization age*.

Gestational diabetes—Occurrence or worsening of diabetes during pregnancy.

Globulin—Family of proteins from plasma or serum of the blood.

Glucose-tolerance test—Blood test done to evaluate the body's response to sugar. Blood is drawn at intervals following ingestion of a sugary substance.

Glucosuria—Glucose in the urine.

Gonorrhea—Contagious venereal infection, transmitted primarily by intercourse. Caused by the bacteria *Neisseria gonorrhea*.

Group-B streptococcal infection (GBS)—Serious infection occurring in the mother's vagina and throat.

H

Habitual miscarriage—Occurrence of three or more spontaneous miscarriages.

Heartburn—Discomfort or pain that occurs in the chest. Often occurs after eating.

Hematocrit—Measurement of the proportion of blood cells to plasma. Important in diagnosing anemia.

Hemoglobin—Pigment in red blood cell that carries oxygen to body tissues.

Hemolytic disease—Destruction of red blood cells. See *Anemia*.

Hemorrhoids—Dilated blood vessels in the rectum or rectal canal.

Heparin—Medication used to thin the blood.

High-risk pregnancy—Pregnancy with complications that require special medical attention, often from a specialist. Also see *Perinatologist*.

Homans' sign—Pain caused by flexing the toes when a person has a blood clot in the lower leg.

Human chorionic gonadatropin (HCG)—Hormone produced in early pregnancy. Measured in a pregnancy test.

Hydramnios—Increased amniotic fluid.

Hydrocephalus—Excessive accumulation of fluid around the brain of the baby. Sometimes called *water on the brain*.

Hyperbilirubinemia—Extremely high level of bilirubin in the blood.

Hyperemesis gravidarum—Severe nausea, dehydration and vomiting during pregnancy. Occurs most frequently during the first trimester. May require brief hospitalization.

Hyperglycemia—Increased blood sugar.

Hypertension, pregnancy-induced—High blood pressure that occurs during pregnancy. Defined by an increase in the diastolic and/or systolic blood pressure.

Hyperthyroidism—Elevation of the thyroid hormone in the bloodstream.

Hypoplasia—Defective or incomplete development or formation of tissue.

Hypotension—Low blood pressure.

Hypothyroidism—Low or inadequate levels of thyroid hormone in the bloodstream.

I

Identical twins—See *Monozygotic twins*.

Immune globulin preparation—Substance used to protect against infection with certain diseases, such as hepatitis or measles.

Incompetent cervix—Cervix that dilates painlessly, without contractions.

Incomplete miscarriage—Miscarriage in which part, but not all, of the uterine contents are expelled.

Indigestion—Inability to digest food or difficulty digesting food.

Induced labor—Labor started, usually by oxytocin (Pitocin).

Inevitable miscarriage—Pregnancy complicated with bleeding and cramping. Results in miscarriage.

Insulin—Peptide hormone made by the pancreas. It promotes the use of glucose.

Intrauterine-growth retardation (IUGR)—Inadequate growth of the fetus during the last stages of pregnancy. Also called *Fetal-growth retardation*.

In utero—Within the uterus.

In vitro—Outside the body.

Iron-deficiency anemia—Anemia produced by lack of iron in the diet. Often seen in pregnancy. Also see *Anemia*.

Isoimmunization—Development of specific antibody directed at the red blood cells of another individual, such as a baby in utero. Often occurs when an Rh-negative woman carries an Rh-positive baby or when she is given Rh-positive blood.

J

Jaundice—Yellow staining of the skin, sclera (covering of the eyes) and deeper tissues of the body. Caused by excessive amounts of bilirubin. Treated with phototherapy.

K

Ketones—Breakdown product of metabolism found in the blood, particularly in starvation or uncontrolled diabetes.

Kidney stone—Small mass or lesion found in the kidney or urinary tract. Can block the flow of urine.

L

Labor—The dilatation of the cervix to make possible the expelling of a fetus from the uterus.

Laparoscopy—Surgical procedure performed for tubal ligation, diagnosis of pelvic pain, diagnosis of ectopic pregnancy and other procedures.

Leukorrhea—Vaginal discharge characterized by a white or yellowish color. Primarily composed of mucus.

Lightening—Dropping or descent of fetus into the pelvis before or during labor.

Linea nigra—Line of increased pigmentation running down the abdomen from the bellybutton to the pubic area during pregnancy.

Lochia—Vaginal discharge that occurs after delivery of the baby and placenta.

L/S ratio—Measurement of the relationship of two substances, lecithin and spingomyelin, in the amniotic fluid. Results give a doctor an indication of the maturity of the baby's lungs.

Lupus—See *Systemic lupus erythematosus.*

Lyme disease—Infection transmitted to humans by ticks.

M

Mammogram—X-ray study of the breasts to identify normal or abnormal breast tissue.

Mask of pregnancy—Increased pigmentation over the area of the face under each eye. Commonly has the appearance of a butterfly.

Meconium—First intestinal discharge of the newborn; green or yellow in color. It consists of epithelial or surface cells, mucus and bile. Discharge may occur before or during labor or soon after birth.

Melanoma—Pigmented mole or tumor. It may or may not be cancerous.

Meningomyelocele—Congenital defect of the central nervous system of the baby in which membranes and the spinal cord protrude through an opening or defect in the vertebral column.

Menstrual age—See *Gestational age.*

Menstruation—Regular or periodic discharge of a bloody fluid from the uterus.

Microcephaly—Abnormally small development of the fetal head.

Microphthalmia—Abnormally small eyeballs.

Milk letdown—Tingling or cramping in woman's breast, experienced when breast milk flows into the breast ducts.

Miscarriage—End of pregnancy. Giving birth to an embryo or fetus before it can live outside the womb, usually defined as before 20 weeks of gestation.

Missed miscarriage—Failed pregnancy, without bleeding or cramping. Often diagnosed by ultrasound weeks or months after a pregnancy fails.

Monilial vulvovaginitis—Infection caused by yeast or monilia. Usually affects the vagina and vulva.

Monozygotic twins—Twins conceived from one egg. Often called *identical twins.*

Morning sickness—Nausea and vomiting, primarily during the first trimester of pregnancy. Also see *Hyperemesis gravidarum.*

Mucus plug—Secretions in cervix; often released just before labor.

N

Natural childbirth—Labor and delivery in which no medication is used, and the mother remains awake to help deliver the baby. The woman may or may not have taken classes to prepare her for labor and delivery.

Neural-tube defects—Abnormalities in the development of the spinal cord and brain in a fetus. Also see *Anencephaly; Hydrocephalus; Spina bifida.*

Non-stress test—Test in which movements of the baby felt by the mother are recorded, along with changes in the fetal heart rate, to assess well-being of fetus.

Nurse-midwife—Nurse who has received extra training in the care of pregnant patients and the delivery of babies.

O

Obstetrician—Physician who specializes in the care of pregnant women and the delivery of babies.

Oligohydramnios—Lack or deficiency of amniotic fluid.

Opioids—Synthetic compounds with effects similar to those of opium.

Ovarian cycle—Regular production of hormones from the ovary in response to hormonal messages from the brain. The ovarian cycle governs the endometrial cycle.

Ovulation—Cyclic production of an egg from the ovary.

Ovulatory age—See *Fertilization age.*

Oxytocin—Medication that causes uterine contractions; used to induce labor.

P

Palmar erythema—Redness of palms of the hands.

Pap smear—Routine screening test that evaluates presence of premalignant or cancerous conditions of the cervix.

Paracervical block—Local anesthetic for cervical dilatation.

Pediatrician—Physician who specializes in the care of infants and children.

Perinatologist—Physician who specializes in the care of high-risk pregnancies.

Perineum—Area between the anus and the vagina.

Phosphatidyl glycerol—Lipoprotein present in amniotic fluid when fetal lungs are mature.

Phospholipids—Fat-containing phosphorous compounds. The most important are lecithins and sphingomyelin, which are important in the maturation of fetal lungs before birth.

Phototherapy—Treatment for jaundice in a newborn infant. See *Jaundice*.

Physiologic anemia of pregnancy—Anemia during pregnancy caused by an increase in the amount of plasma (fluid) in the blood compared to the number of cells in the blood. Also see *Anemia*.

Placenta—Organ inside the uterus that is attached to the baby by the umbilical cord. Essential during pregnancy for growth and development of the embryo and fetus. Also called *afterbirth* when it is expelled following birth of baby.

Placenta previa—Low attachment of the placenta, very close to or covering the cervix.

Placental abruption—Premature separation of the placenta from the uterus.

Pneumonitis—Inflammation of the lungs.

Polyhydramnios—See *Hydramnios*.

Postdate birth—Baby born 2 weeks or more past its due date.

Post-mature baby—Pregnancy of more than 42 weeks gestation.

Postpartum blues—Mild depression after delivery.

Postpartum depression—Depression after delivery.

Postpartum hemorrhage—Bleeding greater than 17 ounces (500ml) at time of delivery.

Post-term baby—See *Postdate birth*.

Pre-eclampsia—Combination of symptoms significant to pregnancy, including high blood pressure, edema, swelling and changes in reflexes.

Pregnancy diabetes—See *Gestational diabetes*.

Premature delivery—Delivery before 38 weeks gestation.

Prenatal care—Program of care for a pregnant woman before the birth of her baby.

Prepared childbirth—Term used when woman has taken classes to know what to expect during labor and delivery. She may request pain medication if she feels she needs it.

Presentation—Term describing which part of the baby comes into the birth canal first.

Preterm birth—See *Premature delivery*.

Propylthiouracil—Medication used to treat thyroid disease.

Proteinuria—Protein in urine.

Pruritis gravidarum—Itching during pregnancy.

Pubis symphysis—Bony prominence in the pelvic bone found in the midline. Landmark from which the doctor often measures during pregnancy to follow growth of the uterus.

Pudendal block—Local anesthesia during labor.

Pulmonary embolism—Blood clot from another part of the body that travels to the lungs. Can cause closed passages in the lungs and a decrease in oxygen exchange.

Pyelonephritis—Serious kidney infection.

Q

Quickening—Feeling the baby move inside the uterus.

R

Radiation therapy—Method of treatment for various cancers.

Rh-negative—Absence of *rhesus* antibody in the blood.

RhoGAM—Medication given during pregnancy and following delivery to prevent isoimmunization. Also see *Isoimmunization*.

Rh-sensitivity—See *Isoimmunization*.

Round-ligament pain—Pain caused by stretching of the ligaments on either side of the uterus during pregnancy.

Rupture of membranes—Loss of fluid from the amniotic sac. Also called *breaking of waters*.

S

Seizure—Sudden onset of a convulsion.

Sexually transmitted disease (STD)—Infection transmitted through sexual intercourse.

Sickle-cell anemia—Anemia caused by abnormal red blood cells shaped like a sickle or a cylinder. Occurs most often in black people.

Sickle-cell trait—Presence of the trait for sickle-cell anemia; not sickle-cell disease itself.

Sickle crisis—Painful episode caused by sickle-cell disease.

Skin tag—Flap or extra buildup of skin.

Sodium—Element found in many foods, particularly salt. Ingestion of too much sodium may cause fluid retention.

Spina bifida—Congenital abnormality characterized by a defect in the vertebral column. Membranes of the spinal cord and the spinal cord itself protrude outside the protective bony canal of the spine.

Spinal anesthesia—Anesthesia given in the spinal canal.

Spontaneous miscarriage—Loss of pregnancy during the first 20 weeks of gestation.

Stasis—Decreased flow.

Station—Estimation of the descent of the baby in the birth canal.

Steroids—Medications of hormone origin used to treat various diseases. Include estrogen, testosterone, progesterone and prednisone.

Stillbirth—Death of baby before it is born, after 20 weeks of pregnancy.

Stress test—Test in which mild contractions of the mother's uterus are induced; fetal heart rate in response to the contractions is noted.

Stretch marks—Areas of the skin that are torn or stretched. Often found on the mother's abdomen, breasts, buttocks and legs.

Striae distensa—See *Stretch marks*.

Surfactant—Phospholipid present in the lungs that controls surface tension of lungs. Premature babies often lack sufficient amounts of surfactant to breathe without assistance.

Syphilis—Sexually transmitted venereal infection caused by *treponema pallidum*.

Systemic lupus erythematosus (SLE)—Connective-tissue disorder common in women in the reproductive ages. Antibodies made by the person act against person's own tissues.

T

Tay-Sachs disease—Inherited disease characterized by mental and physical retardation, convulsions, enlargement of the head and eventual death. Trait is usually carried by Ashkenazi Jews.

Telangiectasias—Dilatation or swelling of a small blood vessel. Sometimes called an *angioma*. During pregnancy, another common name is *spider angioma*.

Teratogen—A substance that causes abnormal development.

Teratology—Branch of science that deals with teratogens and their effects.

Thalassemia—Group of inherited disorders of hemoglobin metabolism, which results in a decrease in the amount of hemoglobin formed. Found most commonly in people of Mediterranean descent.

Threatened miscarriage—Bleeding during the first trimester of pregnancy without cramping or contractions.

Thrombosis—Formation of a blood clot (thrombus).

Thrush—Monilial or yeast infection occurring in the mouth or mucous membranes of a newborn infant.

Thyroid disease—Abnormality of the thyroid gland and its production of thyroid hormone. Also see *Hyperthyroidism; Hypothyroidism*.

Thyroid hormone—Chemical made in the thyroid that affects the entire body.

Thyroid panel—Series of blood tests done to evaluate the function of the thyroid gland.

Thyroid stimulating hormone (TSH)—Hormone made in the brain that stimulates the thyroid to produce thyroid hormone.

Tocolytic agents—Medications to stop labor.

Toxic strep A—Bacterial infection that can cause severe damage; usually starts in a cut on the skin, not as a sore throat, and spreads very quickly. It can involve the entire body.

Toxemia—See *Pre-eclampsia*.

Toxoplasmosis—Infection caused by *toxoplasma gondii*. Can be contracted from handling raw meat or cat feces.

Transverse lie—Situation in which fetus is turned sideways in uterus.

Trichomonal vaginitis—Venereal infection caused by trichomonas.

Trimester—Method of dividing pregnancy into three equal time periods of about 13 weeks each.

Tubal pregnancy—See *Ectopic pregnancy*.

U

Umbilical cord—Cord that connects the placenta to the developing baby. It removes waste products and carbon dioxide from the baby and brings oxygenated blood and nutrients from the mother through the placenta to the baby.

Umbilicus—Bellybutton.

Ureters—Tubes that drain urine from the kidneys to the bladder.

Urinary calculi—See *Kidney stones.*

Uterus—Organ in which an embryo/fetus grows. Also called a *womb.*

V

Vaccine—Dose of medication given to patient to cause production of antibodies to protect against subsequent infections.

Vacuum extractor—Device used to provide traction on fetal head to aid in delivery.

Varicose veins—Blood vessels (veins) that are dilated or enlarged.

VBAC—Vaginal birth after Cesarean.

Vascular spiders—See *Telangiectasias.*

Vena cava—Major vein in the body that empties into the right atrium of the heart. It returns unoxygenated blood to the heart for transport to the lungs.

Venereal warts—See *Condyloma acuminatum.*

Vernix—Fatty substance made up of epithelial cells that covers fetal skin inside the uterus.

Vertex presentation—Head first.

W

Womb—See *Uterus.*

Y

Yeast infection—See *Monilial vulvovaginitis; Thrush.*

Index

$12.95 pb • ISBN 1-55561-143-5
$19.95 Canada
6.125 x 9.25, 384 pgs, b/w illustrations throughout

Your Pregnancy Week by Week
Third Edition

Glade B. Curtis, MD, Ob/Gyn

Completely updated in its third edition, this is the top-selling pregnancy book written by a doctor.

Dr. Curtis designed its unique format to help all women from before they conceive their baby until they give birth. Learn how your baby is developing and review changes in your own body as they happen.

A vast amount of invaluable information about the entire pregnancy is included as well, a bit at a time in each chapter. And a delightful new feature offers a tip-of-the-week to experienced mothers as well as women pregnant for the first time.

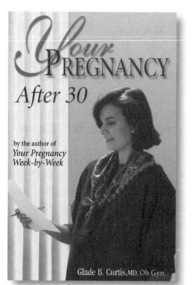

$12.95 pb • 1-55561-088-9
$19.95 Canada
6.125 x 9.25, 384 pgs, illustrated

Your Pregnancy After 30

Glade B. Curtis, MD, Ob/Gyn

The latest in this best-selling series—an important and timely resource for the rapidly growing number of women becoming pregnant after age 30.

Areas of greatest interest covered are:

- Achieving pregnancy after 30
- Multiple births
- Managing fatigue
- Tests for baby and mother
- Nutrition and weight management
- Workplace safety

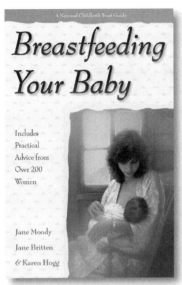

$12.95 pb • ISBN 1-55561-122-2
$19.95 Canada
6 x 9, 234 pgs

Breastfeeding Your Baby

Jane Moody, Jane Britten
and Karen Hogg

Reassuring, comprehensive advice on a subject of increasing interest to a new generation of mothers.

How does breastfeeding work? How do mothers breastfeed premature babies? What's special about breast milk? Can you breastfeed twins? Will I enjoy breastfeeding?

Over 200 mothers describe what helps and what hinders the breastfeeding experience. Written by three breastfeeding counselors, this up-to-date book answers the variety of questions parents have about breastfeeding, so they can decide what's right for *them*.

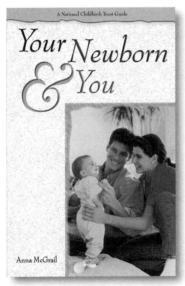

$12.95 pb • ISBN 1-55561-125-7
$19.95 Canada
6 x 9, 254 pages, b/w illustrations

Your Newborn and You

Anna McGrail

What will being a parent really be like? How will I cope with the basics, such as changing diapers? What's the best way to ensure a good night's sleep? How will we manage the change in our lives? Will sex ever be the same again?

Parenting is a hands-on skill—you learn as you go, but you can pick up most from the real experts: other parents. While there is often no right or wrong way to handle things, the suggestions and experiences of other mothers and fathers can help you decide what is right for you and your child.

$15.95 pb • ISBN 1-55561-133-8
$22.95 Canada
6.25 x 9, 208 pgs; 93 color photographs;
34 color illustrations; index

Having Your Baby
The Complete Illustrated Guide

Gill Thorn

Packed with clear explanations, sound advice and color illustrations. Covers the questions and issues a pregnant woman and her partner need to know:

- pre-conception health and pregnancy planning
- how your growing baby develops month by month
- your relationship with your partner
- choices for prenatal care
- getting to know your newborn

$9.95 pb • ISBN 1-55561-128-1
6 x 9, 144 pgs; b/w illustrations throughout

Preparing for Childbirth
Relaxing for Labor ~•~ Learning for Life

Betty Parsons

A voice pregnant women will listen to—encouraging, witty, understanding, calm. During her long career, Betty Parsons has coached more than 20,000 women through childbirth. Now even more women can take advantage of her unique insights. She takes the mystery out of labor, so readers know what to expect, what to do, and how to meet the challenge with confidence rather than fear. This is the book pregnant women will want for themselves, for their own well-being.

$9.95 pb • ISBN 1-55561-114-1
$14.95 Canada
7 x 10, 128 pgs, fully illustrated in two colors

Pregnancy & Childbirth
The Basic Illustrated Guide

Margaret Martin, M.P.H.

For pregnant women and their families, a conception-to-birth guide to pregnancy—written in clear, easy-to-understand terms, with informative two-color illustrations on almost every page. This unique book tells everything you need to know to enjoy a safer, more comfortable pregnancy and welcome a stronger, healthier baby.

With good care, a woman expecting a baby can avoid or significantly reduce many of the common complaints of pregnancy, from backache to nausea, and prevent or reduce health risks to herself and her baby as well. It emphasizes the basics of prenatal care. Simply written for quick, easy understanding—the best in its class!

Also available in Spanish—*Embarazo y Nacimiento*.

Fisher Books is engaged in publishing books
on pregnancy, childbirth and infancy. We also
publish related books on health, self-help and
other subjects. The organization has earned an
international reputation as a leading source of
books that are immediately useful to today's
mothers, parents, educators, caregivers and
healthcare providers.

FISHER BOOKS™

If you have enjoyed this book,
we'd like to here from you.

ENTER NOW!

Fill in the form below and return it to us to receive

our catalog featuring all Fisher Books titles

and enter the monthly drawing for

5 FISHER BOOKS Titles of

Your Choice

No stamp
required

Fold Here — Fold Here

**Return this form to enter the monthly drawing for free FISHER BOOKS titles.
We'll also send you our complete catalog.**

Name _____

Address _____

_____

_____

_____Zip _____

e-mail address _____

How did you hear about this book?

Friend's Recommendation _____

Advertisement (name) _____

Book review (name) _____

Catalog _____

Other _____

Where did you buy this book?

Bookstore (name) _____

Department Store (name) _____

Maternity / Baby Store (name) _____

Mail Order / Internet _____

Other _____

What influenced you in the
purchase of this book?

❏ Cover Design

❏ Contents

❏ Other (please specify)

How do you rate the overall
contents of this book?

❏ Excellent

❏ Good

❏ Average

❏ poor

What did you find most useful about this book? _____

_____

_____

_____

_____

What did you find least useful about this book? _____

_____

Please add any additional comments: _____

_____

_____

_____

_____